NEARLY REACH THE SKY

NEARLY REACH THE SKY

A FAREWELL TO
UPTON PARK

BRIAN WILLIAMS

Biteback Publishing

First published in Great Britain in 2015 by
Biteback Publishing Ltd
Westminster Tower
3 Albert Embankment
London SE1 7SP
Copyright © Brian Williams 2015

ISBN 978-1-84954-805-2

10 9 8 7 6 5 4 3 2 1

A CIP catalogue record for this book is available from the British Library.

Contents

Chapter 1

The family club

THERE ARE PEOPLE who consider football to be a religion but I don't see it that way. Religious faith offers certainty, salvation and, in some cases, virgins. I've never found any of those while watching West Ham United, and I've been following them for fifty years.

Fifty years – blimey, how easy it is to be nutmegged by time. One minute you're a wide-eyed kid, breathless with excitement as your heroes emerge from the tunnel; the next you're a family man with your wife's dad on one side and your little lad watching his first game on the other. Then, before you know it, you're at Wembley being held aloft like a human crucifix high above thousands of jubilant Hammers by your grown-up son as you celebrate the most lucrative goal in the club's history, glancing skywards in the hope that the fantastic fella who was just as much your mate as he was your father-in-law might be looking down from the heavens on this unforgettable moment.

Football: how did I ever get hooked? Because if it's not a religion, it's certainly an addiction. I became a Hammerholic three weeks before my eighth birthday and have never managed to kick the habit. I've seen all the great players who have turned out in claret and blue since the mid-1960s, and rather too many of the not-so-great as well. I've been there when we've triumphed and when we've been humiliated. I've rejoiced over FA Cup final wins, despaired at relegation, celebrated promotion, savoured the sweet and sour pleasure of unlikely escapes ... and looked on powerlessly as the club that means so much to me has been taken to the brink of financial disaster more than once.

Who in their right mind would willingly become a football supporter? And why would you choose to support a club like mine?

Before we go any further, I have an admission to make: I am not a cockney. It is a source of eternal disappointment to me that I wasn't born within the sound of Bow bells, but what can you do if your parents fail to see the importance of such things and choose to move to Bristol in search of better-paid employment and a more comfortable home, then conceive you while they're there? (In their defence, they went back to London when I was still a babe-in-arms, but by that time the damage was done – and to make matters worse they decided to return to their roots on the left-hand side of the capital before moving west again to the Berkshire new town of Bracknell.)

However, I have tried to make up for their geographical failings by marrying into an East End family and, after studying their ways assiduously, I was finally taken into the fold. It was touch and go when I failed to appreciate the wonders of jellied eels, but I went on to master the chirpy walk and then got an A-level in rhyming slang, which was just about enough to see me through.

My wonderful father-in-law, Sid, who was born and bred in East Ham, believed that fate had left him with no choice about which team he had to follow, but he couldn't understand why someone who didn't come from the area would volunteer to shoulder such a burden.

When I was first introduced to my prospective in-laws I was working as a journalist on the business pages of a national daily newspaper that was not exactly renowned for its love of the working man. High finance? Stocks and shares? The City? It was obvious to Sid that my claim to be a dedicated Hammer was simply a devious ruse to worm my way into the family's affections.

I hoped the fact that I understood West Ham followers don't always refer to ourselves as 'Hammers' – the alternative term is 'Irons' – would convince him I was genuine. To prove that I was no impostor, I made it plain that I could tell my Bobby Moore from my Bobby Gould, my Geoff Hurst from my Geoff Pike, my Martin Peters from my Martin Allen. And I shamelessly played my trump card by demonstrating that I know what the rest of the world calls Upton Park is, in fact, the Boleyn Ground. Gradually I won him round – and in doing so it made me realise how my own father had failed me when I was a boy.

When I was a teenager standing on the Upton Park terraces – sorry, Sid, the Boleyn Ground terraces – we used to sing a song to the old music hall tune of 'My Old Man Said Follow the Van' which changed the lyrics in such a way that the advice was to

follow West Ham instead. If only that had been the fatherly coun-
selling offered to me. I was given no parental guidance whatsoever
about football as a child – my old man just wasn't interested. He
was hard-working, sober and rarely beat my mother; but when it
came to the important things, like which team to follow until the
day you die, he was an abject failure.

My choice of club was left entirely up to me – and all these
years later I still wake up in a cold sweat thinking about how
my life could have been ruined at such a tender age. In the early
'60s, Tottenham had won the double; Man Utd were still being
swept along on a post-Munich tide of sympathy; Liverpool were
an emerging force. I could have ended up supporting any one of
them. Imagine the shame!

Luckily for me, the 1964 FA Cup final came at just the right
time. It is impossible to overstate the importance of the Cup final
back in those days. It was about the only game ever shown live on
telly, so people took it very, very seriously. For some reason I've
still not fathomed out to this day, most of the kids where I lived
got behind West Ham's opponents, Preston North End. So, being
a natural born rebel – if not a cockney rebel – I went for the other
lot and the rest, as they say, is history. (Although it's a good thing
we weren't playing the south end of Preston as well that day because,
the way we performed in the first forty-five minutes, they'd have
been out of sight by half time.)

All of which meant that when I had children I wasn't going to
take any chances about which team they supported. Watching
football on the box is all very well, but there's nothing like seeing
it in the flesh – particularly when you're a kid. The thrill of reaching the top of those steps and seeing the stadium spread out before

you for the first time is etched on every fan's memory. Never again will you see grass that green. The whitewash is whiter than white. The precisely strung netting in the goalmouths is just aching to bulge in response to a thunderbolt shot from your favourite player. Combine all that with the roar of the hamburgers and the smell of the crowd and you are hooked 'til the end of your days.

Some parents, in my not so humble opinion, take their offspring to Upton Park too soon. Many of those little 'uns are clearly no more than four, and you can tell by the vacant looks on their tiny faces that they have about as much idea of what's going on as the useless Avram Grant did in his time as West Ham manager. But leave it too long and children start watching TV without you and have fallen in love with the likes of Arsenal, Man U or Spurs before you know it. As a responsible father, I knew it was my duty to prevent that happening.

I reckon the perfect age to blood them is six, and I'm happy to say it's worked for me. Both my kids first went to Upton Park at that sort of age. As a result Geoff, my grown-up son, is now claret and blue through and through. Admittedly Katie, my equally grown-up daughter, doesn't like football – but at least I can look myself in the mirror and know that I gave her every opportunity in life.

Geoff had been pestering me for while to take him before I decided the time was right, so I set him a small examination to make sure he could concentrate for the full ninety minutes. On the day he was born we had played Liverpool. Somewhat unreasonably, I felt, my wife had refused me permission to go, simply because she was having a baby. But, happily, the game was being shown on TV and my best mate recorded it for me while I did my duty in the maternity ward. (Later I had to admit that Di, the mother of my children and custodian of my heart, had been completely right about me not going – the game ended 0–0 and McAvennie missed a sitter.) Geoff's test was to sit through the recording of this game without wandering off or falling asleep – which he passed with flying colours.

His reward was to see West Ham play Bolton Wanderers, newly promoted to the Premier League and still some years away from appointing Sam Allardyce as manager. 'So why not one of the glamour clubs?' I hear you ask. Because I didn't want his first game to end in defeat, that's why. I planned for him to have the lifetime of emotional pain and misery that I have endured; I certainly didn't want him put off at the first hurdle.

It was a proud day for me. Not only was I taking my son for the first time, Sid was with us too. Three generations of Irons sitting side by side – now that's my idea of a family club.

For the record, we won 3–0 with a goal from Berkovic and two from Hartson. Many years later Geoff and I, having failed to find a pub that would let us in, reminisced about the match as we sat on the steps outside the Tesco Express in Empire Way, enjoying the lively atmosphere and a few cans of strictly rationed lager before the play-off final against Blackpool at the end of the 2011/12 season. He reminded me how I had hoisted him into the air after the first of our goals. I thought nothing more of it – until I found myself celebrating Carlton Cole's opener several feet higher than everyone else in the south-west corner of Wembley, courtesy of a rugby-style lift by my 6 ft 3 son. How time moves on.

You never forget your first game, do you? Unusually for someone who supports West Ham, mine wasn't at Upton Park. For three years, comforted only by my collection of *Topical Times* football annuals,

I unsuccessfully tried to persuade family and friends to take me across London to see my idols. Finally, guilt got the better of my father and he agreed I could go on a works outing organised by a group of Chelsea supporters at the factory that employed him. He didn't fancy going himself, and wasn't the least bit concerned that these heathens might try to convert me to their way of thinking. Not that there was any chance of that. By the time West Ham went to Stamford Bridge in the autumn of 1967, the FA Cup had been joined in the trophy cabinet by the Cup Winners' Cup and World Cup. Besides, when I saw Bobby Moore in the flesh for the first time I knew I was in the presence of someone very special indeed.

These were heady days for a boy who had just started secondary school. The BBC had finally realised that it needed to do something about all these pesky kids who wanted to listen to pop music and had revolutionised the way it broadcast to the nation. Exactly four weeks before my introduction to the world of top-flight football, Tony Blackburn had introduced us all to the delights of Radio 1. (OK, trivia lovers, everyone knows that the first record he played in its entirety was 'Flowers in the Rain' by The Move – but what was the next single on the turntable? Give up? Hmmm, thought you might. It was, in fact, 'Massachusetts' by the Bee Gees, which just goes to show that in broadcasting, as in football, nobody remembers those who come second.)

With Radio 1 came Radio 2, 3 and 4, although we had to wait several more years for Radio 5 and the 6.06 programme, which allows irate supporters to vent their spleen on the way home from a match. Not that I had anything to complain about as I walked away from Stamford Bridge that first time. We had won 3–1 and I was ecstatically happy.

Strangely, my overriding memory after all these years is not of the goals – although I can still clearly picture Hurst's header that put us ahead for the second time in the match. Rather, the image that burns brightest in my mind is of Moore, ball under his arm, leading out the team. I was mesmerised. This was no mere mortal – there was a god in our midst and I was duty-bound to worship him.

Behind their captain were West Ham's other World Cup heroes, Hurst and Peters. (And if anyone believes I made a mistake earlier when I said 'we' rather than 'England' won that particular trophy, let me remind you that the score on 30 July 1966 was West Ham 4, West Germany 2.) Also in the team was a man who was to go on to become my favourite West Ham player, although I would have given you long odds against it at the time. Who could ever compare with the likes of Moore, Hurst and Peters in a Hammer's affections? Answer: William Arthur Bonds, aka Bonzo. But more of him later.

I'd like to say that as an eleven-year-old boy I was able to appreciate the tactical genius of Ron Greenwood, but that would be quite a large fib. Luckily, though, the author of the newspaper cutting I have in front of me had a terrific knowledge of the game. According to the peerless Reg Drury of the now defunct *News of the World*, Greenwood had decided to dispense with his wingers and go for the 4–3–3 system that had proved so successful for Alf Ramsey's England the previous year.

The full line-up, for those who care about such things, was: Ferguson; Bonds; Charles; Peters; Cushley; Moore; Burkett; Boyce; Brabrook; Hurst; Dear. Sub (not used): Sissons. With Drury's help, I am able to report that we scored first through Brian Dear, who headed home a Hurst cross. Chelsea equalised through Peter Osgood.

8

Stamford Bridge began life as an athletics stadium and back then it still had the remains of a running track at each end of the pitch. 'The jubilant Osgood kept running a semi-lap of honour behind the West Ham goal before being smothered in congratulations,' wrote Drury. What astonished me was the fact there were people on this Earth who were prepared to celebrate a goal against the team that means more to me than life itself. It wounded me then, just as it wounds me now.

Hurst rectified matters shortly after half time when he headed home after Moore crossed from near the corner flag, then England's World Cup hat-trick hero provided the cross for Peters to score a trademark goal at the near post. Just for good measure, Bobby Ferguson – the goalkeeper for whom Greenwood had paid a world record fee – made some blinding saves. What more could a boy want? What more could anyone want?

That was me completely and utterly hooked on West Ham United. My decision to support the Hammers, made three years earlier, had been totally vindicated. All the players I had idolised from afar had lived up to my heroic expectations – maybe even surpassed them. There was no going back after that game at Stamford Bridge. Together, we have gone in various other directions – particularly up and down – but never back. It's true that over the past five decades West Ham have not enjoyed the success I was fully anticipating when referee Jim Finney blew the final whistle and I joined 40,302 other spectators in the queues to leave the ground, but – as I have discovered over time – true love does not depend on trophies.

So, when the object of the exercise is to win, and it is patently obvious that the overwhelming majority of supporters are destined to spend more time contemplating failure than success, why do otherwise sane and sensible human beings invest so much time and emotional energy in following a football team? It makes no sense – yet all around the world there are millions of disparate souls who do just that (why they don't all support West Ham beats me – but I guess that's just another one of the universal mysteries that will remain forever unsolved).

Ultimately, I believe it has more to do with the people sitting next to you than anything else. Players come and go – even the great ones – but the supporters are in it for all time. It helps if your nearest and dearest share your obsession, or at least understand it, and when you discover that complete strangers feel equally passionate about your team it all starts to make sense.

And, trust me, there's no shortage of passion at West Ham.

If you doubt my word, come with me as we step forward in time from a chilly October Saturday in 1967 to a sunny Sunday in the spring of 1991. We are now at Villa Park for an FA Cup semi-final. You've already met Di and Sid, of course. And Geoff's here in the Trinity Road Stand, too – albeit as a foetus (he won't be born until November). But let me introduce you to Simon, the best man at our wedding and a relatively new convert to the claret and blue cause. He's sitting at my right-hand side, enjoying the biggest match he's ever been to.

There are just twenty-two minutes gone when Tony Gale muscles Nottingham Forest's Gary Crosby off the ball directly in front of us. I can hardly believe referee Keith Hackett has given a foul, and I'm astonished when he reaches for his pocket. You can't give him a yellow card for that! I'm right – it isn't yellow. It's red! This is, quite simply, the worst refereeing decision I have ever seen – and I am not alone in my opinion. Even the Forest fans are baffled.

In the West Ham stands there is nothing but fury. Sitting to my left is my wife. Next to her is my father-in-law. He later admitted that he was completely unaware his beloved daughter even knew the sort of language she came out with at that moment.

As a second division team – albeit one that was destined for promotion weeks later – we were very much the underdogs against a classy first division outfit managed by the mercurial Brian Clough. It was a tough ask with a full team; now, down to ten men, we had no chance.

Yet the lads on the pitch dug in, and their devoted followers got behind them. We had the main stand and the Holte End. There were choruses of 'Bubbles' coming out of both. The singing was punctuated by frequent, desperate calls of 'Come On You Irons'. We weren't asking – we were telling. And our boys responded – getting forward when they could, but then chasing back; all of them throwing themselves into tackles, harrying, fighting for every ball. George Parris even came close to scoring. It was a performance that truly honoured their manager – the awesome Billy Bonds.

Then the cry that was to dominate the afternoon went up: 'Billy Bonds' claret and blue army!' The response came back, with interest: 'Billy Bonds' claret and blue army!' There was still the occasional burst of 'Bubbles', but this wasn't a day to fade and die. Increasingly, the claret and blue army chant took hold.

At half time, astonishingly, we were still 0–0. Out came the cigarettes and the Murray Mints. Some tried to convince themselves we could yet get out of this with a draw, and then stuff Forest in the replay. I don't think anyone really believed it, though.

Clough certainly didn't. He reorganised his team during the break, making sure their eleven would out-pass our ten rather than engage in the sort of street fight that was clearly suiting us.

In our heart of hearts, we all knew what was coming – and we steeled ourselves for it. We weren't any old army: we were Billy Bonds' ultra-loyal claret and blue army, and we weren't going to go quietly. When the whistle blew to start the second half, every West Ham supporter in the ground was standing. And then it started in earnest.

Billy Bonds' claret and blue army! The martial rhythm that underpinned the words was provided by stamping feet and clapping hands. Billy Bonds' claret and blue army! You put your shoulders back, stuck out your chest, declaimed your allegiance and waited for the response. Which always came. Billy Bonds' claret and blue army! And so it went on, the volume increasing slightly with every repetition.

When the same Gary Crosby who had been involved in the incident that had sparked the outrage scored Forest's first, four minutes after the restart, we all knew our duty. As they rejoiced over their goal, we continued to celebrate the magnificence of supporting the most wonderful football club in the world. Billy Bonds' claret and blue army! No one faltered.

The goals kept coming, but we never missed a beat. Billy Bonds' claret and blue army! Louder. And louder. And louder still. By now, we weren't just standing – we were standing on our seats. When Stuart Pearce scored Forest's third after seventy minutes we saw their supporters leap to their feet, arms aloft. But we couldn't hear their cheers: the noise in the West Ham stands was so great we simply drowned them out. It was truly bizarre to watch a large group of grown men and women jumping for joy, while not having to listen to a single decibel from them. With no sound to accompany their celebration, they looked faintly ridiculous – and the pain that always comes with an opposition goal just wasn't there for once. It was as if their fourth and final goal never happened in our part of the ground.

In many ways, it is deeply worrying how you can so easily surrender your individuality to a crowd in the way we all did in response to such incitement. Frightening, but empowering. We may have been losing on the pitch, but we were victorious in the stands.

When the final whistle went, many seemed slightly baffled about what to do next. We saluted our team, gave the referee one last volley of abuse and considered the options. As we shuffled out I heard one guy ask his mate if they should go on into the city centre for a tear-up. 'Nah, let's go home,' was the simple reply.

The journey up to Birmingham had been full of hope – scarves out the window, sausage sandwiches on the motorway, Peter Frampton on the tape deck. Oh baby, I love your way.

Coming back was a different story – more a case of Leonard Cohen than stadium rock. We'd lost, and our Wembley dream was over. Even the gallows humour that inevitably follows on such occasions wasn't enough to lift the sombre mood. It wasn't until later that we realised we had been part of something special.

After the cream of the British cavalry were slaughtered at the Battle of Balaclava, the French general who oversaw the massacre famously remarked that the Charge of the Light Brigade was magnificent, but not war as he understood it. We got a similar response from people who had watched the game on TV. 'If that's West Ham when you're losing, what's it like when you win?' a colleague asked me some days later. He missed the point, of course.

In historical terms this was less Balaclava and more the equivalent of Dunkirk, which in truth was a desperate retreat from a rampant enemy, but came to be regarded as a triumph for the never-say-die spirit that is one of humanity's greatest qualities.

I'm certain there will never be a show of support like that again by the followers of any club, win or lose. What the West Ham supporters did at Villa Park was unique but, as I say, we never stopped to think that our display of defiance was a once-in-a-lifetime experience. That's the trouble with making history. At the time, you have no idea you are actually doing it.

Chapter 2

Home sweet home

ANYONE WITH THE slightest interest in English football will undoubtedly know that West Ham are moving to the Olympic Stadium in time for the 2016/17 season. Apparently, a new bright shiny stadium will herald a bright shiny future for the club. But, to be perfectly honest, I don't want to go.

We are told that what's needed is a ground more accessible for supporters, allowing bigger crowds to watch the games and enabling the club to become a major force in the land. The funny thing is the case being put forward to justify uprooting to Stratford sounds remarkably like the one that took us to the Boleyn Ground more than 100 years ago.

At the turn of the twentieth century, impressively whiskered directors decided that the Memorial Grounds stadium in Canning

Town, where West Ham first played after starting life as Thames Ironworks, was no longer fit for purpose and earmarked a site in the borough of East Ham that would … be more accessible, allow bigger crowds to watch the games and – you've guessed it – enable the club to become a major force in the land.

Ever since it was confirmed that we are to leave the area that has been the club's home since 1904, I've been chalking off each game played there in the same way a condemned man scratches the wall of his prison cell to mark the passing of his last days on Earth – knowing the hangman's noose will inevitably be wrapped around his neck at the end of it all. Frankly, it's not a good way to feel.

Other clubs have moved to new stadiums, I know. The trouble is West Ham isn't another club – it's *my* club. And I'm not sure how to pack up a lifetime of memories that were fermented in London E13 and ship them off to another postal district.

Let me take you on an unofficial tour of the ground. Perhaps, then, you will understand why I am so reluctant to leave.

I'm assuming you got here from one of the smarter parts of London on the District line via Upton Park Tube station and then took the short walk south down Green Street, passing notable local landmarks such as the Queens pub and Ken's café on the way. Each to their own, of course, but I'm not all that keen on the Queens. If you'd fancied a pint on the way you'd have done better getting off at Plaistow and looking in at the Black Lion. Alternatively, you could have stayed on until East Ham, strolled along the High Street until you reached the junction with the Barking Road, and popped into the Denmark Arms, which has a sticky-carpet charm all of its own. What you don't want to do if you come again is make the fatal mistake of alighting at West Ham station – it's a bloody long walk from there.

We are now at the main gates – the John Lyall gates – the ones that were adorned with scarves and shirts and teddy bears and all sorts of other claret and blue stuff when, in 1993, we were robbed of Bobby Moore by that filthy little cheat, cancer. You probably saw the pictures in the newspapers.

If you are not of the claret and blue persuasion yourself, you may well think the theatre of disturbing dreams we are now entering is called Upton Park. Let me put you straight on that one, me old china plate (I told you I was fluent in rhyming slang). Upton Park is the geographical area from which the Tube station takes its name. But the football stadium is officially the Boleyn Ground – so-called in memory of a castle that wasn't really a castle at all.

The 'Boleyn Castle' was a rather strange-looking affair, built in 1544 and boasting vague connections to the woman over whom Henry VIII lost his head before he decided she must lose hers. Some romantics say Anne lived there, others reckon she merely visited from time to time. Sadly, they are wrong – she had been executed eight years before the place was built. However, Green Street House, which stood in the grounds that West Ham had rented from the Catholic Church, became known locally as the Boleyn Castle – hence the name of the stadium that stands before you.

Directly ahead, you will have noticed those two rather large and tacky replicas of castle turrets, which celebrate West Ham's links with Tudor England. Talk about rewriting history! For years the club's owners were desperate to knock down the original building, and finally managed to do so in 1955.

On your right is the players' car park. I agree, some of those motors do look distinctly pricey. (Remind me to tell you about the time I nearly got run over by Mido coming out of there in his

Rolls-Royce. I guess if you are going to get knocked down by a car, a Roller is as good as anything, but you don't want it driven by Mido – he was terrible.)

Over there is the club shop. If you're after a souvenir, I suggest you pop in and get something now. The queues are murder on match day – they have security guys on the doors to ensure that it doesn't get too crowded in there, although I suspect that has more to do with crime prevention than the comfort of the customers.

Right, let me show you where it all started for me. Squeeze yourself through these ridiculously tight turnstiles and join me in the Trevor Brooking Stand.

When I first went to the Boleyn Ground back in the '60s, this was known as the North Bank and it's where I stood. It was cheap to get in and allowed you to look like a hard case without ever running the risk of direct confrontation with the opposition hooligans, who generally parked themselves at the other end of the ground. No one – and I mean no one – ever 'took' the West Ham North Bank, which meant you could stand up straight and confidently sing that you hated Bill Shankly; you hated the Kop and were prepared to fight Man United until you dropped. We didn't give a widdle and we didn't give a wank – we were the West Ham North Bank! They just don't write lyrics like that any more.

This, of course, was many years before Lord Justice Taylor decreed that football grounds had to be all-seater. The North Bank was a concrete terrace, punctuated with metal crash barriers that were there to minimise the danger when the crowd surged forward. What would have minimised the danger even more was if the idiots at the back had refrained from setting off a nerve-jangling human tidal wave by shoving the people in front of them simply for the fun of it, but I suppose folk had to make their own entertainment back in those days. It was tempting to lean on a barrier, but you soon discovered it was better to have it at your back – that way you were less likely to find yourself unexpectedly and unwillingly hurtling down the terracing when the pushing began. For me, the fact that this involuntary cascade was often accompanied by the strains of 'Knees Up Mother Brown' made it no more enjoyable.

There were other problems involved with standing on the terraces – not least the waterfall of urine that started at half time and was sometimes still trickling underfoot at the final whistle. But there were advantages, too. You could congregate with your mates, for one thing. And if you didn't have any mates, you could at least get together with a group of like-minded individuals who wanted to sing their hearts out in the name of West Ham United and tell the world that east London is wonderful, with the reasons why (I won't go into those here because they are somewhat offensive).

There's no doubt that a crowd generates considerably more of an atmosphere when it's standing. But, as things stand, you can't. Stand, that is. Not at a Premier League ground anyway.

The people championing the idea of 'safe standing' – notably the Football Supporters' Federation – are adamant they don't want to see a return to the vast open terraces of a bygone age. And those of us who stood on what were sometimes nothing more than crumbling death traps will say 'hear, hear' to that.

But, more than twenty years after Taylor called for all-seater stadiums, some people do still want to stand at football matches. West Ham supporters do it as a matter of course at away games – and some do it at home fixtures too – notably in the lower tier of the Trevor Brooking Stand.

The answer, says the FSF, is an arrangement that is proving increasingly popular in some parts of the world, particularly Germany, known as rail seating. The technology varies slightly from system to system, but the general idea is that in limited areas of the ground there are seats that can fold up flush with their metal housing, and then be locked in the upright position. The structure that encases the seats comes with a high back and a rail, which gives the row of supporters behind something to lean on.

You buy a ticket for the seat and stand in front of it – unless your club happens to be involved in a Champions League game and then the seats are unlocked and you sit down. Until your team scores, of course, and then there's every likelihood you will stand up again…

The FSF wants to give the idea of safe standing a trial run in the UK, which seems eminently reasonable to me. It will never happen at Upton Park, but there are suggestions it might get a trial run at the Olympic Stadium. David Blackmore, who edits the West Ham fanzine *Blowing Bubbles*, is convinced it will happen after talking to David Gold. The club's co-owner told him:

> We now don't have the violence we once had and already what exists is unsafe standing. At Upton Park, we currently have unsafe standing that is illegal and anti-social. It's time to give something back to the fans. The fans who want to stand should be given an area to do so.
>
> I'd be stunned if we don't have some form of safe standing experiment soon. I think in five years we will see safe standing at football stadiums because, let's face it, it's not very expensive to install and it's safe, very safe, in fact it's twice or three times safer than what we have at the moment.

Blackmore is a persuasive man – he talked me into writing a regular column for him in return for nothing more than a pint from time to time (which, considering I am a professional journalist and the shop steward who is supposed to ensure my colleagues at *The Guardian* and *The Observer* are properly rewarded for their labour, is no mean feat). But he can't persuade me we'll ever get safe standing – the concept has too many opponents.

One of the most powerful voices to speak out against it belongs to Margaret Aspinall who, as chair of the Hillsborough Family Support Group, fought so hard to get belated justice for the ninety-six Liverpool supporters who died in the needless tragedy that was to change the face of English football for ever – and were then blamed by some for bringing about the disaster themselves. One of the victims that fateful day in 1989 was her son James, who was just eighteen. 'There are ninety-six reasons why it should not be allowed,' she says. 'Standing should never, ever come back. I don't think there is anything safe about standing.'

I believe the Hillsborough Family Support Group fought an inspirational campaign to ensure the truth finally came to light. But I'm not sure she's right about this. Neither is Mark, who was in the Leppings Lane Stand that appalling day: 'I knew that the centre pen was dangerous as I'd been in there on three previous occasions (including the semi-final the year before). I was keen to avoid going in there again, so I went to the right of the goal where there was plenty of room.'

Should everyone be required to sit down at a football match all these years on?

I do believe that terracing can be safe. Hillsborough was a result of poor design, planning, stewarding and policing. It was known to be dangerous – the ground didn't even have a valid safety certificate.

If you go to away games you spend the whole match standing. If people stand up safely anyway, I don't see the problem with removing the seats and putting in barriers instead.

It would be nice to have some of the old atmosphere back. But the main reason that I would like to see some standing is that it should be cheaper than seat prices and enable young supporters to get into games. There is going to be a missing generation of fans at some point soon who don't have the money to pay for a season ticket and who haven't grown up with the idea that going to a game every week is part of their life.

It is fair to say Mark is not an armchair fan. Not only does he still rock up at Anfield regularly, he has been to more than 100 other League grounds in England as well. 'I'm not sure I'd want to stand up regularly, but I still stand at lower division grounds occasionally,' he says.

So why not every time? 'My plates are playing me up at the moment,' says Mark. Good to know that, given long enough, you can teach a Mickey Mouser to talk proper.

If there is to be some radical new thinking at the Olympic Stadium, I'd also like to see a section where fans of both teams can sit together – as happens at Fulham.

Generally, of course, there is strict segregation inside a football stadium. Home supporters sit here, the away lot sit there. And never the twain shall meet (unless it's a bunch of Millwall yobbos who've used a League Cup tie as an excuse to hole up in the

Queens with a view to starting World War Three, in which case you, them and a whole bunch of policemen meet in Green Street).

However, it's my guess a lot of us have smuggled an opposition fan into Upton Park at one time or another.

Your mate wants to see the game, but the away end is sold out – so you do the decent thing and invite them to join you in the Bobby Moore Upper instead. You start to regret it the minute the tickets arrive – if this mate of yours doesn't keep his trap shut you are both going to be in for a very uncomfortable afternoon. You are still warning him in hushed tones of the dangers as you surreptitiously check that no one else in the packed bar is listening to your conversation. He's nodding furiously to indicate he fully understands his side of the bargain, but you still feel uneasy. Then a bloke jogs your elbow causing you to spill half your beer and you really begin to wish you'd stayed in bed.

As it happens you both get away with it … this time. But wouldn't it have been so much better if there had been an area set aside where fans of both clubs could go in together and enjoy a laugh with their mates, safe in the knowledge they would emerge at the end of the game with their lives intact? We've got a family section, why not a mixed section? You'd need a few safeguards, naturally. But it would be perfectly possible if there were the demand for it.

Any takers? Or will it just be yours truly, surrounded by Tottenham-supporting friends politely asking me to remind them of one or two of the finer points of the game, like why the fella standing in front of the goal is wearing a different coloured shirt to the rest of the team?

Where were we? Ah yes, the Sir Trevor Brooking Stand, where

– despite it being called a stand – you're supposed to sit down. In all, there are the best part of 6,000 seats – some of which are given over to visiting fans, who generally refuse to use them. The big clubs get the majority of the lower tier, but most just get the left section. West Ham supporters who like to enjoy a little good-natured banter with our visitors take up the right half when they can. Unsurprisingly, there is invariably a generous filling of police and stewards in the middle of this particular sandwich. Above them is the family section, and you can only get a ticket for that if you have a child in tow. (It was in the family section that my son first abused a referee. I nearly died of shame. He called the ref a nincompoop! Of all the insults he could have come up with, he had to use nincompoop. People have been ejected from the ground for using words with that many syllables. I'm pleased to say, he uses much shorter ones these days when analysing a referee's performance.)

The seats in the Trevor Brooking Stand – which, until 2009, had spent the previous fourteen years answering to the name of the Centenary Stand – are part of an overall capacity of just 35,016, which, you will recall, is why we're having to pack our bags and leave. I was on the North Bank to see us draw 2–2 with Spurs when there were 42,322 in the ground, which is the official record attendance at Upton Park (it's likely this figure was exceeded in the '30s but no one knows for sure because many of the club's records were destroyed when the ground was bombed during the Second World War).

In the 1970 game against Spurs, they had the likes of Pat Jennings, Martin Chivers and 'nice one' Cyril Knowles; we had Bobby Moore, Geoff Hurst and the real Frank Lampard. The two teams were evenly matched and both knew how to pass the ball.

Games between West Ham and Spurs regularly attracted crowds

approaching 40,000 back then, but this one was given added spice by the fact it marked Martin Peters' return to Upton Park after a controversial swap deal had taken him to White Hart Lane in exchange for £50,000 and a rather rotund Jimmy Greaves. It finished 2–2, with neither Peters nor Greaves on the scoresheet. Their goals came from Mike England (who wasn't English) and Alan Mullery (who was the first man to be sent off playing for England). Ours were scored by Peter 'useless' Eustace and the not-so-useless Hurst.

The significant thing about Hurst's goal that day was that it made him the second-highest scorer in our history. In all, he went on to score 248 goals in 499 first-team games for West Ham – still some way behind the phenomenal record of Vic Watson, who scored 326 times for the club over fifteen years in the '20s and '30s – but nevertheless a tally that is unlikely to be surpassed in my lifetime, and probably anybody else's. Although I don't recall that being the first thing to go through my head as I punched the air in celebration, showed two fingers to the Tottenham fans (indicating it was the second time we had equalised, you understand) and took several involuntary steps down the terracing as the shoving from the back rippled down.

To your left is the East Stand. You're right: it does seem totally out of place now, dwarfed by the rest of the stadium and looking rather sorry for itself. But it was quite the thing in its day. This was built in 1969, when England were world champions; Harold Wilson was Prime Minister; the Beatles dominated the charts; Moore, Hurst and Peters were still playing in claret and blue – and I was on the North Bank because I didn't know about the shortcut that made it possible to get to the East Stand from Upton Park station without having to trudge all the way down Green Street, turn left at the Boleyn pub and then take the Barking Road far enough east to gain access to the fab new stand from Priory Road.

The trick is to nip off down Tudor Road, which takes you to a footpath that snakes through a gap between the ground and the local bus station. My mate Tony, who wore two-tone tonic suits, showed it to me – and I have been grateful to him ever since.

The East Stand may now be the oldest and smallest in the stadium, but once it was the loudest. And the funniest. What made it different was the terraced lower tier that was to become, in West Ham folklore at least, a legend in its own right: the Chicken Run. (In the interests of accuracy, I should probably point out that the original Chicken Run was an old wooden construction surrounded by fine-mesh wire, knocked down to make way for the new East Stand – which in turn awaits its own appointment with the bulldozer. But a name that good shouldn't be allowed to die when we move to the Olympic Stadium. Let's find room for Chicken Run III.)

I didn't discover this unique part of the ground until the early '70s but, when I did, it was love at first slight. No one was spared the insults that came flying out of there like machine gun bullets – opposition players, officials, even our own players. Actually, it was especially our players – particularly the ones who were judged to be failing to put in the required effort. It wasn't just the barbs themselves that lifted this abuse into an art form; it was the timing with which they were delivered. If taking the piss had been an Olympic event rather than part of the mandatory drugs test, these boys would have won every gold medal going.

The only time you didn't want to find yourself in the Chicken Run was on one of those rare occasions that saw the sun shine on

E13. In fact, it's a problem to this very day in the lower part of the East Stand. Unless you have the foresight to go armed with a peaked cap, you have to spend most of the game shielding your eyes with your hand when it's sunny. From the other side of the ground it looks like a parade ground saluting its commanding officer, which is quite amusing for them, but becomes a bit annoying if you have to do it for an entire game.

Still, that's a small price to pay for all the fantastic humour that came out of there over the years. Funnily enough, a lot of that seemed to go when they ripped out the terrace and put in seats. Did I ever tell you about the campaign for safe standing, by the way? Oh. Seems I did.

If the Boleyn Ground was to have been saved, it would have been done by redeveloping the East Stand, which can only hold 5,000 people. As recently as 2005 this was still very much on the cards, to the extent that planning permission was being sought. The idea then was to use the extra space that became available when the old West Stand went west – both literally and metaphorically. That happened in 2001. It was replaced by a new construction, which was reposi-tioned several yards further back to allow more elbowroom for the playing surface. (I much preferred things when fans were closer to the pitch down both sides, but I can understand why opposition players and shortsighted linesmen didn't.)

But I know that isn't going to happen. No one is going to save Upton Park, not now it has been sold to property developers Gal-liard. Still, if rubbing shoulders with cockneys all these years has taught me anything it's that there's no mileage in feeling sorry for yourself, so let's get on with this tour before someone realises we shouldn't be here and chucks us out.

Opposite you is the imposing Bobby Moore Stand. You will notice that there are two tiers and the 9,000 seats are painted in such a way that they spell out the name of our magnificent club. As far as I know, the contractors who were given the job stuck to the terms of their contract. (Unlike the artist who was charged with painting a giant seagull in the main stand when Brighton moved into their new Amex Community Stadium. He added a little scatological flourish on one of the seats below, which was later painted out because it was considered to be in bad taste.)

It used to be the poor relation in its days as the South Bank, which is perhaps why the away fans were housed there. Back in the heyday of hooliganism, that's where West Ham's serious psychos went in search of aggro. Not that they needed much encouragement, but they got it from time to time from other parts of the ground with the scarily sinister chant of 'South Bank, South Bank, do your job'. There is a story that the Boleyn Ground is haunted by one of Anne's maids. But when I go in the stand that now graces the southern end of the ground and is named after the most famous figure in our club's history, the ghosts I see wear braces, bovver boots and Ben Sherman shirts. To be honest, they are about the only thing I won't be sorry to leave behind.

To your right is the main stand, which can accommodate up to 15,000 Happy Hammers. It also accommodates a whole bunch of happy hangers-on, who are regularly invited by their business chums to watch a game from one of the executive boxes that separate the two tiers. Have you ever watched football from behind glass? It's like having sex with your trousers done up.

This is the stand you saw on the way in – the one with the iffy plastic castles attached to the outside walls. It has been suffering something of an identity crisis in recent years thanks to the wonders of corporate sponsorship. When it was rebuilt it was named the Dr Martens Stand, which must have pleased all those former skinheads who had stomped around in DMs back in the '60s and '70s. That deal ran out in 2009, and for a couple of years it resumed its former unimaginative but geographically accurate title. The West Stand was not to be left in peace, however, and was renamed once more when currency broker Alpari became the club's sponsors. Then they went belly up. We haven't had a lot of luck with sponsorship deals in recent years – this was the second one to end in tears following a debacle involving the XL airline in 2008. As Lady Bracknell would have undoubtedly observed had she been a West Ham season ticket-holder: 'To lose one sponsor may be regarded as a misfortune; to lose both looks like carelessness.'

Anyway, there you have the Boleyn Ground. You'll excuse me if I don't show you the changing rooms and the directors' box and the trophy cabinet (not that that would take very long) – if you want to see that sort of stuff you'll have to take the official stadium tour. No doubt they'll also throw in a few facts I've left out, like West Ham's first game here ended in a 3–0 victory over The Hated Millwall in front of 10,000-odd spectators (the spectators weren't odd, the number is; well, 10,000 is even actually, but I'm sure you get my drift). They might even point to the part of the pitch in the south-west corner that was hit by a Nazi flying bomb in August 1944, forcing us to play all our games away from home until December (apparently we won nine on the bounce, before returning to Upton Park and promptly losing to Tottenham – which is the kind of thing West Ham does).

But I haven't invited you here to listen to a load of facts and figures. I just wanted to show you the place that has meant so much to me and countless others before we have to leave it. To be honest, I should have brought you when there was a game being played – that way you could have really understood the unmistakable feel of this unique part of the world for yourself.

Honestly, there's no place on earth like the Boleyn Ground. If you don't believe me, you really ought to try it for yourself before it goes the same way as poor old Anne.

Chapter 3

One day in the life of…

6.58: I open my eyes cautiously and, as the bright red figures directly in front of me reshape themselves into focus, I become aware of the time. Normally, the alarm clock would be on the point of loudly reminding me of the need to leave my warm, comfortable bed. But I don't have to bend the knee to its tyranny today. It's Saturday. Easter Saturday, to be precise. I have plans, but they can wait.

8.35: Those plans can wait no longer. The extra sleep was welcome, but it's time to abandon the duvet and do the decent thing with the kettle. The slumbering members of my family get their first tea of the day. Getting up is never difficult on match day.

10.16: I turn on the sports channels in search of some early team news. A second cup of tea and a hot cross bun constitutes breakfast. I've showered and dressed. Jeans and a white, short-sleeved shirt with claret and blue trimmings, which commemorates our 1980 FA Cup final triumph against Arsenal, plus the lucky socks – all assembled in the correct match day order. There is a cartoon strip by Charles Schulz in which Charlie Brown is explaining to his little sister that on the day of a baseball game he always puts on his left shoe before the right one, otherwise they would most certainly lose. 'Have you ever won?' she asks him. The final frame depicts Charlie, long after the game has started, still sitting on his bedroom floor looking hopelessly at both of his shoes, unable to decide which one to put on first. Schulz was nothing if not perspicacious (see – it's not just Arsenal fans who know long words). It is true my lucky socks don't always do the trick. But I choose not to think about the *Peanuts* dilemma today.

11.04: Geoff and I are on the train as it pulls out of Brighton. Di has decided to give this one a miss. The sun is shining. My hopes are high. This has all the makings of a great day.

11.15: It's a chance to catch up on how my son's doing at university. This is a crucial time for him: after four years at Warwick he will soon take his master's exams. Then come some life-changing decisions. What career to follow; where to live; whether to take some time out to go travelling or find a job? They are his choices, but as a parent I feel privileged that he wants to share his thoughts with me. Over the years football has given us the chance to talk in a way we may not have done otherwise. Rules could be relaxed when there was a game involved. And on those rare occasions the father–son relationship was strained to the extent we didn't really want to talk to one another, there was always West Ham. Pardew better than Lyall? Di Canio as good as Brooking? Upton Park or the Olympic Stadium? Some issues just have to be discussed, if not resolved.

11.42: Time to check that my mate from south of the river is up for the contest. Mark supports Crystal Palace, today's opponents. We've got a pound-a-point bet about who will have the more successful season. After they had lost nine of their first ten games it looked like I was in for some easy money, but that's not the case now. Palace have gone three points above us after a shock result at Everton during the week. We need to win this one. 'Feelin' lucky?' I ask Mark by text.

11.45: Seems he is. There's even a gag about him having seen our teamsheet, a reference to a minor controversy that's simmering between his side and Cardiff City.

11.48: I resist the temptation to be too bullish at this stage. I took a lot of stick from Mark when Palace won at Selhurst Park earlier in the season, and I'm going to enjoy repaying him in kind today. I keep my reply non-committal, with a limp crack about Allardyce v. Pulis being London's answer to El Clásico. I'll save the rough stuff until later. Keep it simple when we take the lead, then work on something more imaginative for the second goal. That's the point of a bet like ours – it's not about the money, it's about the bragging rights. It's going to be a long summer if we finish below Palace.

Still, no need for negativity. Win today and we go above them on goal difference. After that, with just three games to go, we should be able to keep our noses in front until the end of the season.

12.04: I glance out of the window and catch sight of the Shard, the pointed monstrosity built next to London Bridge station that towers over the capital. In exchange for a small fortune, you can go to the top and take in the view. I ask Geoff if he remembers a more modest construction that we had climbed in search of a vista during the Easter holidays several years ago. Of course he does – that was Zamora's Tower! At least, that's what it's known as in our house. It was 2007. West Ham, looking certainties for relegation, had gone to the Emirates. We'd gone to the Lake District to visit family. On the Saturday afternoon, rather than listen to the Hammers getting stuffed on the radio, we went for a long walk through the Cumbrian hills where we came across an old Roman fortress, no doubt built to keep marauding Scots at bay. A couple of the look-out posts were still intact, so Geoff and I climbed one for no other reason than when a male sees a tower in the middle of nowhere he generally has to scale it. While up there, Geoff noticed it was half time. Nervously, he asked if we should check the score. We feared the worst, but decided to look anyway. Astonishingly, the magic of the worldwide web allowed us to tap into the news from north London. And, even more astonishingly, it turned out we were winning! The solitary goal of the first half had been scored by Bobby Zamora. We didn't find out until later that it was a fluke. Neither did we have any idea that, in our goal, Robert Green was playing a blinder. What we did know was that, having discovered we were winning while up the tower, we couldn't possibly come down until the game had finished. Furthermore, those family members on the ground had to stay there if the spell was not to be broken. Luckily, both Di and her sister Linda had inherited enough of their dad's DNA to understand that this wasn't just mindless superstition; we were dealing with the universal law of the cosmos, and that was not to be messed with when West Ham was involved. So they continued the walk with my brother-in-law and daughter, while we sat it out on the tower. As any football supporter will know, we couldn't look at the score again – that would have surely invited disaster. So we waited until several minutes after we were certain the final whistle had sounded, took our courage in our hands and checked the score. To the cockney boys, 1–0! We had become the first away team to win at the Emirates (having been the last away side to win at the Highbury Library). It was our third victory on the bounce, and we did eventually avoid relegation by the skin of our teeth. It truly was the Great Escape. But it never would have happened if we'd abandoned Zamora's Tower.

12.19: The train pulls into Blackfriars on time. Change here for the District line. On the Tube there are a group of guys discussing where best to get off. I overhear one suggest 'Play-stow'. I can only assume they are Palace fans.

12.53: We arrive at Plaistow – correctly pronounced 'Plar-stow' by the train's computerised Tannoy system. We, too, mind the gap and alight here.

12.57: Geoff and I fight our way into the Black Lion.

13.04: Geoff and I finally get served.

13.06: A quick exchange of texts reveals that an arrangement to meet *Blowing Bubbles* editor David Blackmore has gone awry. Pity. He's an interesting man, is David. He describes *Bubbles* as a fanzine, which worried me at first. To me, the word 'fanzine' conjures up images of badly typed sheets of A4 paper, folded, stapled and handed out by its angry contributors who want to sack the board and get a new manager. Don't get me wrong – I'm always in favour of sacking the board and there's rarely a time when I don't want a new manager. But, at my time of life, I really can't be persuaded to hang around the gates of the Boleyn Ground before kickoff trying to flog something that, more often than not, is going to be used primarily for wiping away the remains of a burger from greasy fingers. Happily, David had something rather more ambitious in mind. His vision was to produce a package for this digital age; not merely a print version, but something that could also be read on just about anything else as well – PC, mobile, tablet … if he could find a way to have a *Blowing Bubbles* chip implanted in your brain, I wouldn't put it past him. However, digital-age technology can't help him at this particular moment in time. It turns out he's on a dawdling Tube at Earls Court and unlikely to be joining us any time soon.

13.30: Geoff and I opt for the second pint, but it's pointless ordering food. There's no chance of getting a table. Again there's a wait before we're served. Next to me is a bloke who is also brandishing a note in the traditional manner of someone who wants to attract the bar staff's attention. They ask him what he wants – but he insists they serve me first because I have been waiting longer. I thank him for his courtesy. He nods briefly, knowing that a man who's done the right thing needs no thanks, and contemptuously points to another fella who didn't observe the time-honoured tradition of waiting his turn and is now sipping illegitimate beer. I concur with his terse assessment of the other man's manners. That prompts a brief conversation in which we agree that Palace fans are a decent bunch but disagree on the question of whether the Premier League should be open to clubs from Wales and Scotland. We part on the best of terms. If you know how a pub works, you will understand football supporters – or, at least, the West Ham supporters.

14.03: Geoff and I quit the Black Lion and join the steady procession through the streets of Plaistow. I don't envy the motorists' fruitless search for parking spaces. I've had plenty of that over the years. Now I prefer to leave the car in Brighton.

14.13: We're in Walton Road. The Boleyn Ground is directly ahead. The 21st-century stadium looms large over the nineteenth-century streets. We reach the junction of Green Street and turn right, which takes us past the tiny house once occupied by Di's Auntie Vi. What I would have given as a kid to have lived directly opposite Upton Park. Better still would have been the flat rented by Auntie Marjorie. She had a place in Priory Court, which overlooked the pitch. And there was me, having to put up with my parents' choice of a centrally heated three-bed semi plus garden and garage in leafy Berkshire. Talk about a deprived childhood.

14.20: Geoff gets a programme. I buy a copy of *Over Land and Sea*, the last of West Ham's old-style fanzines.

14.22: Lunch is two Mad Dogs from Britain's best burger stall, handily positioned for supporters of West Ham United outside the south-east corner of our ground on Priory Road. I usually prefer bacon to a hot dog – even if it is named after a cult hero – but, having had a drink, the sausage seems more appealing. For me, booze and bacon don't work well together.

14.26: As Geoff attempts to wipe the splodge of ketchup from the front of his shirt I idly tune in to some of the chatter going on around us. One bloke wants to see us play two up front – you'll be lucky, mate. Another fella is on his mobile, arranging to meet someone after the game. I recall overhearing a similar phone conversation earlier in the season: to the left of me, one guy had asked the precise whereabouts of the man he was due to meet; to the right of me, his mate had explained that he was standing in front of the Priory Road burger stall. I had looked at one, then at the other, and wondered briefly how much fun it would be to introduce them while they were still speaking to one another. In the end, I let them work it out for themselves.

14.45: We take our seats at the top of the East Stand Upper as four of the 1964 FA Cup winners are introduced to the crowd as part of the fiftieth anniversary celebrations. Eddie Bovington, Ken Brown, Peter Brabrook and Ronnie Boyce wave and accept the generous applause. I resist the temptation to tell Geoff how Boyce headed home Brabrook's cross for the winning goal in the final minute, or that his mother and grandfather celebrated alongside thousands of others outside the town hall the following day as the team started their open-top bus victory tour. He's heard it all before. Come to think of it, I've never told him that the morning of the final was the one and only time I was a Cub Scout. I hated it so much I refused point blank to ever go again. Not a particularly interesting story in itself, but it does explain why my son has never been subjected to the strange practices of paramilitary organisations.

14.55: The teams are out. They've been through the usual preliminaries and are now solemnly lining the centre circle. This is a black armband day. It's the blackest of black armband days. We're not being asked to remember a fallen veteran who has slipped away peacefully after a long and fulfilling existence – sad though that always is. Our grief is for a young man who died only yesterday, having been robbed of his rightful life by testicular cancer aged just twenty.

14.56: The family of Dylan Tombides have requested that he be honoured by a minute's applause rather than silence – and that's what we do. I glance across at the Palace fans and, to their eternal credit, they too are applauding respectfully. Tombides' father Jim and brother Taylor bring out his No. 38 shirt – never to be worn again. The club are to retire the number. The only other time that has happened at West Ham was when Bobby Moore died and the No. 6 was decommissioned at Upton Park.

14.58: As the pitch is cleared for action I allow myself to remember the tragedy of Moore's untimely death twenty-one years ago. The first game at Upton Park after he died was against Wolves. On that sad and mournful day, Moore's claret and blue shirt – complete with number – was represented by a giant floral creation in the centre circle, carefully placed there by Geoff Hurst and Martin Peters. I look to my right at the Palace fans and recall how, shortly before the official remembrance, a Wolves fan had come charging out of the same end and made a dash towards the middle of the pitch. What was this outrage? Did he not know the meaning of respect? And what did he have in his hand? Abuse was heaped upon the interloper from all sides. Then he quickly laid his highly unofficial wreath on the halfway line, bowed his head briefly and, without seeking any sort of applause or recognition, dashed back to join his comrades from Wolverhampton. I've looked out for the Wolves score ever since.

15.00: The mood is still sombre as the game starts. I've never heard 'Bubbles' sung with less enthusiasm.

15.02: The team starts brightly and Stewart Downing gets a shot away. He's not scored all season and is the subject of a sarcastic piece I've written for the latest edition of *Blowing Bubbles*. If he keeps this up he's going to make a monkey of me today.

15.05: All the noise is coming from the Palace end. A section of the East Stand Lower tries to counter, but they're fighting a lone battle.

15.08: Andy Carroll gets his head to a Kevin Nolan cross. For a moment it looks like his effort is destined for the top corner, but it goes just over. The reaction from the West Ham supporters is strangely muted. The Palace fans are asking if anyone can hear West Ham sing. It seems they can't hear a bloomin' thing.

15.11: Mark Noble plays a fabulous ball that allows Matt Jarvis to get to the byline and pull back a wicked cross. Carroll and Nolan are hunting as a pair on the edge of the 6-yard box, but the ball somehow eludes them. More of that please, lads.

15.14: Nolan concedes a corner, which produces a goal-bound header. Carroll blocks it clumsily, and the East Stand Upper breathes a collective sigh of relief.

15.17: Carroll fouls Mile Jedinak in midfield. The Palace man does well not to make more of it. The West Ham support remains hushed. The Palace fans have been inquiring politely if this is a library.

15.18: Palace miss a great chance to take the lead as central defender Scott Dann fails to make the most of a one-on-one aerial contest with diminutive full-back Pablo Armero on the edge of our 6-yard box.

15.19: They take the resultant corner short while the West Ham defence has a little doze. Adrián Mariappa accepts the invitation to enter our penalty area without let or hindrance and has a pop from 12 yards. Kevin Nolan throws his body in the way. Did he stop that with his arm? It looks horribly like a penalty to me.

15.22: Palace's Yannick Bolasie goes down after a robust challenge by Armero. And he stays down. Many of those in claret and blue believe he's making a meal of it. At least it gives us something to shout about.

15.26: Bolasie has recovered sufficiently to set up another Palace attack.

15.27: That's more like it! Mohamed Diamé cuts inside and has a dig with his right foot from outside the box. Palace keeper Julian Speroni tips it over easily enough.

15.28: Palace defend the corner well and break rapidly. Armero is quick to get across and cover, but is forced to put the ball out in front of the Bobby Moore Stand. That's Palace's fifth corner in less than half an hour.

15.29: Diamé gives Palace their sixth corner, swiftly followed by a seventh as Downing heads behind. We haven't defended set pieces at all well this season, and you can feel the jitters in the stand.

15.30: Bolasie's getting booed every time he touches the ball. He goes down easily, takes the free kick and makes a hash of it – earning himself the 'who are you?' treatment.

15.31: The West Ham support has gone back into its shell. Carroll is sent crashing in the Palace box by Jedinak. FFS ref, that's got to be a pen!

15.33: Winston Reid is up-ended in his own half. The howls of protest prompt the Palace fans into taunting us with: 'We forgot that you were here.'

15.35: We remind them of our presence as there's an outbreak of activity in the Palace area. Diamé's shot is saved. Nolan scrambles the ball wide to Downing, who crosses for Carroll. It's a bullet of a header, but Speroni saves brilliantly. That really should have been 1–0. The effort prompts a decent rendition of 'Bubbles' at last.

15.38: It's the thirty-eighth minute and, in recognition of his squad number, West Ham supporters all around the ground are on their feet and applauding the memory of Dylan Tombides. What a tragedy. The poor kid had battled with cancer for three years. It's said he had limitless potential. Few of us in the ground had seen him play – his only appearance for West Ham was as an eighty-fourth minute sub in a League Cup tie against Wigan. But that, of course, is not the point. Football more important than life and death? I don't think so.

15.39: Carroll gets in another header but it's off target.

15.46: After a minute of added time, referee Martin Atkinson calls a halt to proceedings. Palace leave to huge cheers from their travelling support. The home fans keep our thoughts to ourselves.

15.50: No half-time beer, no provocative texts to Mark and no great expectations for the next forty-five minutes. Geoff and I chat quietly. It's agreed we'll have to play better in the second half if we're going to win this.

16.02: Palace show their intent as Mariappa clatters into Noble. The Palace man is wearing a face mask to protect his broken nose. A bloke on my left dubs him Tonto. That's wrong for all sorts of reasons, but it's the first time I've smiled in over an hour.

16.05: George McCartney is booked for pulling back Bolasie. Poor old Linda has been asked to play out of position, and he's struggling. Still the West Ham support lacks its usual passion. It's as if the Tombides tragedy has affected us all.

16.12: Carroll tries his luck with a left shot from outside the box, but it is saved easily. That's his third unconvincing attempt in just over five minutes. You can sense the growing frustration around the ground.

16.14: Palace win a penalty as Armero brings down Cameron Jerome. To my left, the Lone Ranger reckons the decision is 'bollocks'. Hmmm. I think you'll find, Kemosabe, that is a stonewall pen.

16.15: Jedinak smashes the ball past Adrian's right hand into the top corner.

16.16: We kick off again and the home support demands a fight-back with a united chorus of 'Bubbles'. There's some real passion in that.

16.19: Downing tries his luck and wins a corner. It comes to nothing.

16.26: Palace are outplaying us. Manager Sam Allardyce has to do something about this. Carlton Cole is about to come on. Fair enough. But it's Matt Jarvis who's getting the hook – and he's been our most effective player. 'You don't know what you're doing,' Allardyce is told by representatives from all four sides of Upton Park.

16.30: Some people have had enough and are heading for the exits.

16.32: Joe Cole comes on for Stewart Downing. Having started with two out-and-out wingers we've now gone 4–4–2 with a pair of giant strikers and no obvious wide men to supply the crosses. Interesting.

16.36: The exodus begins in earnest. 'Is there a fire drill?' ask the Palace fans. This is precisely the abuse we dish out as away fans. Now we have to sit and take it. It's seriously humiliating.

16.43: After a flurry of substitutions on both sides, Palace bring on former Hammer Danny Gabbidon. I'm pleased that those of us still in our seats give him a decent reception.

16.46: The sign goes up to say there are four extra minutes.

16.50: Carroll is fouled outside the Palace area. He wants to go for goal himself but Noble rightly talks him out of it. This is it, our last chance. Noble floats the ball in, Carroll goes for it … and the whole thing peters out.

16.51: The final whistle. The Palace players are saluted as heroes from their end of their ground. West Ham troop off with their tails between their legs and jeers of derision in their ears.

16.52: My phone tells me I have a message. I know who it's from, but read it anyway. Mark is thanking me for the three points. Worse still, he's being nice about it. He reckons that, according to the reports he's heard, we should have won 5–1. I must have been watching a different game.

17.03: We've escaped the ground and are on Priory Road. David has suggested we join him in the Black Lion, but neither Geoff nor I have much of an appetite for an inquest. We decide to head off to East Ham station.

17.05: We turn into the Barking Road with some serious punditry going on all around us. One middle-aged guy in a hooded fleece and denims tells his similarly clad mates what they already know – if you can't score goals you don't win football matches. But there is more than mere cliché to be heard if you listen carefully. We're predictable; easy to defend against; too ready to hoof the long ball forward if there isn't an obvious pass to be made in midfield. This is a crowd that has been brought up on crisp passing, triangles and a third man running. It knows what it is talking about.

17.15: On the junction of the Barking Road and the high street, the pull of the Denmark Arms proves too strong. I really fancy a pint after the way we've just played.

17.30: Tucked in the corner by the pool tables, Geoff and I check the results from other games. It is still mathematically possible to go down, but the chances are we won't. A run of four straight wins in February, followed by victories against Hull and Sunderland before the present slump set in, are probably enough to see us safe. Fulham have lost, Cardiff could only draw at home and both Sunderland and Norwich have tough fixtures ahead of them. There's got to be more to football than avoiding relegation by the skin of your teeth every year, though.

17.38: 'Dreadlock Holiday' comes on the jukebox and I try to console myself with the thought that the cricket season will soon be in full swing. But for someone who has the fortunes of Surrey and England close to their heart, there's not an awful lot of consolation to be had there.

17.55: We call it a day after just one pint and make for East Ham station. This is not a prosperous area, but there's more to the high street than Poundland and payday lenders. You can still buy a book, get some keys cut and shop for your supper without having to get on a bus. And it doesn't have the ever-growing number of homeless people sleeping rough that affluent Brighton steps over on its way home.

18.03: The District line train has plenty of spare seats and we grab a couple, knowing there won't be many left after Upton Park and Plaistow.

18.35: We get to Blackfriars just in time to see the Brighton train pull out from the mainline station. The ticket barrier guy jokes that the driver didn't wait because he could see we were West Ham supporters. I counter with the suggestion that if he did know who we support, he'd have taken pity on us after the day we've just had.

18.50: The next train to Brighton – and we're on it. Not that it was an unpleasant wait; Blackfriars station spans the river now, and the views are terrific. It's easy to forget what a majestic city London is.

19.10: We pass through Crystal Palace station without stopping. South London is not majestic.

19.12: Geoff is reading – I decide to treat myself to a game of Hearts on my phone. Simple, mindless pleasure. Unlike the card game I got involved in on a football special many years ago. Was it Hull? No – that's where they ambushed us at the station. It was somewhere north, though. I was travelling alone and had bagged a window seat with a table at Euston when I was joined by some lads about my age. They produced a pack of cards and asked if I fancied joining them in a friendly game of Pontoon. It wasn't so friendly half an hour later when most of their money was piled up in front of me. In fact, the atmosphere around the table was distinctly hostile. The game was gathering a crowd. Winning was bad enough. Doing so in front of amused spectators was worse. I was clearly lining myself up for a good kicking. There's no nice way of putting this: these boys were all monumentally stupid. I tried to let them win their money back. I would twist on nineteen and get the two of hearts. Or I'd stick on fourteen and they'd keep twisting until they bust. I don't think they could count up to twenty-one between them. But I suspected they were all good at fighting. In the end I managed to lose enough of my winnings to live to tell the tale. I remember I travelled back in a different carriage. Who the hell did we play that day?

19.23: The Hearts game completed, I turn to my crumpled copy of *Over Land and Sea* (Issue No. 583; Price £2.50). The cover is excellent – it's a *Sgt Pepper's* mock-up, with Sam Allardyce behind the bass drum and a collection of West Ham faces, past and present. I count forty-nine in all. But where's Christian Dailly? I want curly hair, too. I like *OLAS*. It doesn't worry much about spelling and punctuation, but it also doesn't pull any punches. It's had enough of Allardyce and his style of football. It doesn't much care for West Ham's vice-chairman Karren Brady, either. As I say, I like *OLAS*.

20.25: It's good to be home. A glass of red now and supper soon. Di's doing Mexican. *Viva fajitas!*

22.30: No one is interested in *Match of the Day* tonight. We check out the movie channels instead.

23.30: The eyelids are getting heavy. I fear this film is going to join the long list of those whose ending will remain unknown to me for evermore.

00.20: I awake on the couch to discover my concerns were fully justified. But who cares? There will be always be another movie. Just as there will always be another match day. Sure, we lost. Much of the football was pretty forgettable, to be honest. That doesn't stop you going again, though, does it? The game aside, it was a great day out: a chance to spend some time with my one of my kids; quality banter with mates; a couple of beers; a whole range of emotions; a chance to relive past glories – what more could anyone want (other than three points and a team capable of passing the ball to one another)? Win, lose or draw, there'll always be another day at Upton Park. Only there won't, will there? Not when we've gone to Stratford.

00.28: I turn off the bedside light and watch the illuminated numbers on my clock tick over to 00.29. Another minute closer to the end for the Boleyn Ground. Another minute closer to the end for us all…

Chapter 4

Trevor Brooking walks on water

GIVEN A FEW moments, we can all think of the best game we ever watched. But what about the best game you never saw?

If it's goals you're after, there are a fair few to choose from should you be lucky enough to follow the Hammers. But be careful here – goals aren't everything. West Ham's record win is a 10–0 demolition of lowly Bury in the League Cup but, according to those who were there (and not many were), if you weren't able to get along to that you really didn't miss much – although manager John Lyall clearly saw something in Bury's centre half that night because he promptly went out and bought him. So what exactly was the thinking here?

If the extremely shaky Shakers had not had Paul Hilton in their side that night, they would have been beaten really badly.

One game that I would have really liked to have been at was the one in which Geoff Hurst scored six. Yes, I know technically it should have been five – because the first one was handball – but we're talking about a knight of the realm here, not some dodgy character with a history of abusing recreational substances and an arse the size of Patagonia. It's only cheating when he does it and claims it was the hand of God.

West Ham 8, Sunderland 0 makes me dribble just imagining what Upton Park must have been like on that Saturday afternoon in 1968. Any takers for the scorers of the two goals that weren't down to Sir Geoff? Of course, it was Saint Bobby and Sir Trev. You know the times of the goals as well? Oh. I can see I'm going to have trouble with you.

But picking any old game that you missed where we gave the opposition a good hiding would be too easy – and if West Ham stands for anything at all it's about doing things the hard way. So I'm ruling out the massacre of the Mackems and several others like it. For the sake of this rather pointless exercise, you have to select a game that you had actually given some thought to attending but didn't get to for one reason or another. Perhaps it was your wife's birthday, or you had a hangover that merited an entry in the *Guinness Book of Records*. It doesn't matter to me (although I imagine your missus would have something to say if the two coincided).

So I'm going to leave Sunderland behind and move forward a few years to 1976 and the Cup Winners' Cup semi-final against Eintracht Frankfurt. By this time Hurst and Moore were gone, and the shops in Green Street no longer closed on a Wednesday afternoon. But we still had Trevor Brooking. That's Sir Trevor Brooking. The man who's got a stand with his name on it.

If you are of an age that means you were too young to have seen Brooking play, I envy you your youth. But I also feel sorry on your behalf that the odds are impossibly stacked against you ever getting the chance to see a true one-club hero who could make hardened supporters smile knowingly while simultaneously shaking their heads in disbelief at his outrageous skill. It's thirty years since he retired, yet I can still get through grey days by picturing Brooking angling his body to receive a pass, letting the untouched ball slide past him as he used his muscular frame to shield it, and then bringing it under instant control while he turned and powered away from a desperate defender who, seconds before, thought he had everything under control. What made it really special was the fact opponents knew it was coming, but could do nothing within the laws of the game to prevent it happening. These days, climbing stairs makes me gasp. Back then, it was Trevor Brooking.

I will concede that he left something to be desired as a TV pundit (I can say this after fifty years of devotion to West Ham – supporters of other clubs are not permitted to utter one word of criticism of Sir Trev). The problem was twofold, I believe. First, he himself was so good as a player he was unable to believe others could be so inept. And, secondly, he was too nice to be horrid about anyone. So when some useless lump failed to bring the simplest of balls under control, or fired it over the bar from 6 yards out, he put it down to a 'bobble'. It was an expression that was to pass into the lexicon of TV commentary. Before Brooking, 'bobble' wasn't a word you heard all that often – unless it was a reference to that knobbly bit on top of woolly hats.

I do understand that there is nothing worse than hearing a previous generation banging on about how good the players were in their day. I'm sure when Brooking made his debut there was some old boy in the Chicken Run explaining to the bloke next to him that there would never be another Vic Watson. Such is life.

But Brooking really was different gravy and, unlike good old Vic, there is the video footage to prove it. Just take a look at the highlights of the two legs of the Frankfurt game and you will understand why he is so deeply admired by all those who saw him in the flesh.

Before you do that, though, let me tell you how I gave the world the song that really sums up how so many people feel about this man – 'Trevor Brooking Walks on Water'. Yep, that was me.

To be frank, I'm expecting a fair amount of controversy over this particular claim. I can already hear the legions of West Ham stalwarts with bus passes harrumphing that they were singing 'Trevor Brooking Walks on Water' long before Highbury 1975. Honestly, though, over the years I have racked my brains endlessly in an effort to recall a previous occasion when I had heard those words and I really can't come up with anything. Should anyone produce some concrete evidence to prove me wrong – newspaper reports, old videos of *Match of the Day*; sworn affidavits – you can slap my wrist and call me Geraldine. Until then, I'm claiming the copyright.

For reasons that need not detain us here, I was unable to make the great man's final game at Upton Park in May 1984. Apparently, many of those who did go stayed behind for the best part of an hour to salute him, using the hymn of praise I had composed some years earlier. Had I been there, I suspect modesty would have prevented me from telling those around how I'd been the first to put the new lyrics to 'Deck the Halls', but I feel the time has now come. Future generations of historians need to know this stuff.

West Ham were in the Cup Winners' Cup because we had won the FA Cup the year before. (The nation's dealings with Europe were so much simpler then.) The final itself, against Fulham, is remembered more for the fact that Bobby Moore turned out in white instead of claret and blue than for the quality of football – but some of the performances leading up to Wembley had been sensational. Best of all was the quarter-final against Arsenal, which I went to with the wife of a close friend. Sadly they are no longer married so, to spare their blushes, I will change her name to Claire. Why don't you join us in the Clock End at Highbury on an over-cast day in the March of 1975 and I'll give you the full story?

Come to think of it, join us an hour earlier as the Tube pulls into Arsenal station. The Piccadilly line train is rammed with claret and blue – it's standing room only. But the platform is deserted: everybody in north London knows the Gooners are at home to West Ham that day. Everybody except the solitary figure standing on the platform, cradling what can only have been a framed picture bought from one of the local antiques shops. The look of horror on his face as he realised what was about to befall him even before the Tube doors had opened will remain with me for the rest of my life. (Those of you familiar with *The Scream* by Edvard Munch will know what I'm talking about here.)

I can't be 100 per cent certain it was a painting because it was wrapped in brown paper, but it's hard to imagine something that shape could have been anything else. I hope, for his sake, it wasn't a masterpiece. One minute he was standing like a contented human easel, cherishing the artwork nestled in his arms. The next moment he was twisting like a whirling dervish, desperately trying to protect his purchase from the irresistible tide of humanity that had just spewed out of the train and was carrying him back down the sloping tunnel at Arsenal station. I am sad to report he was right to be fearful; it seems that not all West Ham supporters' love of beauty extends to art, and more than one felt the need to stick their fingers through the brown paper while questioning the poor man's sexuality. Expressionism is all very well, boys, but I do think that some of you could express yourselves rather more politely on occasions. Remember, you are an ambassador for the club at away fixtures.

So, where were we? Oh yes, Highbury with my mate's wife. Claire was from South Africa, and had never been to a football match. There was no way my friend was going to take her, so she asked me. Then she asked again. And again. And yet again. And … finally I gave in.

On reflection, a London derby – not to mention a quarter-final of the FA Cup – may not have been the best choice as a debut game for someone unfamiliar with the strangely violent culture that surrounded football in the mid-1970s but, hey, I was young and foolish. (Which I now realise beats being old and foolish.)

You didn't need a ticket to get in back then. Honestly! You could simply turn up and grab a spot just about anywhere that took your fancy. Segregation was a word you only ever heard in conversations about Claire's homeland – it didn't apply to football supporters.

Now I know you'll find this hard to believe, but some West Ham fans often seemed to prefer the bit the rough boys from the other side liked. We weren't always made terribly welcome, but after a free and frank exchange of views (often described as mindless savagery by the popular press) the home supporters would sometimes let us have their favoured part of the ground. Tottenham, for example, always seemed prepared to give us the Park Lane End. Their north London neighbours were generous hosts too but, even so, I was surprised to find myself surrounded by quite so many displaced Gooners, who had been turfed out of their North Bank and now were congregated at the Clock End considering their next move.

It's fair to say they weren't in the best of moods. The Clock End, unlike the North Bank, was uncovered and there was every chance we were all about to get soaked in another heavy downpour. Their humour wasn't improved by an enthusiastic South African screaming 'Come on West Ham' while jumping up and down as she frantically waved a claret and blue scarf. And all this with half an hour until kickoff – and not a sniff of a player on the pitch.

I like to think I've lent my voice to the cause over the years, but there are times when it's better to keep your mouth shut. I tried to explain this to Claire, but she was having none of it. In fact, the more I urged her to button it, the louder she got. It's true that she was an extremely good-looking woman, but I don't think that was why we were being stared at by an increasing number of grumpy Gooners. I remember one, in particular, who was clearly tortured by the idea that he was forbidden by his personal credo from battering a woman, and was obviously considering battering me instead.

On the plus side, Claire was also attracting the attention of other small groups of West Ham fans who, like me, had wrongly expected to find themselves in the majority at that end of the ground. Gradually these small islands of support began to drift our way – drawn by a beacon in the same way that millions have answered the call of the Statue of Liberty. 'Give me your tired, your poor, your huddled masses yearning to breathe free ... send these, the homeless, tempest-tost to me'. The weather-beaten West Ham masses were certainly queuing up to huddle around Claire.

This was the second time I had been to Highbury that season. The previous October I had gone with a bunch of Arsenal-supporting mates from the factory where I was driving a forklift truck – and didn't those boys enjoy themselves as we went down 3–0! It's fair to say they really knew how to have some fun at the expense of a hapless Hammer (when they weren't telling new arrivals at the factory to pop down to the stores to ask for a glass one … or a left-handed screwdriver … or a long stand).

Some weeks earlier, one of the lads was looking for some lost gaffer tape when I reminded him that that particular roll was almost finished and he had discarded it.

'Oh, so I discarded it, did I?' he asked in what he thought was an upper-class accent.

'It's a perfectly good word,' I responded defensively. 'It means to throw something away.'

The accent wasn't so posh when my charge-hand told me in no uncertain terms he was perfectly familiar with the word's meaning. As I recall, there was an odd expletive in there to emphasise the point. And, from that day forth, nothing in that factory was ever thrown away again. All unwanted items were discarded.

'I say, Maurice, I don't suppose you've seen my copy of *Titbits* have you.'

'Why no, Sidney, I believe you discarded it earlier.'

How I laughed.

Two of the scorers in that 3–0 game went on to play for West Ham … with contrasting fortunes. Liam Brady was past his best when John Lyall bought him many years later, but he managed to win over the fans with flashes of brilliance – which underlined the point that, if you have to live within your means as a football club, you are generally better off with a has-been than a never-will-be. (OK, step forward all those who were at Upton Park when Chippy scored with his final kick in his final game as a professional footballer. Oh, it's you again. I should have guessed.)

John Radford, on the other hand, couldn't hit an elephant's arse with a cricket bat, let alone hit the back of the opposition's net. Come on, John, you were supposed to be an international striker – so how do you explain thirty appearances and no goals?

In the name of clarity, can I take this opportunity to point out that, from now on, when I talk about the number of appearances a player has made for the Hammers I give the lot – including substitutions and tuppenny-ha'penny competitions like the Anglo-Italian Cup, Watney Cup, Texaco Cup and Charity Shield. This is because, if I had ever been brought on as a sub for the last five minutes of, say, a Watney Cup game wearing the holy claret and blue, I would to this day be telling anyone who cared to listen that I had once appeared for West Ham. Who wouldn't?

Brady and Radford were both in the Arsenal side for the quarter-final, too. Other notable names on the Gooners teamsheet included Alan Ball, Brian Kidd and Pat Rice. (I always used to enjoy *Match of the Day* highlights of games between Arsenal and Sheffield United, simply because Rice was often required to go up against Tony Currie.)

We made one change from the October fixture – Alan Taylor replaced Bobby Gould in what was his first full game for the club. Taylor had been identified by Ron Greenwood, who had plucked him from the fourth division after the spindly striker scored ten goals in five games for Rochdale earlier in the season. Happily, he wasn't Cup-tied. Better still, he clearly knew what to do when he got anywhere near the opposition's goal. In the first half, that was up the other end – in front of an Arsenal North Bank temporarily under new ownership.

Both sides were struggling to come to terms with the terrible conditions, although West Ham were making a far better fist of this than they had the League fixture. Then young Taylor did what he had been bought to do: he scored. It was a goal you just wouldn't see today – not in the Premier League, anyway. There was a puddle the size of the Serpentine in Arsenal's box, and a scuffed shot from Keith Robson got stuck in the lake. Keeper Jimmy Rimmer had started to come for it, but had to revise his plans when Billy Jennings waded in and retrieved possession. His shot was blocked, but the ball went out to Graham Paddon, who dinked it back in for Taylor to prod home from a yard out.

The West Ham fans in the Arsenal end surged forward – there were thousands of them. At our end, the isolated groups of ecstatic Hammers celebrated, too – none more so than our merry band, conducted by Claire. The Gooners surrounding us looked as thunderous as the sky above.

The pitch really was disgraceful – there were pools of water everywhere. It had the appearance of a paddy field (perhaps that's why Rice liked playing there – sorry, I'll get my coat). A back pass from Billy Bonds came up short in the quagmire and Radford nipped in thinking he would score, before West Ham keeper Mervyn Day took him out in spectacular style. Everyone knew it was a penalty … except the referee! Had Arsène Wenger been there he would have spontaneously combusted with rage.

Despite the conditions, Brooking was imperious. He seemed to float across the sodden ground. Every time he got the ball I felt we could score again. Eventually, following a cheeky nutmeg, he played the killer pass that put Taylor in for his second goal and secured the victory that nobody – except perhaps Claire – had predicted. And during this exceptional display it just came to me: 'Trevor Brooking walks on water, tra-la-la-la-la, la-la-la-la!' No sooner had it left my mouth I realised what an idiot I must have sounded. My singing voice is so bad I was asked to mime in assembly at school, and there were 1,500 kids at my comprehensive. But that wasn't what worried me most: when you sing at a football match you have to do it as a collective; there's no room for solo artists. I expected withering looks from the lads who had gathered in our part of the stand. Instead they took up the song and belted out another stanza of 'Trevor Brooking walks on water, tra-la-la-la-la, la-la-la-la!' Perhaps the fact that Claire was unaware of the social conventions that surround these things and joined in with such gusto helped. Whatever the cause, we soon had up to thirty happy Hammers singing as one. Embarrassed? I was as proud as Punch!

I hoped other groups of West Ham supporters nearby would follow our lead, but I don't remember it catching on that day. In fact, it wasn't a song you heard all that often at subsequent games, if I'm going to be totally honest, but it did get wheeled out from time to time – more often at away fixtures where the travelling supporters always have a greater repertoire than at home. And whenever I heard it (I was never brave enough to try to instigate the singing again) my heart swelled with pride.

I have always been intrigued by the singing and chanting at a football match. In church it is led by a priest. In a soccer stadium it is far less clear-cut who calls the tune.

At West Ham we have some songs that are unique to us. How were they composed in the first place?

Take a particular favourite, still sung in praise of a goalkeeper who last turned out for us in 1998:

> My name is Ludek Miklosko
> I come from near Moscow
> I play in goal for West Ham
> And when I walk down the street
> Everyone that I meet
> Says: 'Hey – big boy
> What's your name?'
> My name is Ludek Miklosko...

Leaving aside for one moment the small geographical error that Miklosko was actually born in Prostějov in the Czech Republic (which is about 1,000 miles from the Russian capital), this is an absolute West Ham classic and, unlike my effort, it could not have happened spontaneously. Who wrote it? And how did they get the people around them to start singing it? They don't hand out hymn sheets at Upton Park. (But if they did, perhaps they could include the correct words to 'Bubbles'. It's 'They fly so high, nearly reach the sky' *not* 'They fly so high, they reach the sky' – please can we all try to get this right in future, everyone?)

Anyway, back to the best game I never saw. From what I've witnessed since on video highlights, the night Eintracht Frankfurt came over for the second leg of our Cup Winners' Cup encounter, Upton

Park was almost as big a mudbath as Highbury had been. But that didn't stop Brooking producing another jaw-dropping display.

I wasn't there to see it because, on the way to east London, I got cleaned up by an articulated lorry on the North Circular. Such was the mess that truck made of my beloved Ford Escort (red; the four-door 1300; good runner but some mild corrosion – near offers accepted) that I didn't get home in time to see *The Mid-Week Match* either.

And ITV was not like Sky – it didn't show the same footage over and over again in a television *Groundhog Day* that lasted all week. You watched the highlights on the night or not at all. So for years I had to use my imagination about what went on under the Boleyn lights as we attempted to overturn a 2–1 deficit from the first leg. I had the newspaper reports of course, and for weeks afterwards I would pester those around me at League fixtures to tell me what they recalled of that magical evening. But it wasn't the same as being there.

While we're on the subject of 'being there', this might be a good time to point out that it doesn't always pay to believe what people tell you about how to get there in the first place. The fella I was going to the game with was something of a hippy by nature and a big follower of a self-styled Tibetan monk called Tuesday Lobsang Rampa, who advocated a method of getting around called 'astral travelling'.

Prompted by my mate – who reckoned he could do it – I tried to master astral travelling myself. The idea is to project your inner self into the ether and then control your out-of-body experience, allowing a ghostly form of yourself to go wherever you like (a sort of spiritual Oyster card). The benefits seemed obvious: for one thing you could float over Upton Park and watch a game for free without actually having to slide out from under your Slumberland continental quilt. And it would take all the hassle out of getting to away games. But I could never do it, which is why I'd saved my hard-earned cash and bought a second-hand Escort instead.

It turned out there was a good reason I couldn't astral travel. The whole thing was total bollocks and Tuesday Lobsang Rampa (real name Cyril Henry Hoskins) was, in fact, the son of a plumber rather than a spiritual guide with an *A–Z* of the cosmos.

Back on the A406, my bullshitting mate and I had come within a whisker of spending the rest of eternity floating in the ether after a juggernaut misjudged the moment to change lanes and solved the problem of my rusting flitch plates once and for all – by obliterating the front half of my car. And while the collision didn't prove fatal for us – nearly, but not quite – it did for my beloved jam jar.

Had we made it to E13 we would have witnessed one of the most truly outstanding West Ham performances of all time.

The highlights I have watched subsequently offer no evidence that anyone trotted out 'Trevor Brooking Walks on Water' that night. But there is a burst of 'Aye-aye-ippy' as we put Frankfurt to the sword. Was there a squadron of Boy Scouts in the ground that night? I've sung some questionable songs at Upton Park in my time (including a highly juvenile version of 'Distant Drums' that still makes me redden with shame at the memory). But 'Aye-aye-ippy'? What were you thinking, guys?

Trevor Brooking scored twice that night. Contrary to public opinion, he did not use his head purely for thinking. Occasionally he would use it to score goals for West Ham. This was one of those nights when he did just that – with a powerful header from close to the penalty spot at the start of the second half.

That made the tie all square on aggregate. Brooking's pass from inside his own half gave Keith Robson the chance to slam the ball home from 25 yards to give West Ham the overall lead. Then Brooking conjured up a little piece of magic that convinced me he truly could have walked on water and replicated several other miracles had he not been such an unassuming and all-round decent chap.

This time he was the one on the receiving end of a pass from the West Ham half. His first touch – with his left foot – gave him the space he needed; his second – with the right foot – eased the ball into the bottom corner. The TV cameras naturally concentrated on Brooking as he ran towards the West Ham bench to celebrate, rather than following the Frankfurt defender who had tried, with a spectacular lack of success, to cover back and had last been seen hurtling towards the Priory Road turnstiles after being utterly bamboozled by that wickedly deceptive shimmy. So we never discovered if he was ever able to find the right money to re-enter the ground.

You really do have to be something out of the ordinary to end up having a stand named after you. And they don't give out knighthoods lightly. Trust me, Sir Trevor Brooking really was different class – take a look at the highlights of the Frankfurt game if you're still not convinced.

That night, as I sat by the side of the road contemplating my mangled Ford Escort, West Ham's favourite son taught the Germans everything there is to know about *fußball*. Although, come to think of it, he had yet to be tapped on the shoulder by the queen. If we are going to be strictly accurate, Sir Trevor was still plain old Mister Brooking back then. But who cares? That's just splitting Herrs.

Chapter 5

The West Ham Way

DON'T BE FOOLED by the sardonic humour at West Ham – we take this football lark very seriously indeed. Believe me, you won't hear people using words like 'footy' in the Boleyn Ground. You'll hear other words beginning with f, but not footy.

And you can forget all this romantic twaddle that we'd rather watch our beloved Irons lose 6–5 in the game of the season than grind out a 1–0 win. Where do people get ideas like that?

Some years ago my ears pricked up when I heard on the radio that Man Utd had won 5–3 at White Hart Lane – a result made even more remarkable by the fact that Tottenham had been 3–0 up at half time. The venerable gentleman who had been watching the game at BBC licence-payers' expense was particularly enthusiastic about United's performance when asked for his summary of the game; in fact, he reckoned the visitors had 'sprinkled stardust' over north London and any Spurs fan who witnessed the event would consider themselves lucky to have been there. I don't think so, my friend. I can't believe there is a supporter in the land who would feel anything but despair after watching a capitulation of that magnitude. (Some say the commentator in question is an institution. Personally, I think he should be in one.)

While we're on the subject of misfortune befalling Tottenham Hotspur (an occurrence dear to the heart of any West Ham supporter), this was the game that spawned news reports of a Spurs fan who was so confident of victory at half time that he took the annoying cliché about 'putting your mortgage on it' and did just that.

The story goes that the guy was keen to impress a new girlfriend, and was no doubt feeling pretty smug when the team he had just introduced into her life trooped off at the interval three goals to the good against the reigning champions. But rather than trying to press home his advantage with a mug of Bovril and a meat pie as any normal man would do, he got on his mobile (which would have been the size of a house brick back then) and arranged for someone to place a six-figure bet, equivalent to the value of his home loan, on his behalf. Forty-five minutes and a liberal helping of stardust later, the bloke had no house. History does not record if he had still had a girlfriend.

Tottenham-supporting friends (I know, embarrassing isn't it?) reckon this is just an urban myth, although I'm not so sure. They like to portray themselves as pessimists, but in recent years they have been a pretty cocksure bunch and I can just picture one of them making that call. Your typical West Ham fan, on the other hand, would be considerably more cautious in similar circumstances. When you've watched your team throw away a 3–0 lead at home to the likes of Wimbledon (1998) and West Brom (2003) you don't start counting your chickens until they are surrounded by roast potatoes having been plucked, stuffed and cooked until the juices run clear. Snatching disaster from the jaws of triumph just doesn't come as a surprise any more – it's simply the West Ham way of doing things.

I should point out that at West Ham the way we do things is not to be confused with the West Ham Way – a phrase generally used to describe a free-flowing style of football that the supporters want to see.

There are those who will tell you there is no such thing as the West Ham Way. Sam Allardyce, in his first season as manager, put forward this fanciful idea after a trip to the picturesque cathedral city of Peterborough. Having been offered some helpful and constructive criticism by 6,000 pilgrims who'd made the journey as well, he responded to the repeated chant of 'We're West Ham United – we play on the floor', by saying: 'There has never been a West Ham Way shown to me. I've spoken to a lot of people at the club and no one can tell me what it is.' Apparently those of us who believe there is such a thing are 'deluded'.

This is the same Sam Allardyce who, the following season, cupped his ear in astonishment as a highly disgruntled Upton Park crowd booed him off after a diabolical performance against Hull. Admittedly we had won and effectively banished any lingering fears of relegation – but West Ham supporters know what we want from our team and had expected better against a side that found itself a goal down and reduced to ten men after barely a quarter of an hour. Allardyce complained it was the only time he'd ever got a response like that after winning – he just didn't get it at all.

Then, just as Allardyce appeared to have seen the error of his ways and changed the system to incorporate two men up front rather than a lone striker (and had West Ham playing some of the best football we've seen in years), his old mate Sir Alex Ferguson chipped in with: 'I hope that, before I die, someone can explain the West Ham Way.' Well, if the crowd of naysayers would care to let me through for a minute or two I'll do my best. You see, WE ARE THE FAMOUS, THE FAMOUS WEST HAM! And we're famous because of a football genius who laid down a (claret and) blueprint for the club that has now become an indelible trademark. His successors ignore it at their peril.

Ron Greenwood was not a man to go out of his way to win friends. He didn't like his own captain (a certain Robert Frederick Chelsea Moore) and he didn't have much time for West Ham supporters or the East End as a whole. 'This community and this area doesn't understand or appreciate anything that this club stands for,' he is quoted as saying by West Ham historian Charles Korr. The problem, according to Greenwood, is that we 'don't understand sincerity and intelligence'.

Maybe not. But we do know a thing or two about football, and we came to appreciate the way he believed the game should be played.

Greenwood joined West Ham from Arsenal in April 1961 – the same month that Yuri Gagarin became the first man in space (personally I'm in no doubt which was the more important event). His footballing philosophy can be traced back to the day he saw the brilliant Hungarian team of the mid-1950s trounce England 6–3 at Wembley – the first time England had ever lost at home – with a performance that revolutionised the way the young Greenwood thought about the game and convinced him he wanted to become a coach when his playing days as a centre half were over.

He said later: 'I knew then for sure that football was a combination of thought and intelligence, and fun and concentration, and vim and vigour, and everything, if you like, even art, if you want to call it that.'

In short, Greenwood's way – the West Ham Way – is about playing open, attacking football by passing the ball quickly and accurately, based on the concept that it is more important to score goals than it is to prevent them. That's not to say defence isn't important: Greenwood built his team around the best defender the world has ever seen and was even prepared to go out and buy some big lads to play alongside him who – in Bobby Moore's words – could 'do some kicking' (as long as they didn't do too much of it).

But the main objective of the game, in the gospel according to Ron, is to break down the opposition using skill plus intelligence and put the ball in the back of their net more often than they put it in yours. And it doesn't always mean playing on the floor, either. While Greenwood liked his players to pass their way through the other side's midfield, repeatedly trying to get two on one so they could play the give and go, he was quite prepared to put the ball in the air – only he wanted to do it in such a way as to produce panic in the defence rather than frustration in the stands.

Sir Geoff Hurst is rather better qualified to explain Greenwood's thinking than me, so why don't I let him do the talking?

'What he took specifically from the Hungarians was the near post cross, a tactic that was to become one of West Ham's trademarks during my time with the club,' says Hurst in his autobiography, *1966 and All That*.

> One day he put cones down in wide positions on the training
> pitch. The cones were to act as full backs, he said. The wingers
> had to run and cross the ball before they reached their cone.
> They had to bend their pass around the cone so that the ball
> landed in the space between the opposing goalkeeper and his
> back line of defenders. It was the task of forwards like me to
> get into that space and attack the ball before the goalkeeper
> or any of the defenders could reach it.

One of the wingers expected to master this particular skill was Harry Redknapp, who was to go on and make his own distinctive mark as a West Ham manager in the years that followed.

If ever West Ham has produced a love-him-or-hate-him character, it has to be H. I know he'll never again be flavour of the month with most West Ham supporters but, for all his faults, I still have a soft spot for Redknapp. But then I like Marmite.

Like most Hammers, I had mixed feelings when he got the manager's job at Upton Park in 1994. The way Billy Bonds was eased out was nothing short of a disgrace. But there was a feeling that Redknapp could take us to the next level. He certainly understood the concept of the West Ham Way.

I wonder what his early predecessors would have made of him? Syd King, West Ham's first gaffer, would have undoubtedly approved – if for no other reason than, like me, he claimed to have a taste for the sort of foodstuffs that divide a nation. In his case it was a stock cube.

'When training, Oxo is the only beverage used by our team and all speak of the supreme strength and power of endurance they have derived from its use,' appeared above his name on the back of a promotional postcard featuring a team photograph in 1904. And you thought commercialisation was something new?

King ruled the club for the best part of thirty years. Arguments about formations didn't take up a whole lot of his working day; teams played 2–3–5 and that was that. But, as with H, King had an eye for a transfer target. Among others, he signed Vic Watson – who will never be surpassed as the club's record goal scorer.

Charlie Paynter replaced King in 1933, remaining in charge until 1950. Like Redknapp, he took over at a difficult time for the club and turned things around. (When isn't it a difficult time at West Ham?) And he, too, was never short of a few words when asked his opinion about footballing matters. I was lucky enough to meet Paynter's daughter Olive, who was still a regular at Upton Park well into her seventies. She was a friend of my parents-in-law, and a lovely lady she was, too.

Next up was Ted Fenton, who had a reputation as a skinflint and was intensely disliked by many of his leading players – not least club captain Malcolm Allison. The flamboyant Allison, who, like so many West Ham players of that era, went on to have an influential career in management, must take some of the credit for changing the football philosophy at Upton Park. Although Fenton was no great tactician himself, he was prepared to listen to new ideas and give the youngsters a chance and, just as Redknapp was to introduce the likes of Rio Ferdinand and Joe Cole to the first team, he promoted John Bond and Ken Brown – who went on to become club legends.

Fenton's successor was Ron Greenwood, who clearly thought enough of Redknapp to give him his chance in the first team. He certainly had a huge influence on the younger man's thinking when he, too, went into management.

Greenwood's West Ham Way is often dismissed by its detractors, since a club that had Hurst, Moore, Peters and Brooking should have won far more than it did. But the lack of trophies is due more to his failings as a man-manager than any flaw in his basic thinking about the way game should be played. He couldn't motivate, and often he couldn't communicate. 'Ron talked about the game at such a high level that sometimes he went straight over the head of the average player,' Bobby Moore told Jeff Powell in his authorised biography. 'Some days I believe there were only a couple of us who understood a word he was on about. He never seemed to realise that he should have been talking down to more than half the team.'

One man who *did* understand Greenwood's way of thinking was his chief disciple, John Lyall – who, many years after his mentor had left the club, came within a whisker of winning the League playing the West Ham Way.

John Lyall is without doubt my favourite manager of all time. He won us two FA Cups, brought us some fabulous nights of European football, masterminded our highest ever League finish and got his teams to produce some breathtaking football. Best of all: he took the time and trouble to write to my wife and me with some very kind words when we got married even though he'd never met us.

Remember Simon, our best man? You met him briefly at Villa Park in the semi-final against Forest. He wrote to Lyall explaining that Di and I were two lifelong supporters who were about to tie the knot and he hoped to surprise us at the reception by including a few words from him when he came to read out the congratulatory telegrams. And the West Ham manager sat down and penned a letter that we both cherish to this day. It's in the album with the photographs if you'd like to have a look. No? Maybe later, then.

The year we got married turned out to be disastrous for West Ham. Two years before, the Boys of '86 had been in with a sniff of the first division title until the penultimate game of the season, finishing in third place just four points behind champions Liverpool. Now the Bozos of '88 were about to embark on a campaign that was to get us relegated and cost Lyall his job after an astonishing thirty-four years with the club.

So, as my old English teacher used to say, let us compare and contrast.

At the start of the 1985/86 season, the game of association football was at an all-time low in England following two appalling tragedies. On 11 May 1985, fifty-six people died and more than 250 were injured as fire swept through the main stand at Valley Parade in Bradford. The disaster was shown live on television. I watched it in the newsroom of the *Mail on Sunday*, surrounded by hard-bitten journalists who could only shake their heads in disbelief at the horror unfolding in front of them. Then, eighteen days later, thirty-nine people died at the Heysel Stadium in Brussels, which was staging the European Cup final between Liverpool and Juventus. Again, the TV cameras were there to record the sickening scenes. In fact, the BBC was heavily criticised for then showing the game while other countries opted not to as a mark of respect to the dead.

There was, however, to be no television coverage of the first half of the new domestic season when it got under way in August.

Football League chairmen, ignoring the falling attendances concerning everyone else, demanded more money from the TV companies to show games that fewer and fewer people could be bothered to watch. They finally had to climb down in December, by which time West Ham had snuck up on the usual suspects and joined the likes of Man Utd and Liverpool in the title race.

November had been a particularly good month. We had won all five games, including a victory over defending champions Everton. Frank McAvennie's goal in a 1–0 win at Coventry took his tally for the season to seventeen – the highest in the entire Football League.

December and January brought mixed fortunes, then in February – just before the weather turned nasty and put a temporary halt to proceedings – a 2–1 win over Man Utd at the Boleyn Ground made the more optimistic among the West Ham congregation start to wonder if this really, finally, could be our year.

After the snow cleared we played Man Utd again in early March – this time in the fifth round of the FA Cup. The first game, at Upton Park, was a 1–1 draw; then the following week we went to Old Trafford and won the replay 2–0. Forget the League title – now we wanted the double!

That little dream went up in smoke three days later when we crashed out of the Cup at Sheffield Wednesday. Hopes of becoming champions seemed to be fading fast too as we lost at Arsenal and Villa. However, revenge against Wednesday at home, followed by a thumping 4–0 win at Chelsea and a 2–1 victory against Spurs at Upton Park, meant the bandwagon was well and truly rolling once more.

Phil Parkes was brilliant in goal. Ray Stewart, at right back, never put a foot wrong. Alvin Martin and Tony Gale, in the centre of defence, were imperious. The tireless Alan Devonshire and an assured Alan Dickens were running the midfield. Mark Ward was causing havoc on the flank. And, up front, McAvennie and Tony Cottee were simply too hot to handle.

At the start of April we were fifth. What a month that turned out to be. It began badly, with defeat at Nottingham Forest. Then came a run of eight games in twenty-two days, which was to prove almost as exhausting for the supporters as it must have been for the players. Di and I were living in west London back then. But if we'd spent any more time in East Ham they would have made us pay the poll tax there.

It was obvious that we weren't the only ones going straight from work to midweek games. Guys sitting near us in the West Stand, who would turn up in jeans and a sweater on a Saturday (replica shirts had yet to become the garment of choice for dedicated followers of football fashion), took their seats on a Wednesday wearing the sharp suits and loud ties that were de rigueur for their loadsamoney jobs in the City. It's funny how a volley of foul-mouthed abuse directed at a referee seems strangely incongruous when it comes from someone who is suited and booted.

After the Forest game there were two home wins, against Southampton and Oxford. Next up was Chelsea and 29,360 of us packed Upton Park ... only to watch us lose 2–1. There has never been much love lost between the supporters of West Ham and those of Chelsea, and after the game the police had their work cut out keeping the rival thugs from kicking the crap out of one another in Green Street. My God, the atmosphere was ugly. Nights such as that can make you question why you go to football matches.

On the Saturday we won at Watford, then, two days later, came a game that will forever stick in the memories of the West Ham fans who were lucky enough to be there. The scoreline will give you a clue as to why: West Ham 8 Newcastle 1. Or, as it used to say on the teleprinter when *Grandstand* broadcast the results as they came in: West Ham 8 (eight) Newcastle 1.

Not only was it a remarkable goal-fest, this game also produced one of the best pub quiz questions of all time:

Q: Who scored a hat-trick against three different goalkeepers?
A: Alvin Martin.

The comings and goings of the Newcastle keepers that night read like a plotline from *Casualty*, so I'll spare you the gory details. But I will just mention Glenn Roeder, who was to go on to manage West Ham and somehow contrived to get possibly the most talented set of players we've ever had at the same time on the books relegated. That night he scored an own goal and conceded the penalty Martin converted to take his improbable place in the record books. To be honest, Glenn, you and West Ham were clearly never meant to be an item.

I'd also like to take this opportunity to tip my hat in the direction of the Newcastle fans who were there that night. As the goals rained in they never stopped singing. It was a fantastic show of support, and I've had a soft spot for the Geordies ever since.

Next up was Coventry, then Manchester City. Both were nervy affairs, and both ended with 1–0 victories that really did put us in with a serious chance of winning the League. Then came Ipswich, our final home game of the season. A capacity crowd in excess of 31,000 was there to see it – blimey, it must have been cosy on the terraces. As ever that season we were seated in the West Stand – at least we were at the start of the match. By the end of it we were standing on the seats, celebrating a 2–1 victory that put us up into second and left the title within touching distance. The bemused, beaming face of my future father-in-law as ecstatic fans poured on to the pitch summed up how we were all feeling better than words ever could. Sid had supported West Ham since time began. This was the first occasion he had stood on a seat at Upton Park.

In the end it all turned out to be a bit of a damp squib. In the penultimate game of the season we did what we had to do at West Brom, but Liverpool beat Chelsea at Stamford Bridge to squeeze us out of contention for the greatest prize in English football. Ah well, you can't win 'em all.

Fast forward a couple of years and it was a very different story. While my wife and I were enjoying our honeymoon, West Ham were in the process of signing two of the worst players who have ever turned out for the club. Striker David Kelly was awful; goalkeeper Allen McKnight was worse. The rest of the team were either past their best or not very good in the first place. The 1988/89 season started badly. And by Christmas it was obvious to most people that we were in serious trouble.

It was certainly crystal clear to the old boy sitting behind Di and me in the West Stand. He came up with the finest piece of analysis I have heard before or since as we watched a Spurs side inspired by Paul Gascoigne tear us to shreds.

It was half time in a game we were clearly destined to lose when Waldorf turned to Statler and announced that he was far from impressed with what he was watching. In fact, he had some quite trenchant views about the capabilities of our brave lads.

In front of me now I have the programme listing the players who represented my beloved West Ham United that day. Before I give you Mr Waldorf's opinions of those warriors (which I can remember word for word), let me give you a flavour of *Hammer* as it was back then.

This particular copy cost me £1.25 and has brought back a legion of memories. The cover features Alan Devonshire, complete with a very questionable moustache and an Avco shirt, doing his best to avoid having lumps kicked out of him by Sheffield Wednesday, who we'd played the previous week. Hmmm, I can see that has whetted your appetite. So make yourself comfortable and we'll flick through the pages of history together.

Inside we are told that this will be the eighty-third meeting between West Ham and Tottenham in the Football League, and Spurs have thirty wins to our twenty-nine.

John Lyall concedes that we could have done with the extra two points in the 0–0 draw against Wednesday, but remains optimistic even though we are second from bottom – and even that is because of goal difference rather than a greater number of points than Newcastle. Norwich are top of the table. Coventry are third. And The Hated Millwall are fifth. Millwall! How shocking is that?

However, there is good news on the south London front. Two weeks previously we had beaten the Lions of Lewisham 1–0 at the Den to record our 1,000th League win – and there is a selection of very iffy pictures in the programme to supposedly prove it.

There are much nicer photographs of a very young Gazza and a very old Phil Parkes, too. Big Phil, in fact, is profiled as Hammer of the Week, even though he wasn't actually playing that Saturday. At thirty-eight, his knees weren't all they should be – but that didn't stop him turning out for the Guinness Soccer Sixes in Manchester, at which we did rather well. Six-a-side soccer, it seems, was about to become all the rage. Wonder what happened to that?

Parkes wasn't the only one in the treatment room according to the programme. Stewart Robson, Ray Stewart and Stuart Slater were all in there with him. There's no mention of Rod Stewart, though.

Page 7 is a particularly good read; in addition to a couple of very upbeat letters predicting an imminent improvement in our fortunes and the Crocker's Corner segment, which records that West Ham's contribution to Children in Need that year was £800, there is also an extremely useful guide to the misinformation surrounding drink-driving. Excuses such as 'the pub only sold alcohol so there was nothing else to drink', 'there was no other way to get home', and 'booze improves the way you handle a car' are all – it turns out – 'drivel'! I can't believe I didn't cut out that panel and stick it on the fridge years ago.

A few pages on, you find details of ticket prices for the forthcoming third-round FA Cup tie against Arsenal (which we would draw 2–2, with the Gooners' goals coming from Paul Merson). Season ticket-holders are asked to apply using Voucher F; paying punters can get in for as little as a fiver.

There are season tickets to be had in the programme as well. The best seats in the house could be purchased for £63. And if you wanted to see out the rest of that miserable season standing on the East Terrace – aka the Chicken Run – you could do so for just £35. And if this offer wasn't tempting enough, they were prepared to throw in a free bottle of wine as well. I think that's a nice touch, although admittedly it wouldn't have gone far if your dinner guests had included Gazza and Merse.

Fascinating though all this is, the real story lies on the back page. No, it's not the fact that the match ball sponsor was TUA of Islington Green (suppliers of quality office furniture), nor that the referee was Daryll Reeves from Uxbridge, who would officiate with the help of linesmen G. H. Bargery (red trim) and A. C. Williams (yellow trim).

It is on the back page where we find the two teams who were being discussed in the row behind me that day. Specifically the team in claret and blue.

'Bloody West Ham – nothing but has-beens and wankers,' was Waldorf's verdict.

'How d'you mean?' asked Statler. It was a question I was keen to hear answered myself. Waldorf then went through the team, one by one, and made his case.

McKnight – wanker. Potts – wanker. Parris – wanker. Gale – has-been. Martin – has-been. Devonshire – has-been. Brady – has-been. Kelly – wanker. Rosenior – wanker. Dickens – wanker. And all this in a calm, measured tone that brooked no argument. The only one to escape his forensic analysis was a certain Paul Ince, who our resident expert conceded was a decent player and therefore wouldn't be at the club much longer. How right he turned out to be.

Try as I might, I couldn't fault his assessment (although Steve Potts, who hadn't yet played thirty games for us, did go on to be a club legend). The professional pundits are paid handsomely to come up with more drivel than a drunk driver facing a breathalyser test – the bloke in the row behind nailed it in a few, short, Anglo-Saxon words. And not a single mention of 'stardust'.

The football we were playing was rubbish, and the man at the helm had lost the plot. Hard on the heels of masterminding the club's highest ever League finish, the dignified and thoughtful John Lyall was facing relegation and, soon after, the sack. It was a remarkable decline in anybody's book, but a roller-coaster ride is part of the deal at Upton Park. It may not be the West Ham Way, but it's certainly the West Ham way.

Chapter 6

Funeral for a friend

THERE CAN'T BE a football supporter in the country who isn't familiar with 'I'm Forever Blowing Bubbles', my club's singular anthem, which suggests fortune is always hiding and dreams are destined for a premature death. Most opposition fans, at one time or another, have twisted the words and sung them back at us as: 'And like West Ham they fade and die.' Those who taunt us may be sadly lacking in imagination, but unfortunately they sometimes have a point.

There is an alternative version of 'Bubbles', sung to the tune of 'Chitty Chitty Bang Bang', which is invariably saved for away games. However, why we sing the song at all has a good deal less to do with a Hollywood film about Caractacus Potts than it does with a soap opera featuring a man with the equally splendid name of Cornelius Beal. And, being an epic saga, this one doesn't appear to be reaching a conclusion any time soon.

The basic storyline involves a music-hall song, a curly haired kid and an advert for soap. The sub-plot is that some eminent historians aren't convinced it's accurate.

Let's start with what we do know to be true. 'I'm Forever Blowing Bubbles' was copyrighted in 1919 in the US and, after crossing the Atlantic, became a hit here in the early 1920s.

This was the time a young lad called Will Murray was making a name for himself at West Ham. Murray had been nicknamed 'Bubbles' by his headmaster, Cornelius Beal. He got the name because, in Beal's eyes at least, he looked like the child whose angelic face had featured in advertising hoardings on a poster known as *Bubbles*. The Pears soap company, which was based in Canning Town, had acquired the rights to a nineteenth-century painting by Sir John Everett Millais of his five-year-old grandson watching a soap bubble float in the air and had added a bar of their own product. This was the *Bubbles* poster that was the centrepiece of a nationwide ad campaign.

What could be more natural than for a football crowd to adopt a popular song with obvious links to the club, first to hail one of its favourite sons, then to salute the team itself? A fascinating booklet, *The 'Bubbles' Legend*, is in no doubt that this is what happened. And its author is certainly well placed to make a judgement – he is Graham Murray, son of Will.

Historian John Simkin, who has been following West Ham for even longer than I have, is not convinced. He says:

> There is a photograph in existence of Murray in 1921. He looks nothing like the *Bubbles* painting. Nor could he, as the

painting shows a five-year-old boy, not a teenager. He has dark rather than fair hair. It is fairly curly, but nothing like the original painting or indeed the Pears adverts that were in existence in the early 1920s.

However, Graham Murray's booklet contains a hand-written reference from Beal that talks of 'W. Murray, the famous Bubbles, who is as good at his work as at his play.' In fact, there are a number of photos of Will Murray in 1921, including one with his teammates of the triumphant Park School side – coached by their headmaster. 'It was Corney Beal, as he was affectionately known, who linked members of his team to popular songs,' says Murray Jnr, adding that Bubbles had acquired his nickname because of his supposed resemblance to the boy in the Pears posters.

But did the West Ham supporters make the same connection? 'Will Murray never played for the West Ham first team,' Simkin points out. 'Is it really credible that the Upton Park fans would sing a song about a player who never made it into the first team?'

Bubbles Murray was certainly a promising youngster and could well have gone on to make a career as a professional if he hadn't opted for the security of a job as a shipping clerk instead. He was a regular on the West Ham Boys sides of 1919–23 and huge crowds turned up at Upton Park to watch them play. 'Perhaps the greatest occasion was in 1921 when they lost to Liverpool Boys 2–3 in the final of the English Schools Championship in the presence of the Duke of York, the future king George VI, in front of 30,000 spectators,' says his son.

So William Murray was clearly a star at the Boleyn Ground when 'I'm Forever Blowing Bubbles' was being popularised in Britain by variety artist Dorothy Ward. When was the song first heard there, though? It is possible to confirm that the Beckton Gas Works Band played it at Upton Park before matches on occasions, although no one knows quite when. But Simkin makes the point that, contrary to popular myth, West Ham fans did not sing 'Bubbles' at the 1923 Cup final, which they surely would have if it had been adopted as the terrace anthem.

He thinks the answer to why we sing 'Bubbles' has been unearthed by fellow historian Brian Belton, who says the song became a morale-boosting favourite with the poor devils who were forced to take shelter in the air raid shelters and Underground stations as the East End took cover from Hitler's Luftwaffe during the Blitz. Simkin says:

> According to Belton, the first time the song was reported to be sung by West Ham fans was during the 1940 League War Cup final at Wembley. This was a game that the Irons won and maybe the fans took it as a good luck omen. Anyway, that appears to me to be the most logical reason.

I wish the legend were true. Will Murray had a famous cousin, Syd Puddefoot, who was unquestionably West Ham's most glamorous star in the '20s. In turn, Puddefoot had a nephew called Den, who became close friends with my father when they served together in the RAF during the Second World War. It was Den who introduced my dad to my mum, which eventually resulted in me. So, by an admittedly roundabout way, I would have family ties with my club's anthem if young Will really had prompted it all.

But it's hard to argue with John Simkin, founder of the Tressell publishing corporation, the brains behind the Spartacus Educational website and a man with three university degrees. The clincher for me is his point that there appear to be no newspaper reports of supporters singing it at all before the Second World War. And that's why I'm kicking myself now. I spent years in the company of a man who could have answered the simple question – did you sing 'Bubbles' at Upton Park between the wars? Because Sid, my fabulous father-in-law, was there. I just never thought to ask him.

'Bubbles' has been heard in some unlikely places. Sheffield Wednesday supporters have taunted their city rivals with it. Apparently, Arsenal fans sang it at Highbury at the end of the 2005/06 season as we were paving the Gooners' way into Europe at Tottenham's expense by beating Spurs 2–1 in the 'lasagne-gate' encounter. (Always happy to help when we can!) And Tony Gale was the choirmaster when it was heard coming from the Blackburn dressing room as they celebrated winning the Premier League title in 1995 after we had denied Man Utd the win they needed at Upton Park. 'I had to teach all those northern blokes the words,' Gale told me. I could have asked Sid about 'Bubbles' then: I was sitting next to him in the Bobby Moore Upper.

The game produced a strange little incident that still makes me smile whenever it comes to mind. News of a Liverpool goal against Rovers, which was all part of the equation if United were to secure the title, sparked a wild celebration among the Manchester fans in what is now the Sir Trevor Brooking Stand just as the ball rolled out harmlessly on the halfway line. From where we were sitting, unaware of – and uninterested in – what has happening at Anfield, it appeared the entire opposition support was ecstatic at being awarded a throw-in. My father-in-law thought it was hilarious.

Sid never did lose his childlike sense of fun. Once, when clambering around in the loft, he put his foot through the ceiling and actually saw the funny side.

Sid was the sort of man who, when required to decorate a room, would paint a giant elephant on one of the walls before getting down to the real job he had been sent in there to do. He'd let his pachyderm dry before emulsioning over it, but even when he covered the wall in the same colour you could always make it out in relief after he finished – much to my mother-in-law's annoyance. What do I mean he was 'the sort of man'? He was the *only* man who ever left the image of an elephant in every room of his house. I can't tell you how much I liked that bloke.

It's a fair bet 'Bubbles' has never been sung anywhere less like a football stadium than St Bride's Church in Fleet Street. The choir's rendition is quite easily the most moving I've ever heard, although – as you'll see if you bear with me for a while longer – I wish above all else that I'd heard them sing it in very different circumstances…

There are a number of West Ham fans who don't like 'Bubbles' because of what they consider to be the defeatist lyrics. Geoff Ellen was one of them. I first met Geoff in 1989 – the year the Berlin Wall came down. Not that our meeting had anything to do with the momentous event that revolutionised Europe – I merely throw it in for a bit of historical context. While the Trabbies were heading west for the Brandenburg Gate in search of a better and brighter future, I had decided to do the same thing by going north across the River Thames – from the *Daily Express*'s building on the south side of Blackfriars Bridge to *The Guardian*'s offices in Farringdon Road.

When I started my new job I thought I had made the biggest mistake of my working life. Unbeknown to me, one of my mates who had made the same transition the previous year had told my new, refined, broadsheet colleagues they were about to be joined by a bruiser from the tabloids who would seemingly be appointed to a fairly junior position but was actually there to sit among them for a month or so, observing their drunken ways, before taking up a senior managerial post and kicking their idle arses into shape.

He had done this a few days before I was due to arrive. Apparently the idea was to allow my new workmates to suffer for a bit, then let them in on the joke before I got there. Unfortunately for me, my 'mate' forgot all about his off-the-cuff prank almost as quickly as he had dreamt it up and failed to tell anyone that this was all just a hilarious gag.

When I turned up to start my new job, the reception I got was a good deal less than friendly. For the first couple of weeks I toiled away knowing there was a big black cloud over my head, but not understanding why it was there. Geoff was on holiday for those two weeks. When he got back he took one look at me and decided that the cuckoo-in-the-nest story was nonsense. Maybe he was an excellent judge of character. Perhaps it was the fact we were both lifelong Hammers. Whatever the reason, we became firm friends right from the off.

Geoff had a heart the size of a house – but he refused to listen to it when it came to having a punt. Bet with your head, not your heart, was Geoff's maxim. While his preferred way of enriching the bookies was via the horses, he wasn't averse to gambling on football matches either. And the fact he was actually prepared to back West Ham to lose really annoyed me.

Not that you could stay annoyed with Geoff for long. He was just too likeable. They say some people can start a fight in an empty room. Geoff was just the opposite. On a trip to Fratton Park one bitterly cold day he insisted that, rather than risk hypothermia by loitering outside for a couple of hours before kickoff, we should find ourselves a nice warm pub. The problem was the only pub we could find was rammed with Portsmouth supporters, who do not enjoy a reputation for being among the most hospitable. Geoff was talking to a group of them straight away, making no bones about the fact that we were there to support West Ham (with that Dagenham accent it would have been difficult to have done much else), but doing it in such a way that no one could take offence. By the time we left I swear he could have got the Pompey lads to have sung 'Bubbles' if he had chosen to do so.

His habit of calling everyone 'mate' helped. Even complete strangers were 'mate' to Geoff. What only a few people knew was he could never remember people's names, so, by addressing friend and foe alike, no one cottoned on when he'd had a temporary lapse of memory. I have to admit, it's a trick I have found myself using more frequently as the years roll on.

Come the start of the 1990/91 season, I was starting to feel quite optimistic about West Ham's chances of securing promotion. The previous year in the second division had been one of turmoil at Upton Park (nothing new there, I hear the cynics at the back of the class say) and we had failed to even make the play-offs. Lou Macari had come and gone as manager; Paul Ince had left too – but not before being inducted into the Hall of Infamy by being pictured wearing a Man Utd shirt while still earning his money as a West Ham player. And the hopes of another Wembley appearance had been washed away in the pouring rain with a 6–0 drubbing at Oldham in the first leg of a League Cup semi-final.

But, as ever, a new season brings new hope and, as Geoff and I discussed the fixture list, I became increasingly bullish about our prospects. There was no one in the division to fear as far as I could see. Charlton, Sheffield Wednesday and The Hated Millwall had been relegated from the division above us, while the two Bristol clubs and Notts County had joined us from the one below. More to the point, Billy Bonds was about to start his first full season in charge as manager – and with Bonzo at the helm nothing could possibly go wrong.

'We'll go unbeaten until Christmas,' I predicted confidently. Geoff looked at me scornfully over his pint of beer (he always wanted to know if I fancied going for 'a pint of beer', rather than just 'a pint') and shook his head. 'I'll give you odds of 100–1 that we don't,' he replied.

His lack of enthusiasm really got my hackles up. 'Go on, then – I'll have a tenner with you,' I said, thinking he would have to back down in the face of that sort of risk. Geoff was a serious gambler and I didn't have to tell him that my £10 would become £1,000 in the unlikely – but not impossible – event of West Ham justifying my faith in them. 'You're on,' he said with a smile. 'What's more, I'll give you League only – it doesn't count if we get beaten in Cup games. Still fancy it?'

Damn right I did. In fact, I couldn't wait for the first game to kick off the following Saturday. Deep down I suspected I'd have to give Judas his pieces of silver, but I really wanted him to sweat first. First up was Middlesbrough at Ayresome Park, and we came away with a point after a no-score stalemate. Then a Frank McAvennie goal secured a 1–1 draw against Portsmouth at Upton Park. The season had started relatively late that year (I think they wanted to give the nation some extra time to mend its broken heart after the World Cup disappointment of Italia '90) and those two results meant I had at least got through August with my bet – and my pride – intact.

September offered more of a challenge. The first day of the month saw us beat Watford 1–0 at Upton Park, thanks to a goal from the mighty Julian Dicks. (Can I just clear something up for those of you who don't support West Ham at this point: Dicksy was not 'Mad Dog' as so many of you seem to think. That was Martin Allen. Julian was 'The Terminator'. Although, should you ever bump into either of them on a dark night, I suggest you stick with plain 'Mister'.)

The following week we went to Leicester and won 2–1, with the help of an own goal and an effort from Trevor Morley. Interestingly – for West Ham fans at least – the Leicester strike force consisted of David Kelly, who had performed so poorly for us in the previous two seasons, and Paul Kitson, who would later do so much to help us avoid relegation when Harry Redknapp, to quote his immortal phrase, reckoned we needed snookers.

Next came Wolves, an early Alvin Martin goal from close range and a 1–1 draw. The highlight for me was watching another young hopeful make his initial appearance for West Ham. Between you and me, I have a bit of a fetish about debuts. The thought that the player you are watching for the first time could go on to be a claret and blue hero always gives me a bit of a tingle (but in a very masculine way, you understand). In this case it was a lad called Simon Livett. Anyone remember him? You do? To be honest, sir, I don't believe you. This was his only League appearance for us. In fact he turned out just four times in West Ham colours and one of those was in a friendly against Panathinaikos at Highbury. Ah, you were at the Makita tournament, too. We must get together and swap memories some time. No, not now, I'm afraid – I'm rather busy just at the moment.

After the Wolves game came a midweek encounter with Ipswich, and we tonked them 3–1. Ian Bishop, Morley and Jimmy 'the tree' Quinn had us out of our seats that night.

Bonzo's team wasn't packed with the starriest names in West Ham's history, but they were starting to play well. Despite my glowing (and gloating) reports of the matches I had been to, Geoff was showing no signs of panic. He was confident that the next two games would win him his money – we were away to Newcastle and then Sheffield Wednesday. I listened nervously to the radio as the results came in. Both games ended 1–1. First Morley, then Dicks, had kept our bet alive.

October's fixture list was packed with winnable games, which is usually a worrying time for West Ham supporters. Oxford were dispatched 2–0 at home, then Hull were put to the sword in a mis-match that has gone down in East End folklore not so much for the remarkable scoreline, but for one of the scorers.

Steve Potts spent seventeen years at Upton Park, making a total of 506 appearances in all competitions, and his one and only goal came in this game. I'd like to tell you it was a 30-yard match-winning screamer that left the keeper grasping thin air as the net bulged behind him. Sadly, the truth is rather different: yes, the shot was from distance, but your mum could have saved it. The Hull shot-stopper, however, failed to fulfil the terms of his job description and let it slip under his body. The ball trickled into the net and we went on to win 7–1.

The following Saturday we were away to Bristol City, who came up with the brilliant idea of trying to dissuade the West Ham support from travelling by organising a 10.30 a.m. kickoff. Nice try! In the event, 5,000 of us bombed down the M4 and saw McAvennie come off the bench to score in a 1–1 draw. The only trouble with starting a game at this time is that it gives a lot of thirsty supporters a chance to adjourn to the local pub afterwards (soft drinks only for designated drivers, of course). And not every city wants to entertain a bunch of chirpy cockneys who've got a few sherbets inside them. You won't make that mistake again in a hurry, will you, Bristol?

I had hoped to satisfy my strange longings to see a debut performance at Ashton Gate, but Bonzo didn't wheel out the newly signed Tim Breaker until the following week at Swindon, and we didn't go to that game. Another effort from McAvennie ensured a 1–0 win, then, in midweek, Ian Bishop scored a blinder, which turned out to be the only goal against Blackburn at Upton Park, before we rounded off the October League programme with a 2–1 home win against Charlton, courtesy of two goals from Mad Dog. We were now second in the table and still unbeaten. Geoff was starting to look distinctly worried whenever I mentioned our bet. This was turning out to be fun!

Although League Cup games weren't part of our financial arrangement, Geoff and I decided to go to the third round tie at Oxford for the simple reason that he lived there. It was just as well for me the game didn't count – we lost 2–1. Even so, I hate to see West Ham lose and the drive back to Brighton was tinged with disappointment. Little did Di and I realise that the next time we would take our VW Golf to the city of dreaming spires, barely three months later, it would be in the saddest circumstances imaginable.

November began with a 1–0 win at Notts County, followed by a 1–1 draw at The Hated Millwall, with Morley and McAvennie doing the honours. Di and I sat those ones out (which meant we missed Chris Hughton's debut) but, let's face it, a girl can have too much of a good thing. We were, however, in our seats in the West Stand on 17 November for the game against Brighton and Hove Albion. We had no way of knowing it then, of course, but one year to the day after that, Di would give birth to our first child – in Brighton. Spooky or what? Stranger still, big Colin Foster got his name on the scoresheet that day. That, and a goal from Stuart Slater, secured a 2–1 win.

The following week, a 1–0 victory at Plymouth (McAvennie again) put us top of the table – a position we cemented on 1 December with a 3–1 demolition of West Brom at Upton Park thanks to Macca, Morley and the legendary George Parris.

That bet was now starting to concern me. It's one thing ripping the piss out of a close friend about the possibility of relieving them of a thousand quid – it's quite another doing it. I knew by then that if West Ham could hold out for just three more games, and go unbeaten to Christmas as I had predicted, I would never ask for the money. But I was worried that Geoff would insist on honouring his obligations – he was a serious punter and would hate the thought of welshing on a gambling debt.

The next game was at Portsmouth – that's the one where we found ourselves in the pub with the Pompey fans. Strewth, it was cold that day. Di, me, Geoff and the wonderful woman in his life, Dee, were huddled at the back of the main Portsmouth stand.

When Morley scored the goal that was to give us a 1–0 win, our enthusiastic celebration was more an excuse to get the blood circulating again than an expression of joy. Even so, it earned us some filthy looks from the home fans.

I don't think I'd thawed out properly by the time we dogged out a 0–0 draw with Boro at Upton Park seven days later. So this was it – one game left and me on the point of winning a grand that I no longer wanted. How could our friendship survive if I won? Geoff would either be offended by my refusal to accept his money, or left flat broke if I did. In the event a Barnsley player called Smith spared me the misery of finding out. His goal meant we went down 1–0 at Oakwell, and Geoff had been proved right – when it comes to gambling you must let your head rule your heart. Mind you, had he not been so obsessed with the form book he might have backed a horse called Upton Park, which was running at Chepstow while we were losing in Barnsley. Geoff reckoned it had no chance. It romped home at 16–1.

Two weeks later, on the Saturday, it was Geoff's forty-second birthday and, by way of a present, West Ham failed to beat Aldershot in the third round of the Cup. The following day I rang to tell him how the West Ham fans had given the visitors a standing ovation after their battling performance. Then, on Monday, I got a call from Dee that left me numbed with disbelief. Geoff had died overnight. He had gone to bed with a headache and never woken up. It was a brain haemorrhage – nothing could have been done to save him. We got the call early in the morning. The enormity of what had happened didn't truly hit me until the afternoon. Di and I were shopping in Sainsbury's when the tears began to fall from my eyes.

It came as no surprise that the funeral was to be a non-religious affair: Geoff was a fully paid up atheist and to have had a Christian burial would have been plain wrong. Equally wrong, in the eyes of many of us who had congregated to say a final farewell to our friend, was the way in which the Socialist Workers Party turned such a deeply personal event into a political rally. Leading lefty Paul Foot gave a tub-thumping speech that made Geoff out to be something he wasn't; they draped his coffin in the red flag then sang 'The Internationale' when his coffin was lowered into the grave. They even had a whip-round at the wake to boost party funds.

Geoff's dad didn't share his son's political views – in fact he was a lifelong Tory (although that didn't stop him giving the Trots a cheque for a hundred quid when they passed the hat round – grief can do strange things to a man). Geoff had told me that politics had sometimes soured their relationship when he was younger, and there were times that the only subject they could agree on was West Ham. His dad was a season ticket-holder and he'd taken Geoff to games regularly.

Although Fleet Street journalists tend to be a fairly secular bunch, we do have our own parish church. It's called St Bride's, and it does a marvellous line in memorial services – which is handy for people who feel the funeral they have just attended is an inadequate way of channelling their sorrow. They like to throw in the odd prayer and an occasional hymn but, in general, they will shape the service to your bespoke requirements. You can even ask the choir to sing 'Bubbles'. Unlike most West Ham supporters, they know the words to the verses as well as the chorus.

For the record, the first verse goes like this:

I'm dreaming dreams,

I'm scheming schemes,

I'm building castles high.

They're born anew,

Their days are few,

Just like a sweet butterfly.

And as the daylight is dawning,

They come again in the morning.

The second isn't quite as snappy:

When shadows creep,

When I'm asleep,

To lands of hope I stray.

Then at daybreak,

When I awake,

My bluebird flutters away.

Happiness new seemed so near me,

Happiness come forth and heal me.

I have seen a version of the lyrics that suggests the first line of the second verse is: 'When cattle creep'. But, let's be honest, have you ever seen cattle creeping in the East End of London? Either way, in the hands of such a brilliant choir the song is magical. By the time they had raised the roof of St Bride's with their unique version, there wasn't a dry eye in the church. As I cleared the lump that was the size of a football from my throat, I looked over at Geoff's parents. No one truly gets over the loss of their children, no matter what age they are. But the look on his dad's face suggested that, for him, the healing process had at least begun.

As I mentioned before, later that year Di and I were to have a child of our own. Some years down the line a colleague, who clearly knows me better than I'd imagined, asked if the fact we had named him Geoff had anything to do with either my boy-hood hero or a sadly missed friend. To be honest, it's starting to look like my son will never score a hat-trick in a World Cup final (although a father never truly gives up hope), but if he can make others feel lucky to have known him, in the way Geoff Ellen did, I will be more than happy. And, I'm proud to say, my son can belt out 'Bubbles' with the best of 'em.

Chapter 7

The ghosts of Christmas

I N A N E F F O R T to do my bit for charity I would like to help an aged joke find a new home by asking if you know why West Ham are like Christmas decorations? All together now: they both come down in the New Year.

Actually, there is rather less to this old chestnut than you might think.

In 1964, the year we first won the FA Cup and the time this all started to matter to me, we finished fourteenth. On Boxing Day 1963 we had suffered the club's record home defeat as we crashed 8–2 to Blackburn, leaving us in sixteenth place. (According to a report in the *Daily Mirror*, West Ham's 'tactics were all wrong and their covering terrible'. Sadly, that wasn't the last time anyone was to say that about the Hammers.) From sixteenth to fourteenth is, of course, an improvement of two places. By the time I had chalked up my golden anniversary of following West Ham, the second half of the season had seen us slip down the League on twenty-two occasions. But we'd also improved our position in twenty-two seasons and finished in the same place we were in on Boxing Day six times.

Admittedly, the reason we don't plummet after Christmas is usually because we haven't got very high beforehand. Our most spectacular decline was a fall of twelve places – from sixth to eighteenth in 1975/76, but that can largely be explained by a fantastic run in the European Cup Winners' Cup, which took us all the way to the final. The previous season – again one that ended with a Cup final – saw us fall eight places from the dizzy heights of fifth on Boxing Day to finish thirteenth. I suspect that was when the 'decorations' gag was first unwrapped.

In our heart of hearts most West Ham fans do not expect to win the League. The highest we have ever finished is third, and I fear that is as good as it's going to get for me. Having watched the team I love get relegated five times, I'm prepared to settle for mid-table security in my old age, maybe with the occasional top-half finish thrown in for good measure (on average they only come around once every three years).

The FA Cup, on the other hand, does offer hope of success once you've got the last of the Christmas tree needles out of the carpet. In my lifetime we've been to the final four times, winning three of them and coming within a whisker of beating Liverpool at the Millennium Stadium in 2006. And, of course, West Ham contested the first final at Wembley in 1923, which is now better remembered for Billy the white horse than the result. (For those of you who like to dot the 'i's and cross the 't's, it finished 2–0 to

Bolton and Billy the horse eventually got a bridge at Wembley Tube station named in his honour.)

The FA Cup really matters to West Ham supporters. We have the tradition, and we sometimes have the realistic chance of winning the six games that earn a captain the right to hold aloft football's most glamorous piece of silverware. So when the draw for the third round is made, many of those in claret and blue hope to get off to a flying start by being paired with a team from the lower divisions. Not me. I'd much rather play the likes of Manchester United than one of the small fry – our record in such games is not exactly spotless.

My first experience of enduring a giant-killing that amused the rest of the nation while throwing me into a well of depression was against third division Swindon in the 1967 FA Cup. I was ten, and took these things personally. (I still do, to be honest.)

West Ham went to the County Ground for the third-round replay with all three of our World Cup-winning heroes. And they came back with their tails between their legs after being turned over 3–1.

I tried to console myself with the thought that this was a once-in-a-lifetime disaster – a team that contained the likes of Moore, Hurst and Peters and had triumphed in Europe only a couple of years before would never allow itself to suffer that sort of humiliation again.

Two years later we went to Mansfield in the fifth round of the Cup. Not only did we have the World Cup winners, we had Trevor Brooking and Billy Bonds as well. What could possibly go wrong?

This time we failed to score against our third division opponents, while they got what was now becoming the customary three by repeatedly pumping the long ball into our penalty area and wait-ing for the inevitable defensive errors. Simple. Ugly. But invariably successful against West Ham back then.

The Swindon defeat had been hard enough to swallow. Mansfield was far worse. My Chelsea-supporting schoolmates were now, like me, two years older – and starting to master the art of taking the piss. I'm not saying they were all that subtle, but they were remorse-less. Not a day went by, until Man City beat Leicester in the final, without me finding a slip of paper – in my desk, in my satchel, in my pocket, even once in my football boots – with the simple message: Mansfield 3 West Ham 0. Children can be very hurtful.

School life didn't get any easier when we went down 4–0 to Blackpool in the infamous third-round Cup tie of 1971.

As soon as young West Ham supporters are old enough to under-stand the spoken word they are sat on their father's knee and told the cautionary tale of being spotted in a nightclub hours before a televised Cup game against a team from a lower division.

Toddlers brought up to be claret and blue sit hushed in dis-belief as they learn how the mighty Bobby Moore and his mate Jimmy Greaves were on their way to their separate beds when a cameraman from the *Match of the Day* team told them the pitch was iced over and there was no chance the game would take place the following day.

Sympathetic dads, who know how easy it is for a quiet pint to be misconstrued, make it plain that there was nothing wrong with rounding up a couple of teammates and heading for a nightclub run by a washed-up boxer. They stress that the lads hardly touched a drop between them. One of their number – the saintly Clyde Best – was actually teetotal. But all that counts for nothing when a bunch of northern mischief-makers scrape away the ice, enabling the game to go ahead ... with inevitable consequences.

Having had this conversation with my own children, I can testify how hard it is to keep the lump out of your throat as the story unfurls. Because what happens next simply serves to underline the fact that you really can't trust anyone in this life.

A number of West Ham supporters who had travelled up for the game were necking pints of Robinsons ale when Moore and co. walked into the 007 club (which was clearly licensed, although not necessarily to kill). No doubt they were thrilled to be in the presence of West Ham's finest at the time – although they got the right hump when the Irons capitulated the following day. They were no happier on the Monday morning, complaining about late-night drinking to the club. Then someone phoned a newspaper and the story became headline news.

Now as a journalist myself I probably shouldn't be telling you this, but one or two of my colleagues are partial to a drink. In fact in 1971 you could be fired for being found sober at your desk. So the idea of a newspaperman with a liver like a lace-up football, flicking the fag ash off his typewriter and settling down to a write a story about young footballers far from home enjoying a few lagers is not without a hint of irony.

Unfortunately for Moore, Greaves, Best and Brian Dear, the fourth member of the party, their manager didn't have a sense of irony. In fact, Ron Greenwood wanted to sack the lot of them. Cooler heads in the Upton Park boardroom talked him out of it, but Dear and Greaves were gone soon afterwards. Best was given the benefit of the doubt, but the already strained relationship between Greenwood and his captain was damaged beyond repair. It's no coincidence that West Ham never looked like getting to Wembley again until both men had been replaced.

Although defeat in the FA Cup is far harder to take than an unexpected exit from the League Cup, you will naturally get a hard time from rival fans if you are on the wrong end of a David and Goliath act in either tournament.

After the Blackpool disaster my final three years at school didn't get any easier. The education authorities had taken the decision to raise the school leaving age from fifteen to sixteen, so when we lost 2–1 to Stockport County in 1972 the kids who would have otherwise left to follow their careers in plumbing, carpentry or petty larceny were still my classmates. They were most disgruntled to still be there – and our defeat at the hands of a fourth division side in a League Cup tie was one of the few things that brightened their lives. Thank you, boys, for sharing your joy with me.

That match is not be confused with the 2–1 defeat at Stockport in which Iain Dowie scored an own goal that is still regarded as one of the finest of its kind by many. There's a 24-year gap between those two games in which we rarely wasted an opportunity to find ourselves on the wrong end of a humiliating defeat by a team from the low-rent end of the Football League.

The pick of the bunch? Hmmm, that's tough – why don't *you* choose one? There are certainly plenty from which to make your selection: Hull City 1 West Ham 0 (FA Cup, 1973); Hereford 2 West Ham 1 (FA Cup, 1974); Fulham 2 West Ham 1 (League Cup, 1974); West Ham 1 Swindon 2 (League Cup, 1978); Newport 2 West Ham 1 (FA Cup, 1979); Watford 2 West Ham 0 (FA Cup, 1982); West Ham 2 Barnsley 5 (League Cup, 1987); Torquay 1 West Ham 0 (FA Cup, 1990); Crewe 2 West Ham 0 (League

Cup, 1992); Barnsley 4 West Ham 1 (FA Cup, 1993); Luton 3 West Ham 2 (FA Cup, 1994). And then, just to make 1996 a really special year, there's a 3–0 defeat at Grimsby on Valentine's Day in the FA Cup – their first win against top-flight opposition in sixty years – to add to the Stockport League Cup debacle a week before Christmas ten months later.

Unfortunately, it doesn't get any better after 1996.

In January 1997, West Ham went to Wrexham for a third-round FA Cup tie that had a touch of the '71 Blackpool game about it. The pitch was covered in snow and barely fit for purpose. In fact most of the country was covered in snow, and almost half of the third-round games were cancelled. But the *Match of the Day* cameras were there, suspecting an upset, so the Welsh club pulled out all the stops to ensure the fixture went ahead. Somewhat surprisingly – and much to the annoyance of the *MOTD* boys who had gone all that way in search of blood – we got away with a 1–1 draw, courtesy of a goal from Hugo Porfirio.

So it was all back to Upton Park for the replay. Third-tier opposition at home after surviving a tricky tie at their place? Surely we already had one foot in the next round, where our opponents would be the lowly Peterborough? Our name was possibly on the Cup once more! But no, that's not the West Ham way. We lost 1–0 after a truly dreadful performance that left Harry Redknapp looking more lugubrious than a bulldog with toothache.

Shall I go on? Look, I'm sorry about all this – I know that those of you with a delicate constitution can't take much more, so I'll spare you the games in which we were humiliated in one of the legs but won the tie overall (such as the 1–0 League Cup defeat at Huddersfield in 1997). But in all honesty I can't really walk away without mentioning the 2–0 setback at Northampton in the same competition the following year – eventually going out 2–1 on aggregate.

The League Cup has never been kind to West Ham. In 2000 we lost 2–1 to Sheffield Wednesday at Upton Park (although, to be fair to the tournament, we were beaten again at Hillsborough in the 2012 FA Cup). In 2002, we lost 1–0 at home to Oldham.

In 2006 there was a 2–1 defeat at Chesterfield. Then there was a 2–1 beating by Aldershot at Upton Park in 2011. And, of course, we cannot omit the fact West Ham lost to Sheffield United on penalties at the start of the 2014/15 season. However, there is a certain amount of satisfaction for all those who hold West Ham dear that this was a giant-killing act – simply because Sheffield United is now considered to be a minnow. It's what Carlos would have wanted.

As I say, defeat to lower-league opposition in the FA Cup is a far more bitter pill to swallow for West Ham supporters. So in 1999 it felt like we'd been put on a course of antibiotics when we lost a third-round replay 1–0 to Swansea in January and then, after the following season's tournament had been brought forward to avoid clashes with an expanded Champions League, we went down 1–0 at Tranmere – thus being on the wrong end of an FA Cup giant-killing act twice in the same year ... which, you have to admit, is unusual. Even by our standards.

Many moons have passed since I left school and I no longer find scraps of paper inserted in inappropriate places reminding me of the score when we lose. But it's still no fun going to work after results like that. Lower-league opposition? Forget it. Give me the likes of Man U any day.

In fact, somewhere in the back of my fast-fading mind is the recollection that the most successful club manager this country has ever seen once stared into the bottom of his glass of Châteauneuf du Pape and moaned to anyone who would listen that West Ham always played better against Manchester United than when we face other teams. I think the word he used to describe the way we raised our game was 'obscene'. Sir Alex Ferguson may have been right. During his reign we scuppered Man U's chances of winning the League twice and turned them over in both Cup competitions. Perhaps there really is something in the notion that they bring out the claret and blue devil in us.

The first ever competitive game between the two sides was in the FA Cup – and we won that one as well. Sadly, history does not record whether the Man Utd keeper of 1911 looked like a man trying to hail a cab when he was beaten (in the way that Fabien Barthez did as Paolo Di Canio slid the ball past him ninety years later). If only they'd had YouTube back then.

West Ham's first League game against Man Utd was on 25 December 1922. The second was on 26 December! Just imagine: back-to-back fixtures on Christmas Day and Boxing Day at a time when rotation was something you did with the vegetables on your allotment, not the delicate little flowers who have agents. (You will be fascinated to learn that in 1922 we won the first game in Manchester 2–1, but lost the return fixture 0–2 at home. How West Ham is that?)

I love the idea of playing twice in twenty-four hours, so – with the help of my son – I am trying to revive this tradition using a format in which West Ham never suffers a humiliating defeat to lower-league opposition: tabletop football.

The idea came to me when I was rummaging around in the loft and came across the Pro-Action Football set Williams Jnr was given as a young lad. It had been many years since Geoff and I had last fought it out over the dining room table – me as Old West Ham versus his New West Ham (he selects any player who has represented the Irons since 1991, the year he was born, while I have the previous ninety-one years to choose from). But we have decided to renew our old rivalry in what I hope will become an annual Christmas showdown.

To be honest, I suggested tabletop football because it is one sporting arena in which I can still compete with him. As a middle-aged man it is only natural that I'm too old and too slow to play football for real. What did depress me, though, was discovering I'm also too old and too slow to play hi-tech versions such as FIFA 2000-and-something. Give me a PlayStation controller and you'd think a diabolical combination of Avram Grant and Gianfranco Zola was running the team, such is the chaos that ensues. But I can still flick a plastic figurine with the best of them.

For anyone of my generation, the top-of-the-table tabletop football game is Subbuteo. And, without wishing to sound unduly immodest here, I was pretty good at it in my younger days.

My first set came with the two-dimensional players that collectors apparently now refer to as 'flats'. The kits were red and blue shirts with white shorts. For no good reason I generally preferred to use the blue players. The trouble was every game felt as though I was controlling an anorexic Everton taking on an equally undernourished Charlton Athletic.

In the year I first saw West Ham play in the flesh, Subbuteo introduced its so-called heavyweight figures, which were three-dimensional and came in different club colours. It was as if a prayer had been answered, and my subsequent letter to Santa couldn't have been clearer. Unfortunately for me, it must have got lost in the post, because rather than getting my beloved Hammers I ended up with Juventus. I think that was when I finally lost all faith in Father Christmas and his stunted workforce.

I begged my parents to help me put right this terrible wrong, but they seemed strangely unwilling to get involved. So I nicked my brother's paints that he used on his pointless plastic Airfix aeroplanes and turned the Old Lady of Turin claret and blue. Well, claret-ish. It was more pillar-box red to be honest, but it was certainly better than black and white stripes.

Encouraged by my success, I tried painting our plastic Homepride flour-grader in West Ham colours too (don't tell me you've never heard of Fred, the little man in a black suit with the bowler hat that unscrewed – what do they teach in schools these days?) but it didn't turn out as well as I'd hoped. My mum thought I'd done it as some form of protest about not getting the Subbuteo side I'd asked for and my pocket money was withheld for several weeks as a result.

However, it takes more than that to discourage a true West Ham supporter and, once my income was restored, I saved hard to buy the team I loved. (There was no such thing as a leveraged buy-out in those days; you handed over your own money or there was no sale.) For the next five years, during my time at secondary school, I never looked back. If there was a Subbuteo game going, I'd be up for it. And – always playing as WHUFC – I won more than I lost (which is more than can be said for the full-sized WHUFC over the same period).

I had a particularly good home record, which probably had something to do with the fact I played on a top-quality surface.

The original idea, when Subbuteo was first sold in 1947, was for players to chalk out a pitch on an old army blanket – but my old man was having none of that. During the war he had been in the RAF, and he didn't like the army or their blankets. So he bought a rather nice piece of green baize and persuaded my mum to get busy with her Singer sewing machine. The result was a beautifully embroidered pitch with permanent cotton lines that cried out for a passing game. (We're West Ham United – we play on the floor.) Few opponents could live with it.

Those of you who recall how quickly the goalmouths at Upton Park became duck ponds in the late '60s and early '70s will note that what I was playing on was somewhat different from the real thing. Still, there's nothing wrong with striving for perfection.

Unlike many West Ham players, I probably retired too early. But you know what it's like when you're coming to terms with puberty – there are so many other things a healthy lad wants to do with his index finger.

It was many years before I played again. It was Christmas at my sister-in-law's and they had bought one of their kids a Subbuteo set. And what a set it was! The only accessories I'd ever managed to acquire were a miniature FA Cup and some plastic hoardings that prevented the players flying off the table and sustaining serious injury when they hit the floor. But this had the lot ... floodlights, stands, supporters, officials, everything you could think of except, perhaps, the mounted policemen who – while you make your way to the ground – look down at you as if you are even more unsavoury than the mess their horses leave behind.

I didn't get to use the claret and blue players on this occasion. My nephew supports Aston Villa (no one knows why) and, given it was his Christmas present, he insisted on his right to the sacred colours. I had no argument with that.

What I did have an argument with was his interpretation of a 'flick'. The rules of Subbuteo are quite clear about how you propel the figures around the pitch. You can't push them, you can't nudge them – and you certainly can't pick them up and put them down anywhere you damn well like.

I like to think of myself as a patient man and I tried to show him the correct technique. I also explained the rules about what constitutes handball, why it's a foul if you smash into an opponent's player without first touching the ball and that you can only score from within a marked zone. But I was obviously wasting my breath.

His first goal clearly shouldn't have stood as he had ignored at least three of the four points I had just made to him. Short of picking up the ball and throwing it into the back of my net, it couldn't have been a more blatant case of cheating. But he was adamant he had scored and determinedly set up the pieces for a re-start.

Looking back, perhaps I should have let it go at that, shaken hands and congratulated him on a well-deserved victory. But I've always had an inherent sense of fair play and I resolved to show him the true meaning of sportsmanship. I went on to produce a mesmerising performance, if I do say so myself. As I recall, I had a healthy lead and was putting together yet another intricate passing movement when he realised the enormity of his mistake and ran off to find his mother. As I explained to her, I think it should take more than losing a game of tabletop football to make a small boy cry. Apparently, for reasons that were never properly explained to me, he didn't play Subbuteo again.

When my son was old enough to take his place at the other

end of the table, Subbuteo had rather gone out of fashion. There was a more popular game on the market called Striker, but that was rubbish. The top-of-the-range model was Pro-Action Football, so – like any parent who wants their children to get more out of life than they have themselves – I happily shelled out for that.

Unlike Subbuteo, you could swivel the players so they are pointing in the direction you want them to kick the ball. (As anyone who has ever played association football will testify, there has never been a better coaching tip than 'play the way you're facing'.) Magnets in the base of the players meant the metallic ball was drawn to their feet and stuck there until you decided to pass or shoot. (Now I know how Trevor Brooking did it.) And when you did want them to get rid of it, you smacked them on the top of the head. (Be honest – who hasn't ever wanted to do that when watching West Ham try to defend over the years?)

The first time we renewed our Pro-Action rivalry the game ended 6–6. The old boys, playing 4–4–2, were: Parkes, Stewart, Martin, Moore, Lampard (Snr), Devonshire, Brooking, Bonds, Peters, Hurst, Robson (Pop). The latter-day legends' starting XI, playing a more modern 3–2–3–2, was: Green, Repka, Collins, Tomkins, Noble, Parker, Tevez, di Canio, Cole (Joe), Cole (Carlton), Zamora. (How that lot got a draw against the greatest players ever to have worn the claret and blue is beyond me.)

That was on Christmas Day. Sadly, the Boxing Day fixture had to be cancelled due to adverse hangover conditions. However, I'm determined to make this a family tradition over the festive period.

After being held at home like that, I think I may have to change my team around a bit, though. Don't tell Geoff, but I'm seriously thinking about presenting him with a team of nicknames the next time we meet. And I'm not talking about the Mooro and Pottsy kind of nicknames – I'm going for proper soubriquets.

On current form, as a 4–3–3, I'd pick: Eric, Muffin, Stretch, Reggie, Pancho, Ticker, Hadleigh (aka Boog), Harpo, Sparrow, Psycho and Sarge. By the time he's worked out who's who, I'll be 3–0 up and coasting.

What do you mean you don't know who Muffin is either? OK, I'll go through them with you – but only you. No blabbing to my son (not that we're competitive, you understand). Those nicknames translate as: Phil Parkes (Eric), John Bond (Muffin), Alvin Martin (Stretch), Tony Gale (Reggie), Stuart Pearce (Pancho), Ronnie Boyce (Ticker), Trevor Brooking (Hadleigh aka Boog), Pat Holland (Harpo), Alan Taylor (Sparrow), David Cross (Psycho), and Paul Goddard (Sarge).

And that's part of the beauty of tabletop football: it gives you a chance to while away time that could otherwise be usefully spent washing the car or mowing the lawn, dreaming up West Ham fantasy teams.

As a man who carries some excess timber myself, I'd be happy to manage a squad that puts up with a bit of overweight too. (There's nothing wrong with having a stout manager – just remember to call him 'Big', not 'Fat', or you'll upset a lot of loyal fans.) The captain's armband for my team of tubbies would, of course, have to go to Frank 'one man and his forklift truck' Lampard Jnr. Waddling out behind him would be Neil Ruddock, John Hartson, Julian Faubert, Luis Boa Morte, Julian Dicks (gulp – did I really just say that?), Mido, Titi Camara, Brian Dear, Jimmy Greaves and – bringing up the rear by quite some way – Benni McCarthy. You'll notice I haven't bothered with a keeper. Quite honestly, you wouldn't need one. Just grease 'em all up and lever any of those salad-dodgers between the sticks and no opposition striker is going to be disturbing the onion bag in a hurry.

If you don't fancy the porkers, how about a team of Alans? Sealey, Devonshire, Dickens, Curbishley etc. Of course, you'd have to play a few out of position – the only defender I can think of is Alan Stephenson. And I'd cheat by including Paul, Martin and Clive Allen (crafty, eh?). But the good news is you don't have to go with Allen McNightmare in goal: there's a guy called Alan Dickie who turned out in the green jersey for us a dozen times in the early '60s and, although I never saw him play, I just know he's better than McNit.

But the biggest challenge when picking fantasy sides is to put together the ultimate team of the most useless players we've ever had. Let's face it, choosing a dream team of West Ham all-time greats is relatively easy. Picking Worst Ham United is far, far harder.

For what it's worth, this is my starting XI from hell: Allen McKnight, Rigobert Song, Steve Walford, Gary Breen, Mitchell Thomas, Freddie Ljungberg, Nigel Quashie, Ilie Dumitrescu, Peter Eustace, David Kelly, Ted MacDougall.

You may well disagree with a number of those selections, and I can understand why. I don't think anyone can put up a serious argument against McKnight – he truly was in a class of his own. But at the back there is a bunch of other players making a strong claim for inclusion: Gary Charles, Ragnvald Soma, Paul Hilton, Calum Davenport and John Cushley all made the shortlist. Some might even suggest George Parris, but I'm not having that. Not George!

And what about midfield? 'No Franz Carr, Andy Impey, Dudley

Tyler or Dale Gordon?!' I hear you cry. 'No Nigel Rio-Coker?' Then there's Matthew Rush, Luis Boa Morte and Florin 'two bob' Raducioiu. As I say, this isn't easy – although Joey Beauchamp did make the task a little less tricky by ensuring he never actually turned out for West Ham during his fifty-eight days at the club, thus ruling himself out of contention in this particular exercise.

Dutchman Marco Boogers, on the other hand, did play for us – making four appearances as a substitute, which included a sending-off for a chest-high tackle on Gary Neville at Old Trafford that did not go down well with a red-faced man drinking expensive French wine. Before the hapless Boogers was finally sent back to the land of his birth permanently, there was an oft-repeated story in *The Sun* claiming he had returned to Holland feeling sorry for himself and was holed up in a caravan. However, it turns out this was not entirely true and the reporter had actually been told that, rather than residing in a *caravan,* he'd gone on holiday by *car again.* An easy mistake to make – it could have happened to any of us.

That aside, what little anyone saw of him convinced us all he was utterly useless, which is why he made the shortlist for one of the two places up front in my Worst Ham side. But, like Mike Small, John Radford, Jimmy Greaves, Sandy Clark and Lee Chapman, he didn't quite get the nod for the first team. Sometimes, as a manager, you just have to go with your gut feeling.

Try it yourself. It's tougher than you think – but you may well come up with something better (or do I mean worse?). Still, I'm standing by my selection. All things considered, I reckon this lot would be certain to go down before the Christmas decorations even went up.

Chapter 8

And we hate Millwall

I UNDERSTAND THAT NOT everybody feels the same way as I do about West Ham. Had I been in any doubt there were one or two clues in the year the hopeless Avram Grant masterminded our relegation. Some of the folk from south of the river, who do not much care for claret and blue, hired a light aircraft to fly over Wigan as our fate was sealed at the DW Stadium trailing a banner that read: 'Avram Grant, Millwall legend.'

At Tottenham – another club not renowned for its love of the Irons – one fan made a banner along the lines of 'Come home, Robbie – mission completed' after loan signing Robbie Keane contributed to our demise by missing a whole host of very scoreable chances.

All very amusing, I'm sure.

Our rivalry with The Hated Millwall, in particular, has prompted a good deal of speculation over the years. Again I am delighted to be able to call on the expertise of historian John Simkin to explain how it all started: 'It has to be remembered that Millwall was established in 1885, ten years before Thames Ironworks and fifteen years before West Ham United. In fact, Millwall were champions of the Southern League when Thames Ironworks was established.'

At that time, the two clubs occupied the same side of the Thames – with The Hated Millwall nestled in the kink of the river that is rather misleadingly known as the Isle of Dogs. Their name comes from the windmills that used to line the western embankment. Sorry, John. Didn't mean to interrupt there. Please, carry on.

The first game between the two clubs took place on 14 December 1895. That day, Thames Ironworks played a game against Millwall Reserves and lost 6–0. A return match was arranged on 25 April 1896. This time the result was 1–1.

Thames Ironworks won the Southern League's second division in 1898/99. That meant that in the following season they were playing in the same league as Millwall. Until then, Thames Ironworks had home gates of between 1,000 (Chatham) and 3,000 (Bristol City). However, for their first game against Millwall in the top division they had an attendance of 12,000. John Powles, the author of *Iron in the Blood* (2005), does not report any crowd trouble. Millwall won the game 2–0.

That season, Thames Ironworks also played Millwall in the FA Cup. This time 13,000 people saw Millwall win the game 2–1. It might be this game that caused the conflict between the two clubs. Tom Bradshaw scored the Hammers' goal. It was the last game he played, dying on Christmas Day 1899. Officially, the 26-year-old Bradshaw died of tuberculosis. However, friends claimed that he had been complaining of terrible pains when he headed the ball. Did he receive a blow to the head while playing against Millwall? Bradshaw was a popular player and if the fans thought this was the case it might have caused considerable anger.

Interestingly, Bradshaw's death also increased hostility towards Spurs. In 1899, Francis Payne, the club secretary, was given the task of finding good players for Thames Ironworks to prepare them for the first season in the top division of the Southern League. His record signing of £1,000 was Bradshaw from Spurs. Hammers' fans were convinced that Spurs would have known he was suffering from tuberculosis when they sold him. Bradshaw only played four games for Thames Ironworks before that fateful game against Millwall.

The third game of that season against Millwall was even more important. Thames Ironworks were second from bottom of the League when they played Millwall on 28 April 1900. The Hammers won 1–0 in front of 8,000 people. This stopped them from being automatically relegated. Instead, they had to play a 'test match' against Fulham. The Hammers stayed in the League by winning 5–1.

The following season Thames Ironworks became West Ham United. For the next fourteen years West Ham v. Millwall was the most important game of the season for supporters, attracting nearly double the attendance of any other game. Crucially, West Ham secured dominance over Millwall during this period. In 1919, West Ham joined the second division of the Football League and, in the 1922/23 season, were promoted to the first division.

After this, West Ham were rarely in the same division as Millwall – although we did beat them 4–1 in the FA Cup in 1930. The next time we played them was in the 1932/33 season after we had been relegated to the second division. Early in the season we beat them 3–0 (two of the goals were scored by the great Vic Watson). The relative size of the two clubs is reflected in the fact that 30,000 attended that game, but the return match at Millwall only had a crowd of 5,000.

Many thanks for that, John – good to know that history proves we really are the bigger club.

They say that if you sit in St Mark's Square in Venice sipping a cup of coffee long enough you will get to see everyone you've ever met in your life. Personally, I think they're wrong (and I'm certain your cappuccino wouldn't be worth drinking by the time every last one of them turned up). More likely, I reckon, is that if you spend long enough supporting a football team you are going to fall out with just about every other club you come into contact with.

I'm not talking about the long-established enmity that West Ham supporters reserve for traditional foes such as The Hated Millwall and Tottenham. This isn't even about that natural human instinct to revel in the failures of the glamorous and successful like Manchester United, Liverpool and Leyton Orient. What intrigues me is how you can grow to dislike so many teams that you once thought would never give you cause to complain.

Take Southampton. There was a time I had no problem

whatsoever with the Saints. The whirling arm of Mick Channon when he celebrated a goal; the one-club loyalty of Le Tiss; the 1976 Cup final underdog win against Man U – what was there not to like? Then, in the season we both came up from the Championship, we had a date with Southampton on Valentine's Day and they behaved so badly that I won't talk to them again until they call to apologise (with chocs and flowers too, I should add).

Yes, our man Matt Taylor was stupid to get involved after we were awarded a penalty. And he shouldn't have raised his hands to an opponent. But Southampton's Billy Sharp went down like he'd been decked by a heavyweight boxer in what looked to me to be a cynical and deliberate attempt to get a fellow professional sent off. The football they played afterwards was no great shakes either and – like the bottle of over-priced Irish cider I had at half time – the whole evening left a very nasty taste in the mouth. So now the south coast side are on the long list of clubs with which I have issues.

Oh, and while I'm at it, on the way to the Southampton game I saw a Saints fan smoking on the platform as he waited for a Tube train – which these days is about as socially acceptable as picking clinkers out of your crack at a family wedding. No one lights up on the Underground any more. Have some people still not heard of the King's Cross fire?

Southampton are not the only team in red and white stripes to have upset me over the years. I never forgave Stoke for 'stealing' Geoff Hurst and I've no intention of ever forgiving Sheffield United for the fuss they kicked up over Carlos Tevez. Yes, we broke the rules and were fined accordingly. I've no problem with that. What does still rankle is the way they sought compensation for being relegated. They went down because they weren't good enough over the course of the season and then lost to Wigan on the last day, not because we had Tevez – who had actually been in the side when we were beaten heavily at Bramall Lane some weeks earlier. Still, no one wants to rake up all that again.

The Argentine will of course be for ever considered a West Ham hero after he gave us the crossed Irons salute upon returning with Man Utd. But I fell in love with him the day he tackled a Watford player with his head. He didn't challenge him in the air – the ball was on the floor when a prostrate Tevez lunged in with his cranium. That, my friends, is how you get to achieve legendary status at Upton Park.

Incidentally, a few days before the Blades played their Sheffield rivals, in the so-called 'steel city semi-final' at Wembley, *The Guardian* ran a story previewing the match. My colleague who was given the copy to edit was no expert on the beautiful game. She felt that, as we were running the piece on a Thursday and the game was on Saturday, it would read better if, rather than mention the days of the week repeatedly, she changed it slightly. Which is how Sheffield Wednesday became 'Sheffield yesterday' in a great national daily newspaper.

While we're in Yorkshire this might be a good time to explain why Leeds is still one of the teams that vexes me greatly. The explanation is simple: Don Revie – the man who set out to win at all costs and convinced talented players they would be better off kicking their opponents instead of the ball in such a way as to be considered entertainment.

One particular moment still gives me the shudders all these years on. Leeds were pressing in front of the South Bank and a speculative cross came into our box. Keeper Bobby Ferguson went for the ball – and, after colliding with defender John McDowell, came crashing down like an Olympic diver performing a double twist with pike. Only Ferguson wasn't throwing himself into a diving pool – he landed head first on hard, unyielding ground. He had clearly lost consciousness – yet the hard, unyielding style that Revie demanded of his teams meant they played on, and would have happily celebrated a goal with a fellow human being lying motionless nearby if a Mick Jones shot hadn't been blocked by the horizontal, but alert, McDowell.

Newspaper reports from the time say Ferguson was out cold for four or five minutes. A witness remembers our bonny Bobby lying there for ten. It seemed much longer. I don't believe there was a single person in the ground who didn't fear he had broken his neck. Back then they didn't quiz managers after a game in quite the same way as they do now, so we never got to hear Revie's thoughts on the matter. It's my guess he wouldn't have batted an eyelid if Ferguson had left Upton Park in a wooden box. (The world record fee we paid for Ferguson certainly didn't prevent him getting battered from time to time. More famously than the Leeds game, he had been carried off the previous season in the League Cup semi-final replay against Stoke at Old Trafford ... but that's another story.)

I realise it's a fair old leap from the art of gamesmanship to artificial pitches, but join me by the long jump pit as I begin my run-up. As I recall, four clubs had the drastic plastic: QPR, Preston, Oldham and Luton. I suppose I should despise them all equally but, hey, no one said life is fair. It's you, Hatters, that really gave me the ache – somehow the beach ball effect at Kenilworth Road seemed even more laughable than at any of the other grounds. I'm not putting you in the same league as loathsome Leeds, you understand – but I won't be buying one of your Luton Lotto tickets any time soon.

And where do you think you're going, Bristol City? I still haven't forgiven you for that 10.30 a.m. kickoff.

Then there's Oxford United. How can anyone fall out with them? Well, I managed it after a rather unpleasant disagreement with one of their supporters following a game at their place. I won't bore you with the details, but I think it's a reasonable guess that the young man with whom I debated the various merits of our respective teams was not an undergraduate at the university that fields the dark blue crew in the boat race.

I never thought I'd have a problem with Coventry – not after they beat Tottenham in a Wembley final. Then, in the Championship at the Ricoh, we had a whole load of tomfoolery about who broke the minute's silence for the city's wartime bombing victims – and now they're on my list too.

I could go on – and I will because I haven't got to Notts County yet. My lack of goodwill towards them goes back to what used to be known as the second division. The only consolation on missing out on the Cup final, courtesy of our old friend Keith Hackett, would have been to have gone up as champions. Only Notts Co spoiled that particular party with one of the most negative displays seen at Upton Park in years. The fact they later appointed Paul Ince as manager only serves to prove that my initial judgement about them was spot on.

Swansea could well have found themselves on this list as well, but their supporters did have the good grace to be genuinely embarrassed by the disgraceful play-acting from Chico Flores that earned

Andy Carroll a straight red and a three-game ban in the 2014 relegation battle. Their manager, the high-class Michael Laudrup, did what so few do and criticised his own player publicly for his actions. (Laudrup's reward? He was sacked three days later.)

There is, I know, a slight chance that I am beginning to sound like a cantankerous old curmudgeon who bears a grudge. As my wife and children will testify, nothing could be further from the truth. Rather it is that I have a strong sense of justice – which is hugely satisfied by seeing the likes of Luton, Leeds and Sheffield United flounder in the lower leagues.

The Italians may have got it wrong about St Mark's Square, but they are right about revenge. Unlike frothy coffee, it is definitely best served cold.

There was a time when, if you wanted a biscuit to dunk in your cappuccino, you'd look to Reading to provide it. But not any more – which explains the reason I don't really care for them either.

Let me be clear about this. I have no problem whatsoever with the good people of Reading – or indeed the town itself. It gave me my big break in journalism. It's just the football club I dislike, even though I used to watch them occasionally as a youngster and have some ancient programmes from 1968 to prove it (Mansfield, Oldham and Gillingham – they're yours if have any use for them).

The thing is, I have no time for anyone who makes up their own nickname (Paul 'The Guv'nor' Ince? Of course this includes you!). Once, Reading were the Biscuit Men; now they like to call themselves the Royals. Talk about social mobility!

Remember Huntley and Palmers? No, they weren't the England full backs in the good old days of two-three-five. They made biscuits. Lots and lots of biscuits. In fact, they made so many biscuits that Reading became known as Biscuit Town. And, without wishing to labour the point, the local football team became known as the Biscuit Men.

At its height, Huntley and Palmers employed 5,000 people in Berkshire's principal conurbation, which is considerably more than the number of supporters Reading FC attracted when I first saw them. I used to go and watch them sometimes after my parents moved us out of London to Bracknell, where my dad had got a job.

I was able to justify to myself these expeditions to support a club other than West Ham with the fact that Reading's goalkeeper – the memorably named Steve Death – had once been on the books at Upton Park. He only ever made one appearance for the Irons, but he was a legend at Reading. At one time he held the record for the longest period in English football without conceding a goal. He went 1,104 minutes without letting one in – that's the equivalent of 12.25 games. He was a brilliant keeper, and I was genuinely sorry when I read that he lost his life to cancer in 2003.

It's no exaggeration to say Huntley and Palmers was one of the main driving forces in Reading's growth as a town. The Quakers who ran the company that bore their names were decent men who gave generously to the local community and offered their employees top-of-the-range working conditions. All of which made the football club's response to the factory's closure in 1976 seem somewhat less than gracious. Rather than revere its proud traditions, the club decided to ditch the Biscuit Men tag and go for a grandiose new nickname instead.

They wanted something that matched the times. And a year later we were all knee-deep in bunting from the endless street parties that marked the Queen's Silver Jubilee as Britain renewed its on–off love affair with the royal family. Berkshire likes to call itself the Royal County, so the big-wigs in the boardroom came up with the brilliant idea of calling themselves – you've guessed it – the Royals! Of course, there had to be a poll of the fans to give this idiotic idea an air of legitimacy – but that was about as democratic as an election in North Korea and 'the Royals' (unlike the family of the same name) was duly elected.

The closure of a factory is no excuse to drop a football team's nickname (we didn't change our moniker when our founding fathers stopped building ships with hammers). And when it involves a company who had done so much for the town that spawned the ungrateful football club in question, it's a real slap in the face.

It's fair to say I'm not a royalist at heart, even though the Queen is a West Ham supporter (I haven't been able to confirm this personally but that's what it said in the *Daily Mirror*, which is good enough for me). Had I ever been a monarchist, all those street parties would have cured that. I'd swapped my forklift truck for a typewriter and a career in journalism but, as a young reporter, I wasn't given the big stories – so I got to cover the street parties. Hundreds of them. In fact, it felt as though I visited every patriotic knees-up held in Berkshire in 1977. Which is one of the reasons I jumped at the chance to swap general reporting for the sports desk soon after.

It was more politics than sport that made me want to become a journalist. Back then I was a bit of a lefty and wanted to change the world for the better. (Still am and still do, to be honest.) But I'd always been interested in sport and was on the verge of captaining England in football, cricket and rugby during various stages of my teens –in my imagination, that is.

The sports desk offered me a chance to learn a range of journalistic skills, and I will be forever grateful to the guys who took the time and trouble to teach me so many tricks of the trade when they could just as easily have been in the pub sinking pints of Courage Best. The acting sports editor in particular was a major guiding light in my early career. He answered to the name of Dibbo.

One of his many talents was to be able to swear in a way I've heard no British subject do before or since. He swore like an American, stringing long phrases together to come up with compound profanities that would make a squaddie blush. Think of Pepsi's lip-smackin' ad campaign of the 1970s, then substitute the most foul-mouthed abuse imaginable, and you'll get the general idea. He was also a fantastic journalist, which is why he was the paper's football correspondent as well as acting sports editor.

However, he was less than popular with the management of the football club whose affairs he was paid to report. Reading's opinion of him wasn't improved by an incident with a director's Tupperware sandwich box, which Dibbo used to answer a call of nature on the team coach when the driver refused to let him off. Then there was the business with the fish and chips, which led to him being banned from travelling on the team bus altogether.

On this occasion, the man at the wheel had been persuaded to stop and allow his passengers the chance to buy something to eat before they hit the motorway for the long haul home, but he refused to pull over when it turned out the fish and chips they had all bought was half-cooked, cold and inedible.

No one quite knew what to do with it all until Dibbo came up with a solution. Once more they implored the driver to stop so Dibbo wouldn't have to put his radical plan into action. And once more he refused. Which is when the football correspondent of the *Reading Evening Post* opened the vent on the roof of the coach and began disposing of uneaten fish suppers through the gap.

Have you ever seen a coach carrying a team of sportsmen on the motorway – or any other road, come to that? They kinda stand out – they've generally got the team's name on the side of the bus for one thing.

The driver of the heavy goods vehicle behind the coach on which Dibbo was now orchestrating the mass disposal of unwanted semi-fried food had certainly spotted the name Reading FC. So he knew exactly where to direct his complaint about what followed next. And, if he is to be believed, the poor man had a fair amount to complain about. One moment he is minding his own business driving south at a steady 70 mph down the M1. The next, his visibility is reduced to zero because his windscreen is covered with flying fish – coated in batter and accompanied by flying chips exploding from their flying wrappings.

By all accounts it was a minor miracle the bloke survived. If there truly was divine intervention that day, some might say it was the due to the piece of cod that passeth all understanding. But I'm not one of them. Anyway, the upshot of all this is the driver was compensated by the club (I believe Cup final tickets were involved) and Dibbo was banned from using the team coach to go to away games.

He wasn't banned from home fixtures at Elm Park, though. That didn't happen until he wrote a highly critical piece about how the club was run, pointing out that loyal fans were being let down season after season by a chairman, directors and manager who didn't have the first idea what they were doing. He was right, too.

As a result, the *Reading Evening Post* was now looking for

someone to cover its local football club. I had done some reserve games, and Dibbo clearly reckoned I was ready for the first team. Much to several people's surprise – not least my own – I got the nod.

Thoughts of using my journalistic brilliance to make this a better world began to fade. Instead, I now saw myself as a leading football correspondent, working for a national newspaper and having the pick of any game to cover – which, naturally, would always involve West Ham.

The day started really well. In the morning I went to the office – which was directly opposite the festival site for those of you who know Reading – expecting to carry out my normal duties before going to the match, but rather than give me a load of stuff to do Dibbo was happy for me sit quietly and do my preparatory homework while he did my work as well as his own. He really was a top bloke.

By the time I got to Elm Park I was armed with enough facts and figures to give Motty a run for his money (not that Motty would ever do a third division game of course – there's not enough stardust for his liking). In fact my head was so full of the sort of vital information my readers would be demanding later that afternoon – the height of their centre half; Reading's goal difference; the ref's inside leg measurement – that at first I didn't notice some of the lads I'd worked with as a forklift truck driver in Bracknell when they started barracking me from the stand as I walked round to the press box.

They were curious about my reasons for being there, and it gave me an immense amount of pleasure to tell them. Because when I had handed in my notice no one at the factory believed I was truly swapping a life in the stores for one in newspapers. They'd heard that sort of bullshit before – people leaving to get a glamorous job playing professional football or training to be an astronaut – and they weren't going to be fooled again. I wasn't exactly ostracised, but it was clear that making up such a whopper hadn't gone down well with my workmates. In my final week they even stopped 'discarding' unwanted items and went back to throwing them away. It was really upsetting.

But now here I was on my way to the press box and grandly offering to take my doubters into the players' lounge after the game. And if they still didn't believe me, they could buy a copy of that evening's *Post*, which, on the front page of the football special, would be displaying my byline. I tried not to sound arrogant as I explained that I had to be going now because I had work to do. Although I may have had an extra spring in my step as I skipped up the concrete stairs to take my place in the exclusive area reserved for the fourth estate.

You would think someone who was destined to be the country's leading football writer would remember their first League game in the press box, wouldn't you? Particularly as it turned out to be their last League game. But, for the life of me, I can't recall the opposition that afternoon.

I do remember how extraordinarily difficult it is to write a running report of a football match for an evening paper, however. Unlike the reserve games I had covered, this wasn't just a case of sitting back, observing proceedings, composing your thoughts and then typing up a few well-chosen words. To make the five o'clock edition a reporter must file copy as the game is being played. You don't sit back, and there's no time to compose your thoughts. You watch the match – and dictate your report over the phone as you do so. The problem is, the action unfolds quicker than you can put together the grammatically and factually correct sentences that are required for a newspaper. As a result, you have to remember accurately what is taking place in front of your eyes while reporting what happened several minutes beforehand. It's a bit like patting your head and rubbing your tummy at the same time – knowing that several thousand people will be all too keen to point out any mistakes you have made the following day.

After the game I hung around briefly in the hope of picking up a couple of decent quotes for the piece I would be required to write for Monday's paper, then hurtled back to the office to get a copy of that evening's edition and see my report in print.

Dibbo was still at his desk when I got there. 'How did I do?' I asked.

'How many people called Bennett were actually playing in this game?' he wanted to know, squinting at me over the top of his glasses, which he was forever having to push back over the bridge of his nose.

'Funny you should ask that,' I told him. 'There was one on each side. It made life quite difficult actually.'

'Hmmm, thought it must have been something like that,' he said quietly.

I enquired nervously if there had been a problem, and he rummaged around in the metal tray at his side before finding a copy of my story. He turned to the second sheet and began to read: 'After winning a crunching tackle on the edge of the penalty area, Bennett laid off the ball to Bennett, who dropped his shoulder and waltzed round Bennett before putting in the perfect cross for Bennett to power home the header. Visiting keeper Bennett stood no chance.'

I waited for the tirade of abuse that was about to follow. It was some time before I could say anything. Sorry seemed as good a place as any to start.

'What did you do – about all those Bennetts, I mean?'

Dibbo just smiled and shrugged. 'I looked at the teamsheets and changed the names. No one will ever notice. Come on – let's go and have a pint, you look like you need one.'

He was right. On both counts. A more senior colleague was asked to keep the good people of Reading apprised of their team's fortunes for the rest of the season and the following year my mentor was allowed back in by the chairman, so I never did go on to be the nation's No. 1 football correspondent.

I did finally get to see West Ham from inside a press box though. That, too, was down to Dibbo.

It was the 1980 Cup final. I couldn't get a ticket for love nor money and, although I no longer worked for the *Post*, Dibbo got me in on a press trip organised by the paper's owners. We had lunch beforehand with Daley Thompson (who two months later would win the first of his decathlon gold medals at the Moscow Olympics) and then went on to Wembley – with seats that offered the best view in the stadium.

Naturally, I'd have rather been on the terraces with the rest of the West Ham fans (honest, lads, it was hell having to accept all that corporate hospitality), but I tried to make the best of a bad job. If I recall correctly, some fella called Brooking scored a goal that day. Or was it Bennett?

Chapter 9

Supping with the devil

I HAVE A TERRIBLE admission to make, and now seems like as good a time as any to own up to my sins: I have supported Manchester United.

It's true: I was once a cockney red. In my defence I never stopped loving West Ham while I was seeing another club. Furthermore, I was very immature at the time. But I know now that it was wrong.

Before you judge me, let me try to explain. As a fresh-faced nineteen-year-old I had been sent to south Wales by my immediate employers to learn the basics of journalism – they clearly didn't want to do it themselves, which was odd considering I had been taken on by a newspaper. There I found myself sharing a house with an even fresher-faced young man (unlike me he didn't have a stylish Zapata moustache), who came from somewhere called The North. His name was Bob. It still is, in fact.

It's fair to say we were wary of one another to begin with. We had been allocated a student house on the outskirts of Cardiff with four other young wannabe members of our chosen profession and none of us had the faintest idea what the immediate future held for us.

As with any strangers trying to find some common ground, one of the first topics of conversation was football. We had all been instructed to turn up some time during the first weekend of January – which for any self-respecting supporter means the third round of the FA Cup. I was jubilant: the previous day West Ham had won at Southampton. Bob, on the other hand, was not so chuffed – it turned out he was a Man U supporter and they had been held to a draw at home by lowly Walsall. Three days later he was even more displeased when the Mancs lost the replay. Perhaps, looking back, I could have been more sympathetic at what must have been a difficult time for him.

What finally broke the ice was *The Sweeney* – the TV programme rather than the Flying Squad itself. Bob couldn't understand a word of the rhyming slang that littered each episode, so I translated. And, as he gradually got to know his dog and bone from his dickie dirt, our friendship grew.

One of the many things we had in common was a pathological dislike of the city in which we now found ourselves living. So to cement our friendship we started going to Ninian Park on Friday evenings – which isn't quite as silly as it sounds because, for much of that season, that was when Cardiff City played their home games. We supported whoever Cardiff were playing. (By the end of that season we were to take this to international level and, as two lone

Sassenachs, found ourselves in the midst of a baffled Tartan Army roaring on Scotland against Wales.)

Until this point I always thought of myself as a one-club man. But we were a long way from Upton Park, and once you start fooling around with other teams it's hard to stop yourself. So when Bob suggested a threesome – him, me and Man Utd – it didn't seem quite as grotesque as it sounds now. However, I wasn't prepared to turn my back on West Ham completely; we had been in a relationship for many years by this time and you don't give that up lightly. After examining my conscience I decided it would be OK to explore the exotic charms of the Red Devils if Bob was prepared to try a blind date with West Ham. We had ourselves a deal.

The year in question was 1975. We were on our way to Wembley. The mighty Manchester United, who only a few years before had been champions of Europe, were now in the old second division. It turned out to be a fascinating few months.

The first game we went to under our pact was West Ham v. Swindon in an FA Cup fourth-round replay at the County Ground. It was a mudbath. In fact, my overriding memory of West Ham's Cup run that year is mud. It was as if we'd cornered the market in the stuff. The records show that there were 27,749 people in the ground watching Trevor Brooking and Patsy Holland score the goals that secured us a place in the fifth round and many of those were there to support West Ham. Be fair – that's not bad for a wet Tuesday night in Wiltshire. It was certainly several thousand higher than Swindon's average attendance in the third division.

Man Utd weren't getting bad gates themselves. The glory years of Charlton, Best and Law were behind them, and the previous season had ended in a humiliating relegation. But former Chelsea boss Tommy Docherty – the man once described as having more clubs than Jack Nicklaus – was putting together an exciting young side and the fans were turning out in huge numbers to support them. It is estimated that in the 1974/75 season Man Utd took 15,000 fans to Cardiff, 20,000 to Sheffield Wednesday and a staggering 25,000 to Bolton. At Old Trafford they never got fewer than 40,000, and in November more than 60,000 turned up to watch them play Sunderland. And all that in the second tier of English football at a time when attendances were falling because many people preferred to stay away rather than risk getting caught up in the violence making headline news with dispiriting regularity.

Manchester United's travelling support – the so-called red army – had a reputation for causing trouble wherever it went. But then, so did West Ham fans. It's true there were some serious headcases among both sets of supporters, just as there were at every club in the country, and no one is trying to defend how the violent minority behaved on occasions. In mitigation, though, it should be pointed out that the reception we got from the police as away supporters in the '70s did nothing to ease the tension. We would be met at the station as the football specials pulled in and marched to our destination as if we were on a chain gang. You didn't break ranks to get a pint or a bag of chips – it wasn't permitted if you supported one of the nasty clubs. Local people would turn out to watch us go past – some hostile, others simply curious. Defiantly, we'd sing and we'd chant … usually with one eye on the police dogs you knew were itching to get their teeth into your denims and the other eye on the police horses ready to happily crush every bone in your foot if you failed to stay in line. If you did catch the eye of one of the policemen you realised just how much they wished you were somewhere else.

It's a strange sensation, but when you're made to feel like a criminal even the most law-abiding of citizens can be tempted to believe they are entitled to behave like one.

Before we go any further, let me make it perfectly plain that neither myself nor Bob, who is now a highly respected sports journalist, are, or ever have been, football hooligans. But Bob could look after himself. I knew his northern accent wouldn't cause him any problems as a temporary member of the claret and blue army – we have recruits from all over the country after all. I, on the other hand, was concerned that my southern pronunciation would not go down well in Manchester. Bob told me not to worry, explaining that Man United have always had a large following in London and the cockney reds were much respected by their Mancunian brethren – mainly because they included some of the most terrifying individuals in the country at that time.

However, I come from a long line of cowards. In fact, cowards run in our family – and none of them run faster than me (boom boom!). Actually, when you've been given a chasing around a strange town by a bunch of morons intent on giving you a good kicking it really is surprising how rapid a person can be.

In the '70s, after an away game, as you made your way back to the station and cattle trucks that passed as football specials, you'd think carefully before answering anyone who asked you the time – especially if the person making the enquiry was wearing a watch. Your best bet, if you found yourself alone and confronted by a group of young gentlemen with scarves tied around their wrists asking you some pointless question with the sole purpose of determining whether you had a local accent, was to sprint back in the direction from which you'd just come, then head off down the side roads.

Left here, right there, each turn an instantaneous decision – not knowing nor caring which direction you were going in, just trying to stay two steps ahead of your pursuers and hoping the patron saint of away supporters would look after you.

Old Trafford, for me, was about to become a home ground. Even so, the prospect of standing on the Stretford End pretending to be harder than the hard cases who surrounded me was not something that appealed greatly. Couldn't we sit in the main stand instead? Apparently not. It's the terraces for you, my lad – and let's hear no more about it.

God knows how I got away with it – perhaps it was the camel hair coat (which will never truly go out of style while the real hard-men are still allowed to buy their own clothes); maybe it was the fact I kept my trap shut as much as possible. What limited experience I've had of truly dangerous people is that they say little and stare a lot. But, for whatever reason, I increasingly found myself in the midst of the red horde and being treated as one of their own.

Sometimes I'd be offered a cigarette, which I'd take with a curt nod and wait for someone to light it for me. And on the rare occasions we found ourselves anywhere near the fighting that was becoming synonymous with Man Utd I'd look at the skirmish as if weighing up the possibilities then simply shake my head – implying it was too minor for a cockney red to become involved and we'd leave this to the Manc infantry.

I was starting to wonder if there was a career in method acting for me. At the time it was looking more likely than a career in journalism. I was not enjoying the course I had been sent on, and got a reputation as a troublemaker when I tried to convince my fellow students to join the National Union of Journalists and take industrial action to improve our terms and conditions. (Not only was 1975 a vintage year for hooliganism, it was pretty good for strikes too.)

Bob felt the same way as I did – we wanted to be real reporters, not schoolroom scribes trying to master the libel law and the workings of local government. And we didn't like the nightlife in Cardiff. We'd walk into a pub and the place would go silent. Or we'd try our luck at one of the city's discos and invariably draw a blank.

Up until then I hadn't had been much of a one for discos. Some people just aren't meant to boogie. On the rare occasions I had been to clubs with my mates in the past I'd forgone the dancing and stood with a pint looking like a really interesting sort of bloke, waiting for the girls to come to me. As a strategy it was spectacularly unsuccessful. But Bob taught me a few steps – I still use them today when the occasion demands – and with a sophisticated panache guaranteed to turn heads we'd hit the floor to the sounds of 'Kung Fu Fighting' and 'Lady Marmalade'. *Voulez-vous coucher avec moi, ce soir?*

I can't think why we didn't have more success with the opposite gender: I remember telling one beguiling Welsh wench that, being a journalist, I was an expert in shorthand and ready to take down anything she said at a moment's notice. Rather than giggle knowingly at this astonishing witticism as I had anticipated, she lamped me with a right hook.

Things got so bad we decided to forget about Cardiff altogether and a bunch of us jumped into Bob's canary yellow Opel Kadett and headed for the other side of the Severn Bridge. We ended up in a pub in Bristol with the two roughest-looking strippers who have ever disrobed in the name of eroticism. I don't want to be unkind here, but these two troupers were so repulsive they could make beer curdle.

We were still laughing about it on the way back to Cardiff when one of the guys sitting in the back dropped his cigarette down the side of the seat. As he was sitting closest to the petrol tank the general mood of hilarity changed quite quickly when he told us what he'd done. Bob was forced to make an emergency stop on the hard shoulder and we tore out the back seat to get to the smouldering Player's No. 6 before it became necessary to look up just what the 'fire' part of a third party, fire and theft insurance policy really covers.

I realise the odds are heavily stacked against Hollywood super-star Steve Martin being on the M4 that night, but some years later he and John Candy re-enacted a scene that took our local difficulty to its ultimate conclusion in *Planes, Trains & Automobiles*. Makes you think, doesn't it?

In a desperate attempt to be fair here, the journalism course did have its moments. On one occasion we were taken to a police training school – I think the object of the exercise was to make it plain to all concerned that journalists and police are born to mis-trust one another. It's genetic.

The best day of all was when we went down a pit – at least the blokes did: the girls weren't allowed. Being something of a trouble-making rabble-rouser, my sympathies had been with the miners during their struggles with Ted Heath's Tory government, which had been voted out the year before. But if they hadn't been I'd have still become their most ardent supporter after spending a day underground in a mine. You really cannot believe the conditions in which those guys had to labour unless you've seen them for yourself.

And talk about taking your work home with you! That coal dust gets everywhere, and I mean everywhere. Your ears, your nose, your … well, you get the picture. And you don't get rid of it in a hurry – it was weeks before I could get in a hot bath without the water instantly turning black.

These excursions notwithstanding, most of the time spent learning the rudiments of our chosen craft was desperately tedious. But at least we always had the football at weekends.

When West Ham's season had kicked off in August with a thumping defeat at Manchester City I never dreamed that a few months later I would be queuing up to get into Old Trafford to support the red half of the city. But here I was, regularly doing just that. To be honest, all these years on and the games we saw have become something of a blur. But one that readily comes to mind is the Cardiff fixture. Such was our dislike of the Welsh capital we made a special point of going to Old Trafford to watch them play there. United won 4–0 and I saw Steve Coppell make his Man Utd debut.

There were a couple of United players from that team who ended up at Upton Park. Bustling striker Stuart Pearson would, among other things, later provide the cross-shot that Trevor Brooking headed home to beat Arsenal in the 1980 Cup final, while midfield general Lou 'Lou, Skip to My Lou' Macari was destined to be West Ham manager for all of six months. Who'd have bet on that? Come to think of it, Lou might. He was accused of betting on just about everything else.

While Man Utd were tearing up the second division, West Ham were starting to put together what would turn out to be a triumphant Cup run. After beating Swindon we were drawn against QPR in the fifth round, a game we won 2–1 at Upton Park. Then it was Arsenal at Highbury in the sixth round and, unless you skipped Chapter Four, you will now know this was the first time it was officially noted that Sir Trev walked on water.

The semi-final against Ipswich at Villa Park was one of the worst games I've ever seen. It finished 0–0, and both sides were lucky to get nil. It didn't help that both Bob and I had monster hangovers, brought about by spending most of the previous night drinking vast quantities of Bull's Blood (the Hungarian wine rather than the actual blood of a bovine male). We were in the North Stand and it was so packed we couldn't force our way on to the terracing itself and had to stand on a sloping walkway instead. Try that for two hours and see what it does to your hamstrings.

The most memorable part of the day was the drive back to Cardiff. Bob was behind the wheel – it was his car after all – but he decided I should steer from the passenger's seat while we polished off a bottle of vodka between us. So that's the way we did it – for 100-odd miles. It was probably the most stupid thing I have done in my life – and certainly one of the most dangerous. Almost as dangerous, however, was watching Man U clinch the second division title at Notts County.

Between you and me, I much preferred supporting Man Utd at Old Trafford than on the road. Bob's mum and dad always made me feel tremendously welcome whenever I stayed in their warm, cosy, comfortable home. Usually Bob's mum would feed us royally, but on one occasion his dad gave us the money to treat ourselves to a meal in the Grand Hotel. It was the first time I ate duck à l'orange, which, preceded by a prawn cocktail, was without doubt the pinnacle of style in 1975. Many years later I went back to the

Grand with Di after we'd been to see a game in the north-west. We stayed overnight – partly because we didn't fancy the drive back south, but also because I wanted to rekindle the memory of those wonderful times. We got woken up by a bunch of workmen in the adjoining room at 6 a.m. and, after our complaints to reception that no one should be hammering this early on a Sunday morning were relayed to the horny handed sons of toil next door, we were subjected to a stream of abuse through the paper-thin wall until we finally got up and went down for breakfast.

Anyway, there was no getting out of the trip to Nottingham – not with Manchester United on the verge of the title. Again we drove up from Cardiff – this time with Bob firmly in control of steering wheel as well as pedals. But soon after parking the car we became part of the phalanx of Man U fans making the slow march to the game under the watchful – and nervous – eye of a huge police escort.

Inside the ground there was the usual mixture of emotions that you get with any football crowd; expectation, tension, bravado – even some humour. But that day there was a sense of insanity too. One guy shinned up a floodlight pylon and got a huge cheer for his efforts. Another idiot decided to follow suit and clambered up the pylon in the other corner. But instead of being saluted for his efforts he was urged to jump – and for several worrying moments I really thought he was going to give in to the baying crowd below.

Bob recalls how he was finally talked down. 'It was a convincing and compelling piece of advice from the highly trained police negotiator: "Come down here, you thick twat".'

I can't pretend to remember much about the game itself, although United were two up at half time and got the point they needed. We all ended up on the pitch afterwards. Even those of us who didn't want to go found ourselves there; to be honest, you don't have much of a say in the matter once the common consensus is for a human stampede. Depressingly, what should have been a celebration became another wrecking spree as hundreds of Man Utd fans tried to tear apart Meadow Lane with their bare hands.

My overriding memory of the game is the sound of unidentified objects flying past my head at various times throughout the match. I had witnessed coins being thrown before, but this was something different. The missiles were clearly heavier and more menacing – they hissed in flight. It wasn't until the following day, when the Sunday newspapers were full of pictures of a 5-inch metal kung fu star embedded in a policeman's helmet, that I realised what had been whistling past my unprotected cranium. Had one of them hit me I doubt I would here to tell the story now. It seems some of the more enterprising yobbos had been making them at school, painstakingly filing down lumps of metal into the shape of a star with several razor-sharp prongs. I wonder what those characters are doing today? No doubt they are family men with strong views on law and order. Perhaps one of them even went on to be a metalwork teacher.

Fleet Street went to town on the red army. The *Daily Mirror* was still frothing at the mouth on Monday. Under the front page headline 'Savage animals' it reported that six kung fu stars had been recovered and two supporters were still in hospital. On the back page Tommy Docherty was quoted as saying: 'What these mobsters will do next season has me really scared.'

A fortnight later Bob and I were at Wembley to watch West Ham beat Fulham 2–0 in the Cup final, courtesy of two goals from Alan Taylor – and the chances are I never would have got to see the game if it hadn't been for my northern soulmate. Being an all-London final, tickets were like hen's teeth in the capital but, luckily, there were some to be had in the north and Bob's dad managed to lay his hands on a couple in Manchester. I've no idea how he did it – but I will always be grateful to him for that.

The following season Bob and I were both back on our respective papers, trying to put into practice what we had learned in Cardiff. But although we could no longer go to matches together on a regular basis we were determined to see both West Ham v. Man Utd games that season. Which is why I watched in horror as some of the worst crowd trouble ever witnessed at Upton Park was played out in front of me – believing my mate was in the thick of it.

It was widely expected there would be trouble between two sets of supporters who detested one another. The shops and pubs near Upton Park had closed for the day and the sale of alcohol was prohibited. Some eyewitnesses have reported they saw skirmishes before the game, but I don't recall encountering any trouble after Bob and I parked the Kadett in a side street and made our way to the ground. With three times the usual number of police on duty, anyone who fancied a pre-match tear-up was certain to get nicked.

As usual in those days, the away team were given the South Bank – and they didn't get all of that. Bob had decided he wanted to be with his fellow supporters in their end of the ground rather than join me on the North Bank, where he would have been required to remain seriously schtum for the duration of the match. We went our separate ways at the junction of the Barking Road and Green Street.

The atmosphere was tense from the outset. After six minutes a massive Mervyn Day goal kick landed on the edge of the Man Utd penalty area and, as their defence dithered, Alan Taylor nipped in to score. On the North Bank we forgot about abusing the opposition fans for a while and concentrated on celebrating the goal.

West Ham were still 1–0 up at half time. Then, nine minutes after the interval, Man Utd supporters began to spill on to the pitch. Exactly what happened down their end is still a matter of debate. Go online and you will find any number of accounts from people who were there. Some put the disturbance down to fighting, others reckon it was simply because too many people had been herded on to the South Bank terracing.

Eugene says:

> I was at that game in 1975, the ground was rammed full, hundreds of Manchester fans had kicked in one of the turnstile gates to get in after the gates were closed, there was a big crush on that terrace. The crowd were swaying everywhere, fans got on the pitch to escape the crush, there was no fighting. There was a lot more in that ground that day than the stated attendance of about 38,000. The Manchester fans had a bad name then, they came to Upton Park in their thousands. It was pay on the gate, there was just not room for them all.

But Steve disagrees. 'This was violence. I was there. West Ham were in the ground hours before us and ambushed us on the way in. They were throwing bottles and milk crates at us. There were quite a few fans locked outside, WHU and reds.'

This was a time when the fans of both clubs reckoned they were the heavyweight champions of British hooliganism. The red army was notorious after its exploits in the second division; West Ham's Inter City Firm had yet to be formed but there were plenty of other, smaller, groups (some of which were later to be marshalled under the ICF banner) who were ready and willing to dish out a liberal dose of West Ham aggro when called upon to do so. The Mile End Mob; the Teddy Bunter Firm; the South Bank Crew – you really didn't want to mess with those boys. It was these 'firms', say some, who caused the mayhem.

Stepney says:

> I was there that day on the South Bank. Man Utd at that time had a reputation for wrecking trains and town centres everywhere they travelled. They came down in large numbers that day hoping for a repeat of 1967 when they swamped the North Bank and beat the Irons 1–6 on the pitch.

His comment is appended to online footage of Brian Moore's calm, measured, analytical commentary of the mayhem that was taking place in the south-east corner of the ground. He adds:

> What you see on this video is the result of them having been attacked relentlessly by the TBF [Teddy Bunter Firm] and the South Bank Crew. They were forced over the corner by the Chicken Run and were trying to get away to safety. Many of them suffered further attacks at the hands of the West Ham mob on their journey back through the East End on the District line. Man United supporters were despised by West Ham in those days.

Pogo12xu saw things in much the same way.

> About thirty minutes before kickoff Man U had been run
> on the pitch from both the South Bank and the west side.
> Police made them get back on to the South Bank terraces
> and tried to keep rival fans apart. Shortly after kickoff, a
> turnstile door was broken down and several hundred more
> joined an already overcrowded terrace, West Ham steamed
> in again forcing everyone at the front to spill on to the
> pitch.

Whatever the cause, one thing is certain. If there had been fences, as there were at Hillsborough fourteen years later, there could well have been a tragedy on a similar scale.

As the chaos played itself out, referee Peter Reeves was left with little choice other than to take the players from the field. He set a time limit of twenty minutes for order to be restored, after which he proposed to abandon the game. Ron Greenwood, recently elevated to general manager, went on the pitch in his gabardine Mac to see if he could help the hard-pressed police sort out the mess.

Years later, Richard went online to say: 'I was there that day as an eight-year-old with my dad sitting safely in the West Stand. It was my first game at West Ham and I remember thinking, "Is this normal?" I remember John McDowell of West Ham leading a child off the pitch.'

In the event, the players came back with two minutes to spare – and Manchester United promptly scored via a Coppell free kick and a Macari header.

Our second goal – which turned out to be the winner – came on seventy minutes and was also the result of a set piece. Trevor Brooking picked out Graham Paddon, who had been brought down to win the free kick, and his low cross was fired home by Bobby Gould. Deep, deep joy for all those in claret and blue.

What I didn't know at the time was that, by a huge stroke of luck, Bob had managed to avoid the man-made maelstrom that could have cost him his life. I'll let him tell the story himself.

United took massive crowds to all games and this one was no different.

After we split up I located the massed ranks of United fans and stood in line to get in. Everybody seemed pretty chilled – West Ham were always decent opposition, but it wasn't seen as a powder-keg game: that was reserved for the likes of Liverpool, City and Leeds.

After about twenty-five minutes I hadn't moved and nor had anybody else.

The rumour went round that the end was full so I decided to do the unthinkable – go and stand on my jack in the West Ham end. My grasp of cockney was limited only to the few months I'd known this London fruitcake in Cardiff: apples and pears, giving it large, you're having a laarf – that sort of nonsense. I knew that if I tried to sound remotely southern I'd do a worse impression than Dick Van Dyke in *Mary Poppins*. So all I could do was keep my mouth shut.

Surprisingly, when I got to the Hammers' end, there was no queue and no stewards or coppers checking supporters in. So I handed over my cash and in I went.

I manoeuvred as far to the left side of the stand as I could get.

My plan to be incognito, though, was immediately compromised by a group I had unknowingly stood next to: 'U-N-I-T-E-D, United are the team for me, with a knick knack paddy whack give a dog a bone, why don't City fuck off home?' Oh no. I had stood next to a group of seemingly suicidal reds.

Heads turned in our direction, so I suddenly made a discreet exit to a relatively safe area. It was around about now, thankfully, that everyone's attention was drawn to the other end. It was chaos. United fans were grouped in several factions but seemingly below West Ham supporters who had the high ground and were able to charge down at them.

Police crowd control was pretty basic in those days. But to have no segregation at all – absolutely nothing at all – was mind-boggling. Occasionally you would see United and City fans mingling in a derby at Maine Road, but I can't ever remember seeing such a ticking timebomb anywhere else.

It was sickening watching the scrapping – and the utterly useless, spineless, leaderless response from the police.

As the game developed and we were thankfully losing, the last thing I needed was Lou Macari getting a goal to make it even more edgy. The Manchester lads in the West Ham end, pretty quiet during a disappointing game from our perspective, suddenly spurted into life and it kicked off again.

Maybe, in the light of Bob's account of events that grim day, Gould's winning goal was even more important than it seemed at the time.

The victory put us level with QPR and Man Utd at the top of the table, separated only by goal average[1] and with a game in hand on the other two. Normally I would have been ecstatic at beating my mate's team and being in such a dizzyingly high League position, but for once I didn't rub it in. Not after what we had just seen.

Instead, we listened to the reports of what we'd witnessed on the car radio as we headed for home. 'Talk about uninformed gibberish,' says Bob.

> It was all the maniac Mancs' fault, of course. The local station fell completely for the stereotype: northern monkeys coming to the big city for a punch-up. Not a word on the complete shambles brought about by a lack of organisation by the police and the club. Journalistically, it was an important lesson for me. The anger I felt then shaped how I went about my business afterwards, and to this day. Assume nothing – rather than follow the obvious line, dig under the surface to find the full facts. Don't be a lazy tosser.

---

1 From the time the Football League was formed in 1888, rather than separate sides who were level on points by the self-explanatory goal difference used today, their positions were decided by dividing goals for by goals against. It wasn't an 'average' at all, but that's what it was called. Not only was it hard to work out in your head, the system promoted defensive football (2–1 is a better result than 6–4 while a clean sheet is priceless) and it was finally junked at the end of the 1975/76 season. Sadly, the violence that was also part and parcel of the game back then took rather longer to eradicate.

For anyone thinking of taking up a career in journalism, can I just say that is better advice than anything Bob and I were ever given in Cardiff.

History hasn't been kind to the '70s, and after days like that you can see why. But it wasn't all football hooliganism and industrial unrest. Unlike now, people didn't fear for their jobs, the cost of housing was affordable for the vast majority and there was a general feeling life would improve for everyone. Much of the fashion was a bit ropey, but some of the music will live on for ever (including 'Lady Marmalade'). And what about the food? Prawn cocktail and duck à l'orange – it doesn't get much better than that. Not to mention the Black Forest gateau to follow. Like the decade itself, that never got its just desserts either. For all its faults I still look back on 1975 with fondness. Let's face it, any year's a good year when you're nineteen and you've still got your entire life in front of you.

Chapter 10

West Ham 'til I cry

I F YOU'VE NEVER been to a chilli festival, put that right the next time there's one in your neck of the woods. You'll be hard-pressed to find anywhere else you can have as much fun while still fully clothed.

The highlight of these events is the chilli-eating contest, in which a group of brave souls, encouraged by their so-called 'friends', take to the stage and set about a number of chilli peppers ranging in strength from something you'd happily give your granny to a thermonuclear variant that could take out half of Doncaster.

There is a strange pleasure to be had watching people voluntarily torturing themselves in such a way. Unless there is a complete wimp up there they all generally manage to negotiate the first round, which is when you get the initial indication of form. That fella in the studded leather jacket, who's 6 ft 3 and chiselled out of granite, looked curiously troubled by the basic pimiento, while the unassuming guy in the lamb's wool sweater at the other end of the table dispatched it without blinking. He could well be the one to watch here.

By the time you've got up to the jalapeños some of the contestants are starting to look distinctly nervous; one or two may even be running up the white flag at this stage. There will certainly be casualties on the cayenne leg, and when they start bringing out the Jamaican hots and Scotch bonnets the body count really begins to rise. Judging by the way Leather Jacket Bloke left the stage clutching his stomach, the chances are he won't be going to work tomorrow. Still, at least he wasn't struck down by the dreaded 'chilli claw' in which the body goes into spasm and certain muscles contract to temporarily leave the unfortunate victim with a hook instead of a hand. He'd never be able to ride his motorbike like that.

The relative strength of chillies is measured on the Scoville scale. Devised in 1912 by an American called Wilbur Scoville, the basic idea is to take the substance that puts the fire into chillies – capsaicin – and dilute it in sweetened water until it is no longer detectable. The more sugar water you need, the hotter the chilli. So a basic red pepper scores zero, while the innocent-sounding Dorset Naga requires a million parts water to one part capsaicin – and thus rates 1,000,000 on the scale. (Should you ever have the misfortune to be on the wrong end of police pepper spray you will be looking at well over 2,000,000 Scoville units, but I suggest you keep this knowledge to yourself or you're likely to get another squirt for being a clever-clogs.)

As a system of measurement it's all a bit imprecise, but I believe it has something to offer the game of football. What we need is a similar method to judge decisions made by referees, so I have written to FIFA suggesting that, now it has got to grips with goal-line technology and found something useful to do with a can of shaving foam, it adopts the Hackett scale – named after the man whose memory will forever burn with a white heat of anger more fiery than the hottest habanero in the hearts of all those who follow West Ham.

It was Keith Hackett, you will recall, who gave Tony Gale a straight red card for an innocuous challenge in an FA Cup semi and effectively ended our chances of reaching the 1991 final. Ironically, the roots of this awful decision can be traced back to a previous Cup final involving West Ham, and the birth of the 'professional foul'.

In 1980, against Arsenal, West Ham's Paul Allen was clear through on goal and had every chance of being the youngest ever scorer in a Wembley Cup final when he was unceremoniously upended by Willie Young, a man who truly put the Goon in Gooner, in what was seen as a blatantly cynical foul even by the more physical standards of the time. Referee George Courtney felt, under the laws of the game, he could do no more than award a free kick and Young stayed on the field. I witnessed this from the press box at Wembley and even seasoned hacks were outraged. It was one of those rare moments when the entire footballing world came together and agreed that something had to be done! Trouble was, they couldn't agree on precisely what.

So, in the best traditions of these things, a sub-committee including some of the most famous names in football was set up to make a few recommendations – which they duly did. And, in exactly the same traditions, those recommendations were rejected. However, we now had the concept of the professional foul which, unlike your common-or-garden foul, is 'an act of foul play, usually to deny a goalscoring opportunity'.

In England, the Football League instructed the referees to start sending off players considered to have committed a professional foul in the early '80s on the basis that the perpetrator was guilty of serious foul play, which merited a straight red card under the existing laws of the game.

FIFA, on the other hand, took a rather more leisurely approach to the tricky question of what to do about players who deliberately kick their opponents up in the air rather than stand back and applaud sportingly as they score the goal that gets their manager the sack and ensures they themselves will be playing non-League football for the rest of their careers.

The world's governing body waited until Italia '90 before it decreed that refs should send off players for a professional foul. The following year, FIFA's position was endorsed by the IFAB, the guardian of football's laws. And, according to Mr Hackett, there was to be no leniency for offenders.

He has been quoted as saying:

> The thing that nobody knew was that the Thursday prior to the match [in which he sent off Tony Gale] referees were told at a meeting the law had not been applied properly. We were told a simple foul was all that was necessary for a sending-off. Gale was sent off for a foul that would not have got a yellow card a week before.

The massed ranks of West Ham supporters certainly didn't know about that particular meeting as we looked on in astonishment while he brandished the red card at Villa Park three days later. 'My decision dramatically affected the game and ruined a lot of people's day out,' he concedes. Well, you've got that one right, mate.

Gale feels hard done by to this day. He told me: 'I still can't believe the sending-off. I've got pictures of it at home, and whenever I look at them I get the right hump. It was the only time I was sent off in my career.' This was a man who made more than 700 senior appearances throughout his career and, by his reckoning, he was only ever booked seven times. 'I wasn't a dirty player,' he insists.

> There were only twenty-two minutes gone and we were up against it after that. I had to go to the dressing room – you have to leave the field of play if you are sent off, and that includes the bench. I just sat there quietly and waited for the lads to come in at half time.
>
> As they went out for the second half, Billy Bonds told me to come with him. We were walking side by side in the tunnel when an official from the FA tried to stop us. 'You can't go out there, Tony, you've been sent off,' he said.
>
> Billy just glared at him. 'Don't you think you've taken enough liberties?' he asked the bloke. 'He's coming with me.'
>
> So I spent the second half on the bench!

According to Gale, his manager emphasised the point about where he felt they could and couldn't go with some rather robust industrial language but we needn't quote that verbatim here.

'The best thing was the response of the fans,' Gale goes on. 'They didn't stop singing for the rest of the game.

'I've never forgiven Hackett. I'm convinced to this day he wanted to be the first person to implement the new ruling that had come out that week.'

So you haven't kept in touch then? 'Funnily enough, I got a call from him recently. It was the first time we'd spoken since the incident. He asked me if I'd like to appear with him in a video about refereeing. He wasn't joking either!' As with Bonzo's reply to the FA official all those years ago, Tony Gale's response to Mr Hackett's invitation is best left unreported in full. (Clearly Gale's bark is worse than his bite because he and Hackett did go on to make a short film together. Very watchable it was too.)

Martin Allen, cousin of the baby-faced Paul who had been hacked down at Wembley all those years before, hasn't forgotten that day either. According to one newspaper interview with Mad Dog:

> A couple of years ago managers were invited to a meeting of the Referees' Association before the season. The first person introduced was Hackett. It was the first time I had seen him since he ruined my FA Cup final dream.
>
> I remember the cup and saucer I was holding shaking. The coffee spilt over my trousers. I was getting a lecture from Keith Hackett! I never heard a word of it. All I could do was imagine him holding up that red card.

The point about Mr Hackett wanting to be the first person to apply the new ruling is an interesting one. Looking back on the game, it was as if he wanted to be the star of the show – which is just about the worst offence a referee can commit, I reckon. So, on the new scale, Gale's dismissal rates the maximum one million Hacketts – not just for the decision itself but also because the man who ruined one of the most important games of the season shrugged it off with barely a hint of an apology.

It's curious how many former West Ham players have been involved in incidents that would register on the Hackett scale if it had been introduced earlier.

Freddie Sears never fully recovered from the diabolical decision that robbed him of a perfectly good goal for Crystal Palace at Ashton Gate during a loan spell in 2009. His shot clearly hit the back of the Bristol City goal, but he'd struck the ball so sweetly it came flying back out. Referee Rob Shoebridge disallowed the effort and Sears seemed to lose all self-confidence after that. For the damage it did to young Freddie's career, Shoebridge gets 400,000 Hacketts for that clanger.

Something strangely similar had happened to another member of the Allen clan. In truth, Clive is Tottenham through and through. But he did score the goal that secured our promotion at the end of the 1992/93 season, so for the purposes of this discussion he is one of our own. (There is a bonus point on offer here for anyone who can remember who scored the other goal in that 2–0 win over Cambridge. Right then, you sir – the man in the Dagenham Motors shirt with his hand up. No, it wasn't Trevor Morley; the answer I'm looking for is David Speedie. Better luck in the music round.)

Just like Sears, Allen also scored a perfectly good goal for Palace that the referee missed. This was back in 1980, against Coventry. His free-kick hit the right-hand stanchion inside the goal, only for the ball to bounce back out of the net. Referee Derek Webb consulted his linesman – and then ruled no goal. I'd rate that 300,000 on the Hackett scale.

As a rule, any decision that goes against Frank Lampard Jnr would be Hackett-free. But as he was playing for England against Germany when he had a legitimate goal chalked off, the blunder by Uruguayan referee Jorge Larrionda does register this time. Lampard's effort, of course, was in the 2010 World Cup in Bloemfontein and would have been the equaliser had the ref or his assistant Mauricio Espinosa seen the ball cross the line after it ricocheted off the bar. I'd rate that at 200,000 on the scale. The Germans argued that this merely evened things up for Sir Geoff Hurst's controversial goal in the 1966 World Cup final, which they still maintain never crossed the line. Please don't think there's any bias involved here on my part, but I'm sorry, my friends – you are wrong about this. Check the record books: I'll think you'll find that it did.

Roy Carroll stumbled around between the sticks in West Ham colours from 2005 to 2007. Before that he had plied his trade at Manchester United. Sir Alex Ferguson's decision to move him on was no doubt hastened by a horrible fumble in the dying moments of a game against Spurs in which it appeared Pedro Mendes had scored a shock winner with a long-range shot he had unleashed from a different postcode. At least it appeared that way to everyone except referee Mark Clattenburg and lino Rob Lewis, who both failed to notice that the ball had crossed the line. Normally an error of that magnitude would merit 150,000 Hacketts, but as it denied Tottenham three points the sentence will be halved on this occasion.

Curiously, Mr Hackett himself was at Old Trafford that night. 'From my seat in the stand I could see what the match officials couldn't. I had the advantage of elevation. The match officials at ground level had no chance. I felt sick about what happened. Sick to the stomach, in fact. I was frustrated that I couldn't help.' Thanks, but no thanks, Mr Hackett. You've done enough already.

Paul Gascoigne, of course, never played for West Ham, but he is that rare breed of player who somehow seems to belong to all of us. His booking at the hands of referee Dougie Smith shows precisely why we need a system that measures the stupidity of officials. When Mr Smith dropped his yellow card, Gascoigne picked it up. And, Gascoigne being Gascoigne, he couldn't resist the temptation of brandishing it as if booking the ref before handing it back. Everyone saw the funny side – except the ref, who immediately booked Gazza for attempting to make people smile. In my book that rates 999,999 Hacketts.

The worst decision at Upton Park in recent years – worse even than the sending off of Carlton Cole by the hopeless buffoon Anthony Taylor in the game against Everton three days before Christmas in 2012 – was the red card shown to Andy Carroll by Howard Webb in a controversial encounter with Swansea in January 2014.

Despite what the rest of the football world felt about the decision, Webb was right according to his former colleague Graham Poll. Apparently the people who judge such things reckon Poll is one of the best refs this country has ever produced. In fact, he was in line to take charge of the 2006 World Cup final until he made a slight error in a crucial qualifying game and booked the same Croatian player three times before sending him off. Nice one, Graham. Why don't you and Mr Webb both take a wheelbarrow full of Hacketts and sling your hook before I get cross again. Oh, and you can take Anthony Taylor with you.

On a rather less notorious occasion we got away with one at

Upton Park in the 2005/06 season when Alan Pardew surprised everyone – me especially – by guiding what appeared on paper to be an under-strength squad to a top-half finish. Three of the fifty-five points we notched up that year were down to a controversial O.G. at Upton Park by Middlesbrough's Chris Riggott. His deflection, following a Paul Konchesky free kick, was ruled to be a goal by the assistant ref despite Boro keeper Mark Schwarzer smothering it at the second attempt. We could see from the East Stand that the ball hadn't crossed the line. Heaven only knows what referee Steve Bennett saw. We waited for him to overrule the lino, and could hardly believe our luck when he pointed to the centre circle. The laughter that accompanied our celebrations was down to the fact that a dodgy decision had actually gone our way for once rather than merriment at Riggott's misfortune. (Not that we're immune from taking the mick out of a hapless defender who puts the ball in his own net – we just didn't do it this time.)

I have never been a huge fan of Steve McClaren, who was the Middlesbrough manager at the time. But on this occasion the Wally with the Brolly had a point. 'It took me thirty seconds to go to the back of the stand and see it wasn't a goal, so why can't officials do the same?' he asked. 'If the technology is there we have to use it. Other sports exploit it.'

You're right, Steve – goal-line technology has got to be an improvement. But when has football ever bothered to learn anything from those other sports you mentioned? Ever tried arguing with a rugby ref? You don't do it a second time. Similarly, you won't see a cricket umpire surrounded by stroppy prima donnas waving their arms around like a demented copper directing traffic after the lights have failed simply because a decision has gone against them. It's drilled into you as a kid, the umpire is always right – even when he's wrong. A bit like yer dad.

I've not done a lot of refereeing myself (two five-a-side games, to be precise) but it seems to me that, rather than merely follow the rules slavishly, there's room for some creative thinking. You are no doubt familiar with the rap duo Rizzle Kicks. Well, I once put my theory into practice by asking a nice young man called Mike to kick Rizzle as hard as he could while I was looking the other way – and it worked like a charm.

Geoff and Jordan 'Rizzle' Stephens were schoolfriends for years. Despite being an Arsenal supporter, Jordan is a lovely lad – but it's fair to say he's never been short of an opinion and he's certainly not shy when it comes to expressing himself. So I wasn't overly surprised when he questioned my first decision in a five-a-side game at the local sports centre which was part of my son's fifteenth birthday celebrations. To be honest I was a bit surprised when Geoff asked me to ref it, but I felt vaguely honoured too. I even went out and bought a whistle.

Jordan never went so far as to tell me where to shove my whistle – he's far too well-brought up for that – but it was clear from his frequent protests that he believed he should be protected from some of the more robust tackling that was a feature of the game. I'm a bit old-school myself and I like a decent challenge. You can't have spent as many years admiring the likes of Billy Bonds and Julian Dicks as I have and not appreciate the defensive side of our beautiful game, so I was perhaps letting a bit more go than you'd see on *Match of the Day* in this antiseptic age of minimal contact and boots like slippers and balls that don't have laces which you can head when they're wet without concussing yourself. Kids today? They don't know they're born!

Several polite requests asking Jordan to keep his lip buttoned fell on deaf ears, which prompted my next move. When the ball was down the other end I called over Mike, who was playing at the back for the other side. Naturally, I got the 'What me, ref?' look as I beckoned him, but I explained that not only wasn't he in trouble, but I also had a little task for him. His look of bewilderment turned to a full-beam smile as I explained what I wanted: namely, the next time he was anywhere near Jordan he was to clatter him as hard and as unfairly as he could. In short, he had one free foul and he was not to waste it.

He didn't. Jordan was miles from the ball when Mike sent him flying with a villainous tackle from behind. When he picked himself off the floor he turned to me in search of justice, and found me strangely unsympathetic. 'Sorry, Jordan, just didn't see it,' I told him. And as he looked me in the eye in total disbelief, the penny dropped. He was as good as gold from then on and we all had a fantastic afternoon. If I remember correctly I engineered a questionable penalty shoot-out which ensured Geoff got the winning goal. Well, we were paying for it, after all.

The men in black like to tell anyone who will listen that they have a tough job, but I'm not convinced. They don't even have to wear black any more (although at least they ditched that awful green they used to wear in the early days of the Premier League. I'm no fashion icon, but lime green? Per-leeze!).

When the Football Association was founded in 1863 there were no referees. This was a game for gentlemen and, as they weren't going to attempt to gain an unfair advantage by deliberately employing underhand tricks, nobody could see the need for a ref. Instead, the FA went for two umpires to interpret the laws of the game – one provided by each side. By the 1880s it became clear these two honourable gents couldn't always agree, so they brought in someone to whom their quarrels could be referred. That's why they are called 'referees' (although I have heard them called other names at Upton Park over the years, not of all which are entirely complimentary).

The following decade it was decided to put the referees on the field and – quite literally – sideline the umpires. That's when they found themselves demoted to mere linesmen. (Note to the FA: efforts to upgrade their job description by rebranding them 'assistant referees' are fooling no one; they are linos and everybody knows it. If they were proper referees they would get a whistle instead of a flag.)

But they can console themselves with the thought they don't cop anything like the abuse that the man in the middle has to take. My mate Steve tells me that he once saw a long consultation between a ref and a linesman, which resulted in a controversial decision going Derby's way. At which point a section of the crowd adapted a Glen Campbell classic with 'He is a linesman for the County.' And that was at Chelsea – who'd have thought they could come up with something as good as that?

The laws that govern association football have evolved since 1863. There are now seventeen. I think there should be an eighteenth – one that prohibits people crying in public before, during or after a game. Of course there will be exceptions – I'm a reasonable man, after all. So young Callum Mann, who was picked out by the TV cameras as West Ham were drubbed 5–0 at Nottingham Forest in the third round of the 2014 FA Cup and was reduced to tears, has nothing to fear.

Furthermore, in line with UK statute governing the age of criminal responsibility, anyone under ten will be exempt from punishment if they are caught sobbing on camera as their heroes are relegated. I am even prepared to extend this amnesty to juveniles as a whole if one of the 'heroes' concerned is seen on a mobile to their agent seeking a transfer before the final whistle has sounded. But that's about it.

And, tearful fans please note, there is a significant difference between being relegated and failing to secure promotion through the play-offs – particularly if, like Blackpool, your miserable little club is unable to sell its allocation of tickets and then refuses to make those unsold seats available to ticketless opposition supporters who would have walked barefoot to get to a Wembley final.

Weeping is not the West Ham way (except perhaps when you see how much the owners have upped the price of tickets again). Admittedly, there were some runny eyes when we were relegated at Birmingham with forty-two points in 2003, but the pollen count was exceptionally high that day and I put it down to widespread hay fever.

Did we cry when we were hammered 6–0 by Man Utd in the FA Cup? We did not. We thanked our Mancunian hosts for their hospitality and went about our business whistling cheerful cockney ditties. Did we cry when we were humiliated by the same score in the Premier League at Reading? We did not. We offered our brave lads some heartfelt and constructive advice about the importance of the shirt instead. Did we cry when we were thrashed six-zip in the first leg of a League Cup semi-final at Oldham? We did not – we did a conga round the godforsaken terracing that stood in the shadow of Saddleworth Moor while one of our number stripped off and danced chubbily in the pouring rain. Did we cry when history repeated itself at the Etihad years later as our boys threw in the towel against a rampant Man City and surrendered any hope of reaching Wembley before the return tie at Upton Park? I think you get my drift.

But hit the internet and you'll see clips of lachrymose supporters from all corners of the country wiping away the tears as their hopes of going up/staying up/winning something (delete where not applicable) vanish before their very moist eyes.

This sobbing business is a relatively new phenomenon. When football was played in black and white, supporters – as the Pathé newsreels will testify – would spin their rattles and throw their flat caps in the air when they won. And, if they lost, they'd merely shrug their shoulders, go home in an orderly fashion and give the dog a good hiding. Not that anyone condones violence against defenceless animals, of course. But there has to be a better way of taking defeat than boo-hooing in public.

The whole thing reached its nadir when, in the 2011/12 season, Man City fan John Millington was seen sobbing as his multi-squillion-pound team lost to Swansea because he thought they'd blown their title chances. They still had ten games to go, for – well, I was going to say 'crying out loud', but we're trying to man up here, so I'll instead go with – 'pity's sake'.

At first Mr Millington denied he was blubbing. 'I wasn't crying, I was just frustrated and very tired. There may have been a tear in my eye but I was just exhausted and frustrated,' he was quoted as saying in the *Metro* newspaper.

But later he went on to claim that his failure to maintain a stiff upper lip during the run-in was actually wot won the Premier

League for Citeh. He told the *Manchester Evening News*: 'I really think it made the difference. Mancini said they had to win it for me and I think the players realised that. They saw me in tears and realised what it meant to all the City fans. United's players must have seen it too and it seems to have put the pressure on them. I like to think I started the mind games back then and it seems to have done the trick.'

The crying game took an even more bizarre twist during Euro 2012 when a German woman was shown on telly supposedly in tears because the Fatherland had been rinsed by Italy in the semis. She later complained, saying the footage was misleading because it had been shot earlier and she was actually crying when the teams came out.

What sort of excuse is that? Blimey, I've often wanted to cry when I've seen the teams come out at Upton Park, particularly when Allen McKnight and David Kelly were in the same side. But you don't, do you? It's just not the done thing.

And the reason you don't want other people seeing the tracks of your tears over something as trivial as a lost game (or even a lost relegation campaign) is that, as at all clubs, there are the occasional moments of shared grief that truly warrant an open show of emotion.

Bill Shankly famously once said that football is more important than life and death. A great quote, but nonsense nonetheless. Which is why I shed a tear when I heard the terrible news that Bobby Moore had been taken by cancer (and another when I saw the tributes outside the main gates in Green Street), but merely confine myself to kicking the cat and re-programming the satnav when we go down.

Which brings us, albeit in a roundabout way, back to our chilli festival. To avoid the embarrassment of being seen dabbing the old mince pies with a tissue inside a football stadium, remember to wash your hands after touching those fiery little devils – failure to do so will almost certainly end in tears if you rub your eyes in disbelief at yet another baffling decision by the ref. But the next time it happens simply make a note of the howler's Hackett rating and drop it in the post to the Referees' Association. I'm assured they will be delighted to hear from you.

Chapter 11

A book of two halves

WE ARE NOW halfway through this book. I've added a bit on for deliberate time-wasting plus injury to any feelings that may have been hurt, but there goes the whistle for half time. So you've now got fifteen minutes to kill in the best way you see fit.

You could try nipping off for a pint and something to eat, but the prices are extortionate and the queues will be endless. Chances are, by the time you've gulped down the last mouthful you'll have missed the start of Chapter 12.

Not that sitting there and waiting to be entertained will do you much good. This isn't the good ol' US of A with marching bands and toothy majorettes twirling batons as if their lives depended on it. The best you can hope for is a couple of ancient rock classics mangled by a low-grade PA system and, if you're lucky, a brief update on the half-time news from elsewhere. (At the mid-point of *Fever Pitch* Nick Hornby is indoctrinating his half-brother into the strange ways of Arsenal, and in *The Damned United* Brian Clough is preparing for his first home game as manager of Leeds at Elland Road.)

There have been efforts to jazz up half time at Upton Park with a bit of American-style glitz and glamour courtesy of the Hammerettes, a group of local lovelies who once brightened the interval with some energetic dance routines. But you get the feeling the club's heart isn't really in it these days.

As any painter and decorator will tell you, a Hammerette is not to be confused with Hammerite, which is the stuff they slap over metal railings to prevent rusting. The girls strutted their stuff at the Boleyn Ground until they were given the bullet four weeks before the start of the 2006/07 season. To be honest, I wasn't their biggest fan. However, you had to give them top marks for effort. And as our back four could never move in unison, it's probably unfair to have expected the half-time dance act to have done so.

What followed was certainly worse – watching anti-corrosive paint dry would have been more entertaining than the penalty shoot-outs for toddlers and the various other 'community events' (the club's words, not mine) that replaced the Hammerettes.

I realise we live in an age of austerity, but whoever thought that four members of the London amputee football team having a kickabout at half time in the game against Everton qualifies as entertainment should think again. Brave though these people are, this was never going to be much of a spectacle. And someone at the club must have realised there would be feedback from certain sections of the crowd – not all of which would be positive. The remarks suggesting West Ham would be better off dropping the much-maligned Modibo Maiga and playing one of these lads up front instead, although accurate, were as inevitable as they were unkind.

To be fair to the mastermind who fathered this particular brainchild, I will admit that it was at least better than the world final of something called Match Attax, staged at half time against Chelsea some years ago, whereby two pimply youths went head to head over a small table in the centre circle and played an unfathomable card game before our disbelieving eyes.

It shouldn't be like this. By all means give the players a break and allow the manager a chance to remind his highly paid superstars that the general idea is to pass the ball to someone clad in a shirt similar to the one they themselves are wearing. But what about the paying public? We've forked out a small fortune for our tickets, so in this day and age is it unreasonable to want every minute packed with high-octane entertainment? Association football is supposed to have moved on since the idea of an enforced break of fifteen minutes was incorporated into the original laws of the game in 1863, yet supporters who actually pay to squeeze through the turnstiles might find that hard to believe.

Those who have studied such esoteric subjects as why football really is a game of two halves have concluded it is down to the nineteenth-century toffs who liked to kick a ball around at public school before emerging into the real world and giving the working classes a kicking of a rather different nature. Changing ends at half time was part of the deal at Eton and Winchester among others, while the likes of Rugby and Harrow changed after a goal had been scored. Schools such as Eton and Rugby played by different sets of rules – Eton's being closer to soccer and Rugby's being more like, well, rugby. The advantage of the fixed break halfway through a game was that, when the schools encountered one another, each could have a half playing the game with which they were most familiar. Well done, chaps – that all sounds jolly sporting to me. But where does it leave the plebs in the stands?

Sure, you get the chance to stretch cramped legs after being stuffed into an undersized seat for forty-five minutes (or to sit down if you are an ageing away supporter). And, of course, there's an opportunity to take a leak. While we're on this rather indelicate subject, could someone in authority at Wembley explain to me why, the last time I was there to support my beloved Hammers, the men's toilet closest to us was set up like a ladies' – cubicles only and no urinals? Trust me, that is not the quickest way to get a herd of blokes in and out of a public lavatory (although some of my fellow supporters did try to speed things along by using the basins – don't forget to wash your hands afterwards, lads).

I think supporters deserve a bit more. A spot of live music would go down well, and at West Ham we've got enough big-time musicians who support the club to stage our own version of Live Aid at half time.

It's not as if Upton Park has been used solely to stage football matches in its illustrious past. There's been boxing, for one thing. And religion. My fellow journalist and union activist Tim Dawson was there to see the American evangelist Billy Graham whip up a storm some years ago.

He recalls it to this day. 'My one visit to Upton Park left me with a single overwhelming conviction: there is no God,' says Tim. (We know how you feel, mate.)

Tim goes on:

I had gone to the stadium to see Graham conduct a 'revival meeting' in 1989. My attendance, however, was as a newspaper reporter not a seeker of salvation.

Graham was the best-known of the TV evangelists. He toured the world spreading his gospel of booming certainties. His was a faith that reduced the Bible to homilies, promoted a belief in miracles and centred on an absolute conviction in being 'born again', stripped of sin and offering up one's soul to Jesus.

I arrived at Upton Park to find its stands packed to capacity – that was my first surprise. On the pitch was a stage in front of which was a huge empty area. A parade of warm-up acts struggled to enliven the crowd.

When Graham finally took to the stage, however, it was clear that we were in the presence of a man who understood how to work a crowd. Looking like a late-period Johnny Cash, he had the quality of an Old Testament prophet. And simple as his stories were, he invested them with a fervour that resonated even at the top of the West Stand.

The climax of Graham's sermons had always been the same. 'Come on down,' he would demand – encouraging his audience to leave their seats and gather in front of the stage. Graham would then lead his congregation in a 'sinner's prayer' – the cornerstone of born-again Christianity where all would either reaffirm or embrace faith anew.

So it was at West Ham – although Graham did not rely on oratorical skills alone. As his sermon reached its explosive conclusion and he called on us to come forward, a small army of stewards suddenly appeared among the audience. Soon they were pushing and cajoling us down the gangways and on to the turf.

In the interests of journalistic inquiry, I followed. Now the stewards were tending to those of us on the pitch individually. 'Are you ready to make a sinner's prayer?' one asked me. I declined, but noticing that those who did bend to their knees were being given a package of literature, I asked if, as a representative of the press, I might be given one. 'They are only for the converted,' I was told.

My professional instincts kicked in – that pack might be the key to a decent story, I figured. So I picked among the throng and found another steward. 'I'm ready,' I said. The steward held my hands, pushed me to my knees and asked that I repeat these words: 'Forgive me of my sins, Lord, I accept Jesus as my master.'

Graham's performance had not really moved me – but now, bent down, hands clasped in the steward's sweaty grip, I knew that, if a thunderbolt from the sky was ever going to strike me, this was the moment. Seconds passed. I opened my eyes, my fingers were released and I looked up. The light momentarily dimmed as I was handed my information pack, but forked lightning – there was none.

The moral that I left with was this: like West Ham themselves, Billy Graham, on song, could put on a show with the power to transport crowds to a different realm. If you are looking for miracles and evidence of the existence of God, however, you will have to go a lot further than the end of Green Street.

Many thanks for that, Tim. Although I would say here that, had you ever seen Trevor Brooking at his best, you might not be quite so sceptical about the miraculous.

Not that I'm advocating a revivalist meeting at half time (except in the dressing room when we're 2–0 down). Besides, the devil has all the best tunes – which is why I'm going for a concert.

The original Live Aid, in 1985, famously kicked off at Wembley with Status Quo 'Rockin' All Over the World'. Should I ever find myself in the Midge Ure role of organising the whole thing while someone else takes all the credit and gets a knighthood, I would have to rule out Parfitt, Rossi and co. because they don't support West Ham. But there are plenty of rock stars who do.

Now, before we go any further, let's be clear about this. Music at half time is fine; music when the players run out is just about acceptable (as long as it's not something really naff like *The Great Escape* theme); music when a goal has been scored is an outrage. Clubs that do it should be made to forfeit the game immediately.

OK, now we've got that out the way I'm going to ask David Essex to open our Upton Park showpiece gig with his 1978 hit 'Oh What a Circus' which, as a title, is as valid now as it was then. He gets the honour for a number of reasons, most notably the fact that he is not just a lifelong supporter, he was once on the books and actually played for the youth side.

Another former member of the youth team who made his name on stage rather than on the pitch is Iron Maiden founder Steve Harris. In the spirit of Live Aid, when some members of different bands teamed up specially for the occasion, I'm going to ask Harris, who is principally a bassist, to line up in a West Ham fan band with Def Leppard lead guitarist Phil Collen, multi-talented

Foo Fighter Dave Grohl on drums, the Cure's Roger O'Donnell on keyboards and Prodigy frontman Keith 'Firestarter' Flint doing the vocals. I reckon the song for them is Iron Maiden's classic 'The Number of the Beast' which, as anyone who ever had the pleasure of being marked by Julian Dicks will tell you, is three.

Next up is Billy Bragg, doing a duet with Pixie Lott. I realise this is an unlikely pairing, but as a partnership it does at least have more chance of success than John Hartson and Eyal Berkovic ever did. I'd like to hear their rendition of Bragg's 1996 single 'Upfield', done as a tribute to the subtle clearances from the back four that we have come to know and love in recent years.

We're going to have to find a slot for Jack Steadman of the indie rock set-up Bombay Bicycle Club, not least because he's the great-great grandson of Arnold Hills. But I'm afraid you won't be seeing Katy Perry or Morrissey at this particular concert, even though – in their separate ways – both have turned heads by famously wearing West Ham colours in public. The Smiths' lead singer fuelled speculation that he might be a closet Hammer by appearing on the cover of his single 'That's How People Grow Up' in a shirt that bore the club badge and suggested he was a member of the West Ham Boys Club, but Morrissey later made it plain that while he may wear the odd tie-dye T-shirt, he was not a dyed-in-the-wool fan. Perry, meanwhile, had the tabloids drooling by taking to the stage at the 2009 MTV Awards in claret and blue lingerie from the club shop – but since her marriage to West Ham season ticket-holder Russell Brand ended in bitter acrimony she has given the Boleyn Ground a wide berth. I guess that now she has to get her frillies from Marks & Sparks like everyone else.

You will, however, be getting West Ham diehard Nick Berry

with his number one single 'Every Loser Wins' (if only that were true at Upton Park). And to close the show, let's give it up for the Tremeloes – not so much because they are massive West Ham fans, but because they gave us the anthem that runs 'Bubbles' a pretty close second in the Upton Park hit parade (for younger readers, that's what we used to call the charts when the Tremeloes topped them).

Opposition supporters must be baffled when we burst into 'Twist and Shout'. Why would a bunch of cockneys sing something that is so closely associated with a lovable bunch of mop-tops from Liverpool? Everybody knows 'Twist and Shout' is a Beatles classic. Actually, it had been a hit for the Isley Brothers, and the Beatles covered it. So did the Tremeloes, who were from Dagenham.

In 1962 both bands had auditioned on the same day with Decca in the hope of signing a major record label deal – and the Essex boys got the nod. Clearly, they were going to spearhead the pop music revolution in Britain – it was in all the papers! The hits started to roll off the production line quicker than the new Ford Cortinas coming out of the Dagenham car plant and the following year the Tremeloes, fronted by Brian Poole, took the charts by storm with 'Twist and Shout'.

Liverpool's Fab Four, meanwhile, were staging a concert in East Ham in 1963. Rosie, my sister-in-law, was there. 'It was at the Granada in the Barking Road,' she tells me:

> I queued from early morning with dad – who insisted on accompanying me, even though I was what I thought was a very grown-up thirteen years old. I paid 7s 6d for the ticket in the circle – I was subsequently offered the vast sum of £10

for it by a wealthy girl at school, but wouldn't have sold it for a million.

This was just before the release of their first album, *Please Please Me*, and they did pretty much all the numbers from that LP, including 'Twist and Shout'.

The concert was incredible – I think. I say that because the screaming was so loud that it was almost impossible to hear the music! I do remember the Beatles were showered with jelly babies. One of them (I seem to recall it was Ringo) had rashly said on TV that he liked jelly babies, and so we all trotted along with a bag-full which we then threw at them!

That was in March. In the summer the Tremeloes released 'Twist and Shout' as a single, while the Beatles included it on what was known as an EP, which stood for extended play and in this case was made up of four songs and cost twice as much. The rivalry between the two bands was intense. In the eyes of many, this particular battle was being won by Brian Poole and his mates. And what could be more natural for a bunch of football supporters to use something like that to their advantage when the opportunity arose?

At the start of the 1963/64 season West Ham went to Anfield and, thanks to goals from Martin Peters and Geoff Hurst, found themselves 2–0 up at half time. Cue the travelling supporters, who felt the most appropriate way to mark the occasion was with a hearty rendition of 'Twist and Shout'. *Twist little girl.*

In the second half Liverpool pulled one back, but goalkeeper Jim Standen saved a penalty to ensure a famous 2–1 victory – and a good deal more singing from the cockney contingent. *Twist so fine.*

We still sing it to this day. *Twist a little closer.* There are some pedants who say that the Beatles went on to achieve considerably more success than the Trems, and that West Ham's subsequent record on Merseyside means Liverpool actually had the last laugh. But I don't agree. *Let me know that you're mine.* The minor detail that, at the time of writing, we haven't won at Anfield since 1963 is neither here nor there. We've still got 'Twist and Shout'. *Ooooooooh!*

Without wishing to boast, I am one of that rare breed of individuals who has seen West Ham a goal to the good against Liverpool at their place. Not that we were in the lead for very long. And, to be perfectly honest, I wasn't too upset when they equalised – it's why I was able to get out of there in one piece. But at least I can tell my grandchildren, should I ever be blessed in that department, that I was there when it happened.

It was the mid-1970s and I had gone north with my mate Big Mick – a fellow forklift truck driver and my minder in the factory's five-a-side team. Rather than take the football special, we beat the Inter City Firm to the idea of travelling in comfort and took a regular train. By the time we pulled into Lime Street the Liverpool supporters were there in large numbers waiting to 'welcome' the football trains that were due in a few minutes after us. The police were there, too, but we didn't stop to ask directions to the ground. We kept very, very silent and walked past the lot of them looking for all the world like a couple of merry Mersey-siders who knew precisely where we were headed.

We didn't, of course, but after a quiet pint in a quiet pub, the quiet landlord pointed us in the right direction and we got to the not-so-quiet ground with our lives intact. The only trouble was we came at it from the wrong side and the police wouldn't let us through their cordon to join the other West Ham supporters in the Anfield Road end. We were left with a choice of the Kop or the Main Stand. After deliberating for all of three picoseconds we opted for the latter. Much as I love the Liverpudlian sense of fun, I felt the Kop might not be quite as hospitable as some pundits would have you believe.

Obviously we weren't wearing colours. By saying less than a Trappist monk on Strepsils while pretending to be engrossed in our programmes, we managed to escape any unwanted attention before kickoff. And I knew the drill once the match started. As with any away supporter who has smuggled themselves into the home crowd, I was quite prepared to cheer a Liverpool goal in the name of self-preservation. More importantly, I told myself that in the unlikely event of us scoring I would remain unmoved – allowing myself no more than a secret smile and a quick nod in Mick's direction once I had wiped the smirk from my face.

I most certainly was not going to punch the air with both fists, throw back my head (complete with Rod Stewart haircut) and tell my beloved Irons that I truly worshipped them in the most raucous tones imaginable. So when, after eleven minutes, Keith Robson converted a Billy Jennings cross-cum-shot it was hard to say who was most surprised when I did just that – me, Mick, or the thousands of sulky Scousers who surrounded us.

You know what it's like when your team scores – for a brief moment you enter a private world of ecstasy, oblivious to all around you. That's fine when you're with your own kind, who are celebrating in a similar fashion. It is not so good when the people around you have got the ache because you have scored against their team. And it's even worse when your mate and personal bodyguard has vanished while you have been enjoying a brief taste of heaven here on earth. I was now alone in a sea of red.

As the game re-started I could almost touch the hostility. I knew I was being stared at by the people behind me. The hair on the back of my neck was bristling with alarm. This could turn very ugly indeed, especially if West Ham scored again. I needn't have worried. A minute later, Liverpool's Tommy Smith picked up the ball on the edge of the area after we had failed to clear a corner and slammed it past a helpless Mervyn Day to make 1–1 and restore a sense of normality to proceedings. I even applauded politely, happy to no longer be the centre of attention.

That day I used half time to find Mick and ask him precisely where he had disappeared to after we'd scored. He assured me we got separated when the crowd surged forward in response to the goal, and he'd tried to work his way back but couldn't pinpoint my exact location. Sure, Mick, I believe you. Who wouldn't?

When I first went to the Boleyn Ground the half-time music was provided by brass bands from the likes of the Salvation Army or St John's Ambulance who firmly believed that Britain in the swinging '60s still wanted to hear 'The Dam Busters March' and 'Colonel Bogey' on a Saturday afternoon. The programme in front of me, from the game against West Brom in August 1969, reveals the band that day was supplied by the British Legion.

On the back page, club announcer Bill Remfry reveals West Ham are expecting bigger crowds at reserve games and he is planning to provide what he calls a 'Music Parade' made up of 'music from the shows and films, big bands of yesterday and today, and composers of the popular classics (such as Suppé, Rossini, Offenbach, etc).' No offence, Bill, but I reckon my Live Aid idea beats yours hands down.

One thing that hasn't changed over the years is the stampede to the bar a few minutes before the ref actually calls a halt to proceedings on the pitch. This wasn't so much of an issue when we all stood – people simply pushed their way through the crowded terraces causing the minimum amount of inconvenience to those around them. It's a different matter entirely when everyone's seated, though. Packed in as tightly as we are, it means that if someone wants to leave their seat everyone in their row has to stand to let them out. When the people in front stand, you have to as well. And the ripple effect goes on behind you.

To compound the felony, the ones who leave early are invariably the last ones back, resuming their seats after the second half has kicked off and repeating the disruption they caused at the end of the first period. They are also the people most likely to head for the exits a few minutes before the end of the game in what they will always tell you is an attempt to 'beat the traffic'.

However, the next time you find yourself going up and down quicker than my blood pressure, do what I do and console yourself with the thought that their lack of consideration for others is costing these people a small fortune. In the Premier League there are nineteen home games. If in every one of those games someone heads off for a half-time pint three minutes early, returns two minutes late and then leaves five minutes before the final whistle they will miss a total of 190 minutes over the course of a season. That's more than two full games. And, as you will know yourself, they are not exactly giving away the tickets these days.

What baffles me is that the early risers are quite happy to risk missing a potentially momentous event, like Ravel Morrison's first goal for the senior side. Actually, I nearly missed that myself. It came forty-one seconds after the start of the second half in a League Cup tie against Cheltenham, and Geoff and I just got to the top of the steps as Morrison collected the ball on the edge of the area, turned inside, then out, wrong-footing the entire defence before curling the ball low into the bottom corner. But before you start giving my son and me that pained look of someone who has to shift themselves to let us through, let me point out that as everyone was standing to salute the goal we were able to take our seats in the Bobby Moore Upper without annoying anyone.

For those who remain in their seats, the programme is often the only source of entertainment. For many it is an intrinsic part of the day. And there was a time, long before anyone had ever heard of mobile phones, it was vital if you were interested in the half-time scores from other games.

The way the system worked was pretty basic: nailed to the perimeter walls were a set of boards with a letter on them which represented other matches being played around the country. At half time the scores went up, and the programme contained the key revealing what game corresponded to which letter. Unless you were the Rain Man and could memorise the entire first division fixture list in alphabetical order, you had to pay one shilling for a copy of *Hammer* to know what was going on in the other games (that's 5p in the new-fangled currency that was introduced eighteen months after the aforementioned West Brom match – which we lost 3–1 by the way. For the life of me, I can't remember the half-time score, I'm afraid).

Was F Leeds v. Newcastle or Liverpool v. Burnley? And what the hell were K and L, which were always the two games featuring London clubs in a lower division? See what I mean? No *Hammer*, no hope.

But if a programme is an essential part of the proceedings, I am yet to be convinced about another so-called football ritual. Before you answer the next question I would like to remind you that you are under oath and the penalties for perjury in this country are severe. So think back, then answer clearly and concisely: when did you last have a pie at a game?

Aha – just as I suspected! So why is there this myth that football and pies go together like Frank McAvennie and Tony Cottee? The idea seems particularly popular with affluent, middle-class supporters who suddenly turned into instant experts on the game when it became fashionable to start going to the 'footie'. Is it, I wonder, the glory-hunters' revenge for Roy Keane's crack about the 'prawn sandwich brigade'? If so, this nonsense has gone on long enough.

Just take a stroll down the Barking Road before any home game. Immediately behind the Bobby Moore Stand is a row of shops including one that sells pie and mash and another that does fish and chips. They're two doors apart. Sure, Nathan's pies are popular, but the queue for the Ercan Fish Bar is reminiscent of the snaking lines of people who wait for days outside polling stations in those courageous countries that have thrown off the shackles of dictatorship and won the right to democracy for the first time. Ably assisted by my son, who has a master's in computer science, I have done some highly sophisticated analytical research here – namely standing by the nearby programme stall and noting the length of the queues for well over a minute. Trust me, the chippy has got this one wrapped up … so to speak.

Personally, I prefer the brilliant hot food on sale in Priory Road. Anywhere that offers a Mad Dog, a Terminator and a Stevie Bacon burger cannot be ignored by anyone who truly has West Ham in

their heart (and cholesterol in their arteries). This wonderful institution simply has to be rebuilt, brick by brick, outside the main
gates of the Olympic Stadium.

When I first started going to the Boleyn Ground in the late
'60s, I would invariably travel by Tube and alight at Upton Park.
Had I turned left when I came out of the station, rather than
go south and head for the ground, I may well have encountered
Linda, my future sister-in-law, who had a Saturday job in the
pie and mash shop that used to be further up Green Street, on
the opposite side of the road to the station. In fact, I might have
met the woman I would one day marry, because Di sometimes
worked in there too. The shop made its own pies, but the example set by the manager to his staff is something that I adhere to
now. 'Mike would never touch the pies,' says Linda. 'He knew
what went in them.'

Incidentally, should you have ever wondered about the green
liquor that is practically mandatory with pie and mash, it apparently takes its colour from parsley. That, at least, is the official
explanation.

Now, if I'm not going to have a pie on familiar soil I'm certainly
not going to risk it at away games. Why? Because, as I drive home
after a match in some far-flung part of the nation which has culi-
nary traditions all of its own, I have no wish to hammer down the
motorway with one eye peeled for a service station as my small
intestine makes increasingly alarming noises, that's why.

To be strictly honest here, I did break my own rule by having a
Seagull pie at the new Amex Stadium in Brighton. But then I live
in Brighton (yeah, yeah, my boyfriend knows I'm here … and I'm
sure you can see us holding hands) so I wasn't so concerned about

being struck down with gastroenteritis half an hour after the final whistle. And, just in case you were wondering, no – they don't put seagulls in Seagull pies. I have tried to elicit compensation from the club for contravening the Sale of Goods Act (as Amended), but at the time of writing I have drawn a blank on that front.

Anyway, to return to my argument that it's the clever dicks rather than the true fans who are obsessed with pies, I have categorical proof that I am right and everybody else is wrong (as my wife will tell you, this is not always the case).

We are at St Andrews, watching our brave lads teach the Blue-noses a thing or two about how to pass and move. A chubby gentleman, clearly of the Birmingham persuasion, has spent most of the first forty-five minutes single-handedly abusing us from the adjacent stand and then decides to beat the half-time rush. As he heads for the exit he is sent on his way with the spontaneous chant of 'Home for his dinner, he's going home for his dinner.' But he didn't go home – he came back after the interval. And this is where the proof of the pudding, or rather the pie, can be found.

'Only went for a burger, he only went for a burger,' was the greeting from the travelling claret and blue support as our Brummie friend took his seat.

A burger, you will notice. Not a steak pie. Which just goes to show the first thing on the menu that pops into the typical football supporter's mind doesn't come wrapped in pastry but is generally found between two slices of some form of bread (for me it's a bacon sandwich – the Great Dane – if I'm in Priory Road). Case proven, I think you will agree.

Perhaps it will all be different at the OS. If the proponents of the move are to be believed, this will be the promised land offering a half time of fine dining and service with a smile. The queues, sir? Ha-ha, we don't have those here – they are so E13. This is Stratford.

Come to think of it, I won't be sorry to leave queuing behind. And I suppose if I want a bit more live entertainment on the pitch at half time it's only right I learn to live with some theatrical traditions in the stand as well. Did you know that at the theatre it is possible to pre-order half-time drinks even before the play has kicked off? They leave them on a table in the bar with your name on them. And when you go to get them at the interval they are still there!

They also give you a bit of warning that the second half is about to begin so you can return to your seat in plenty of time. Gadzooks, is that the two-minute bell already? Excuse me while I polish off the last of this dry sherry – I'd hate to be late back and annoy the rest of the audience.

However, if the Olympic Stadium is to be a theatre, please don't use an old theatrical expression to wish someone good luck before they go out and perform. Knowing West Ham's luck, tell one of our players to break a leg and they probably will.

Chapter 12

Stick yer blue flag up yer arse

A S I SAT outside the Neasden branch of Tesco sipping my second can of Carlingsberg Extra Stripe and feasting on a sandwich stuffed with sausage, egg and what was almost certainly bacon, I was supremely confident that nothing could ruin my day.

We had just beaten Blackpool in the play-off final at Wembley and, while my plan to find a welcoming pub away from the ground and sink a few celebratory pints had gone awry, I was looking forward to getting home, ordering a curry, opening a bottle of red and watching the game all over again – safe in the knowledge that Blackpool squandered their chances before Ricardo Vaz

Tê smashed the ball into the roof of the net in the eighty-sixth minute to put us back in the Premier League.

Two hours later the wine was poured, the ruby was on its way and I was sitting expectantly in front of the TV, aching to relive the ecstasy of our glorious afternoon in the sunshine. What could possibly spoil that?

I will tell you what spoiled that. Chelsea – the team I detest like no other – won the Champions League. And I was forced to watch them do it to appease my son who, although a claret and blue loyalist, was adamant we had to watch the biggest club game of the season before replaying our own triumph. Anyway, he insisted, Chelsea would lose to Bayern Munich, making our own victory that much sweeter when we watched it on Sky Plus. Only Chelski didn't lose, did they? And to make matters worse they dragged it out into extra time and a penalty shoot-out before they picked up the trophy that made them, if only for one season, the best side in Europe. (Geoff now insists that we had to watch the game live because there was no room left on the Sky box due to the number of *Columbo* episodes I had recorded – but, as the world's greatest fictional detective would undoubtedly prove if given the chance, there is no truth in that whatsoever.)

For me Chelsea's triumph was harder to swallow than the dead rodent found by the unfortunate Katie Crabtree in her Tesco sandwich some weeks before I bought mine. (According to Ms Crabtree, who was expecting chicken and bacon rather than chicken and a small furry animal, she bit into something that 'was black and had hair'.) But that's Chelsea for you. Just when you think they can't depress you any more than they already have, they go and do just that.

Those of you with grey hair and long memories will remember that back in 1970 Chelsea played Don Revie's Leeds in the FA Cup final. It was one of those games I really wanted both sides to lose. As a naive thirteen-year-old who went to a school where most of the kids supported Chelsea I tried to convince myself after the first encounter at Wembley was drawn that they would slug it out for a couple of months in replay after replay, then the authorities would call the whole thing off with neither team being awarded the Cup because England had more pressing matters in Mexico that summer. But those hopes were dashed when the west London outfit won the second game at Old Trafford.

Had my wish of a never-ending Cup final been fulfilled Chelsea keeper Peter Bonetti wouldn't have been in goal for the national side and made the fateful blunders that turned a 2–0 lead over West Germany into a stomach-wrenching 3–2 World Cup quarter-final defeat. That all came about because England's real No. 1 – the matchless Gordon Banks – was stricken with food poisoning (which undoubtedly had nothing to do with a Tesco sandwich because in those days the supermarket chain didn't have an Express store in Leon). Had we won that game we'd have surely beaten Italy in the semi and given the world the encounter everyone wanted to see – a re-match of Pelé versus Bobby Moore in an England–Brazil final.

Where was I? (You'd be surprised how quickly Memory Lane turns into Alzheimer's Avenue when you get to my age.) Ah yes, Chelsea.

There was a time when the club I loathe and the one I love were evenly matched. Take the game at Stamford Bridge in the World Cup-winning year of '66. Chelsea 5 West Ham 5 – you don't get more evenly matched than that. But that same year, in the Russian city of Ukhta, Mr and Mrs Abramovich were digging out their best bottle of vodka to celebrate the birth of their son, and we all know how he went on to tip the balance of power.

The day I celebrated my fifteenth wedding anniversary – 1 July 2003 – Abramovich founded his unholy Roman empire at Chelsea (we got a babysitter and had a nice meal out in one of Brighton's many excellent restaurants – thanks for asking). As all romantics will know, this was our crystal wedding anniversary. Fortunately no one gave us a crystal ball as a present; had they done so and enabled me to see what the immediate future held for us, in comparison with the newly formed legions of glory hunters at Stamford Bridge, I would have probably jumped off the end of the Palace Pier (don't ever let anyone tell you it's called Brighton Pier).

By this time, West Ham had been under the tender care of one Terence Brown for a little over a decade. Brown, the chairman and majority shareholder, effectively owned the club but it's fair to say he wasn't getting a lot of thanks from his ungrateful flock on the terraces. To be honest, Terry was despised by most supporters.

He became chairman after West Ham were relegated in May 1992. His first year at the helm saw us win promotion under Billy Bonds, but it meant we had missed the debut season of the new Premier League. As this is when the modern era in English football is generally considered to have begun it is an obvious starting point to compare the latter-day fortunes of two clubs originally separated by ten miles and now distanced by several billion pounds and an entire football culture.

In '93/94, our first season back in the big time, we finished thirteenth, with Chelsea fourteenth in what was now the FA

Carling Premiership. At the start of the '94/95 season, in which four teams would be relegated as part of the process of slimming down the top division from twenty-two teams to twenty, Brown gave Bonds the tin tack. Bonzo's assistant Harry Redknapp was promoted to the managerial hot seat made vacant by the unseemly departure of his best mate, but H shrugged off the controversy that surrounded the move and steered us to fourteenth – three places behind Chelsea. The following year he got us to tenth, with Chelsea eleventh.

After that, Redknapp never managed to finish above Chelsea, but during his time in charge the gap was never more than nine places – and that came in the season that saw Brown lose patience with his garrulous manager after a fearsome row about the transfer kitty and replace him with the rather more tight-lipped Glenn Roeder who, in his first season, took us to seventh place – just one behind Chelsea.

In all, West Ham and Chelsea were in the Premiership for ten seasons before we vanished through the trapdoor once more. Of the twenty League games between us we won nine, Chelsea eight and there were three draws. Pretty even-steven, I'd say.

The 2002/03 season will haunt the West Ham supporters who were forced to live through it 'til the end of their days.

It had begun with such promise. We'd had three players in the England squad at the World Cup in Japan and South Korea. The side was a nice balance of experience (James, Sinclair, Kanoute) and youthful brilliance (Cole, Carrick, Defoe). We had captured the mighty Gary Breen after he'd starred for the Republic of Ireland in the Far East. We had a young manager with fresh ideas. And we had Paolo Di Canio. Too good to go down? We were destined for a place in Europe!

The reality turned out to be rather different. It would be wrong to pin the blame on Roeder for everything that went wrong that year, and we are all delighted he recovered from the terrible brain tumour that struck him down minutes after the Middlesbrough game had finished. But he does have to shoulder his share of the responsibility for the shambles that was on display week in, week out.

There were a lot of games from that season I'd like to forget. One particular encounter that I would pay a competent psychiatrist good money to have scrubbed from my memory is the débâcle against Leeds at Upton Park one Sunday afternoon in November.

They had earned themselves a place in Europe by finishing fifth the year before (we were seventh, remember), but had just been knocked out of the League Cup and were struggling in the Prem. Manager Terry Venables, like the hapless Roeder, was under mounting pressure. One newspaper dubbed this game the P45 derby.

If we were going to start the long climb out of the relegation zone and drag Leeds down into the mire with us this would have been as good a place as any to start. However, as a rule, teams rarely improve their League position by conceding four goals in the first half.

The booing started long before Leeds got their fourth. They opened the scoring with their first attack after eleven minutes as Ian Pearce made himself look a chump by misjudging a hopeful punt from their keeper that led to a cross which left David James no chance with the header that followed. We pulled one back through Di Canio, who nipped in to reap the benefits of a shot from Michael Carrick that was only partially saved and rebounded to the ever-alert Italian. Then we chose to re-enact the ancient Japanese ritual of hara-kiri (which is not to be confused with Harry Kewell, who scored twice for Leeds that day).

Tomas Repka was having a dream of a game, only it was the sort of dream that ends with a screaming fit and a pool of icy perspiration in which the tormented soul who's having it is left to quiver with fear at the horrors that have just been dredged up from the deepest, darkest levels of the subconscious mind. When he wasn't kicking Leeds players he was failing to mark them in our penalty area. To say he went missing doesn't even begin to cover it. He was having a long weekend when they scored their second from a corner and had gone on a full-blown sabbatical when they volleyed home their third. He was lucky not to be subbed before half time.

The fourth goal, in stoppage time, was just too much to bear for hundreds of West Ham supporters, who headed for the exit rather than take any more of this cruel and unusual punishment (only it wasn't so unusual that season). Christian Dailly failed to notice one of Leeds' chunkier strikers as he attempted a back-pass to James, and the Australian with a surname that sounds like an unpleasant foot complaint charged down the attempted clearance before rolling the ball into an unguarded net. Try enjoying a pie and a pint at half time after that.

We did stage something of a fight-back in the second half but, as with everything else we did that season, it was too little, too late. Like so many of the fans, Repka didn't come back after the break. Di Canio did though, and won a penalty which he then converted. The masked Trevor Sinclair, who had somehow managed to break his face in circumstances I can no longer recall and was wearing a protective device that made him look like a bug-eyed monster, then gave us hope – the cruellest of all the emotions, as West Ham fan John Cleese observed in the film *Clockwise* – by scoring with a quarter of an hour left, and Pearce would have salvaged a point in injury time if his header had been on target.

The scoreline flattered West Ham – 3–4 doesn't sound so bad if you say it quick. And it spared Roeder the humiliation of being called into Terry Brown's office and getting his marching orders. I was pleased about that in a way.

I recall arguing with a bloke I knew that, given time, good old Glenn would get it right. What's more, I pointed out with some pride, he was a really decent fella who conducted each post-match interview with dignity and gravitas. 'Get shot of him or he'll get you relegated,' grunted my acquaintance, who clearly had more football acumen than I gave him credit for. You can probably guess which club he supported. The fact he had to store his blue flag where the sun don't shine for a couple of games as we did the double over his team proved to be of little consolation as he was proved right and we slipped out of what was now the Barclaycard Premiership – albeit with dignity, gravitas and a record points total for a side relegated from the top flight.

Que sera, sera, whatever will be, will be. Yes, we really were going to Grimsby. (Only we weren't, as it turned out – they went down the relegation snake too.)

Now, while you all take a moment or two to ponder the mystery of how a collection of so many top-quality players could contrive to finish in the bottom three (ours, not Grimsby's), I will use the time to slip on my bullet-proof vest and a hard hat before writing the next sentence. I believe Terry Brown saved West Ham from total disaster after we were relegated in 2003.

Yes, that's the same Terry Brown who presided over the ill-fated bond scheme, under which incredulous supporters were asked to part with the thick end of £1,000 for the privilege of being allowed to buy a ticket. Yep, honestly – I'm talking about the much-maligned £1.2 million-a-year Terry Brown, who later left the club with a ticking timebomb by agreeing the Tevez and Mascherano deal with Kia Joorabchian, and then walked away with £33.4 million after selling us to an Icelandic businessman whose financial affairs smelled worse than a beached trawler full of rotting cod. So, we're clear about this: I am defending Terry Brown, whose worst offence in the eyes of many fans was to fence West Ham's crown jewels after we were relegated. Guilty as charged, Your Honour. But at least he sold them for decent money rather than letting them go at criminally low prices.

Brown held his nerve when a fire sale looked inevitable. The signs were ominous when Lee Bowyer and Les Ferdinand were allowed to leave on free transfers almost immediately the season had ended. The pressure to offload highly paid players who would actually fetch some cash was enormous – and it grew day by day as managers who knew we needed to sell bombarded Brown with requests for the likes of Cole, Carrick and Defoe.

The crucial deal was the sale of Glen Johnson to Chelsea for £6 million halfway through July. It was the first signing they made under Abramovich. Yes, we all knew the boy had bags of potential but he was still an unknown quantity in terms of top-flight football. In short, Chelsea were prepared to take a punt – and Brown made sure they paid top dollar.

By setting the bar at that level he was able to extract £2.5 million from Manchester City for a fast-fading Trevor Sinclair six days later. Then, at the beginning of August, he persuaded Tottenham to part with £3.5 million for Kanoute, who had spent all season looking like he would rather be anywhere than Upton Park.

Sadly, one more still had to go. Sadder still for most of us, that other one was Joe Cole, who joined Johnson at Stamford Bridge for £6.6 million. The following season they finished runners-up to the Arsenal 'Invincibles' in the Premiership, while we failed to secure automatic promotion. It was hard to take: made harder still by our inability to beat Palace in the play-off final – which ruined my entire summer – but, on the plus side, we were still solvent. And when you see what has happened to the likes of Portsmouth and Coventry after relegation, that is a very big plus.

Of course, we weren't as solvent as Chelsea, who were now owned by a Russian multi-billionaire with money to burn on little things like winning Premiership titles, FA Cups and the Champions League. While they were doing that we were bouncing up and down between divisions like an ageing punk rocker who refuses to admit that the Sex Pistols have had their day.

It was certainly going to be a long time before we beat Chelsea again. That finally came after a ten-year wait in our first season back in the Premier League under Sam Allardyce. Carlton Cole got his first goal against his former club then, with four minutes left, Mo Diamé drilled home the second. When Modibo Maiga wrapped it up in injury time, those of us with claret and blue in our hearts celebrated from Afghanistan to Zanzibar (honestly – you can't go anywhere in the world without bumping into a Hammers' fan). The final score was West Ham 3 Chelsea 1 – as it was in the first game I saw between the two teams back in 1967. This victory felt every bit as good as it did then.

Now we await the next win at Stamford Bridge. But if we keep turning in the sort of heroic performances that José Mourinho dismissed as nineteenth-century football in January 2014 it can only be a matter of time (Radio 5 suggested we parked the horse-drawn carriage; great gag, guys – I wish I'd thought of that).

Chelsea aren't the only team to have benefited from a mega-rich benefactor over the years. When Manchester City clinched their first Premier League title so dramatically as they came from behind to beat QPR in the dying minutes of the 2011/12 season you could practically hear fans up and down the country thinking the same thing; why can't a billionaire buy our club and transform us from a bunch of no-hopers into title contenders?

In the words of the old adage, be careful what you wish for.

We at West Ham had a brief taste of the high life when a couple of chancers from the land of ice and snow decided to pluck us from obscurity. At the time it seemed as if all our prayers had been answered. But as we know now of course, unlike mum we shouldn't have gone anywhere near Iceland.

Many people still think of Eggy as the owner but I suspect that's partly because Eggert Magnússon is a damn sight easier to pronounce than Björgólfur Guðmundsson, who actually put his hand in his pocket towards the end of 2006.

That transaction really did put an end to the idea that West Ham were a family-owned club, rather than a high-risk business venture. Brown had been a bridge between the past and the future, but at least he had one foot in an era of continuity that lasted more than a century.

The Cearns family connection with West Ham can be traced all the way back to 1900 – Jimmy Cearns was one of the founding fathers. Martin Cearns, who was on the board when the club was sold in 2006, was the third member of the clan to have been chairman at one time or another. Another one of the directors who approved the sale to Guðmundsson was the great grandson of Arnold F. Hills, without whom there would be no West Ham United. We can only guess at what he would have made of his successors.

For a comprehensive portrait of the man who is generally considered to be the father of the club, you can't do much better than Charles Korr's excellent book, simply titled *West Ham United*. Read it when you get the chance. In the meantime, here's a potted history.

Hills joined his father's firm – the Thames Ironworks and Ship-building Company – after graduating from Oxford University and took over after the death of his dad.

He was vegetarian, teetotal and a decent sportsman in his younger days, playing for the university football side and becoming England's champion runner over a mile. He was one of those upper-class, well-educated Victorians who knew what was best for the hoi-polloi – Hills believed with a missionary zeal that what the likes of us need most is hard work and clean living.

To be fair, after leaving Oxford he chose to live near the factory in Canning Town where he began to get an idea of what life was really like for working men. He was particularly concerned about the lack of recreational facilities in the area. However, he was also a hardnosed industrialist, who was quite prepared to sack those workers who took part in the illegal strikes organised by the General Labourers' Union (all strikes were illegal back then). The final decade of the nineteenth century was a torrid time for industrial relations, particularly in the East End, and there was a series of bitter disputes that affected Hills' business just as they did the docks and other factories in the area.

In 1895 he set up a company newspaper – the *Thames Ironworks Gazette*. It gave him the chance to argue the case that the massive and hugely overcrowded Essex suburb of West Ham should become part of the County of London. And in the June of that year, under a headline that read: 'The importance of co-operation between workers and management', he used the paper to announce he intended to set up a football team. This, Hills believed, would heal the wounds in his factory caused by the repeated stoppages and dismissals.

That team, of course, was Thames Ironworks FC and it was made up of Hills' employees. They paid the princely sum of 2 shillings and sixpence to join and trained on Tuesdays and Thursdays under gaslights at a church hall in the Barking Road. After attracting more than fifty members they were able to put out two teams in their first season.

Not only did Hills finance the teams, he took an active interest in their results. He even took the trouble to share his thoughts on how the game should be played with every member of the new club: 'As an old footballer myself, I would say, get into good condition at the beginning of the season, keep on the ball, play an unselfish game, pay heed to your captain, and whatever the fortunes of the first half of the game, never despair of winning, and never give up doing your very best to the last minute of the match. That is the way to play football and, better still, that is the way to make yourselves men.' Hear, hear, Mr Hills.

The first season was good; the second was even better. Membership was up and Thames Ironworks were now able to field three teams. The fixture list included thirty first-team matches and six Cup competitions. In these early years the home ground was near the factory, in Hermit Road, but they were thrown out by the land-lords for breaking the terms of the tenancy agreement by building a fence and charging people to get in.

Once again Hills came to the rescue. In a massive show of faith, he found the money to fund the building of the magnificent Memorial Grounds, which was to be the club's new home. The stadium really was something to behold. The capacity was well over 100,000 – for an amateur factory side, remember. Not only was there a football pitch, the grounds included a running track, tennis courts and a swimming pool. (Olympic Park, eat your heart out.) The year it opened, 1897, was Queen Victoria's diamond jubilee – and she's the one being remembered in the 'Memorial' part of the name. However, with a staggering lack of gratitude, the ruler of an empire on which the sun never set failed to stump up the 5s 6d reduced price for a ladies' season ticket (blokes had to pay ten bob). Unlike Queen Elizabeth II, she was not a West Ham supporter.

Thames Ironworks continued to do well, beating all the other amateur sides in the area and rising steadily – joining the Southern League in 1898 and immediately winning promotion to the first division. But success on the pitch was not matched by support on the terraces. This was essentially a works side – albeit one that was attracting top players – and the wider community who weren't employed by Arnold Hills simply didn't warm to it.

Hills himself didn't want to hire professional players, whom he referred to as 'mercenaries'. His factory ran several different clubs, not all of them associated with sport, and he wanted anything bearing the company's name to be made up of his employees. But those handling the day-to-day running of the football club thought differently. They strived to attract the leading talent of their day.

And just to show that there is nothing new about double standards in football, Hills swallowed his principles and announced in 1899 that: 'It may be necessary to introduce a little ferment of professional experience to leaven the heavy lump.'

The big bang moment for West Ham United came in 1900. It was brought about by a combination of Hills' increasing disillusionment at what he had created and a need to raise money to enlarge his business interests. This involved turning his firm into a limited company to raise capital and, with shareholders to answer to, he felt unable to plough other people's money into his football team. He had no choice but to wind up Thames Ironworks FC.

But rather than simply walk away from the whole idea he proposed a new club, which would itself be a limited company with him as the major shareholder. He realised that if it was going to stand on its own two feet it would need his help until a new and, hopefully, larger group of supporters made it financially viable. He offered to personally buy one share for each share sold to the public and he allowed the new club to continue to use the Memorial Grounds, where we stayed until moving to the Boleyn Ground in 1904.

A little over 100 years later Guðmundsson stumped up £85 million to become owner of West Ham – small change to a man who was one of the richest geezers on the planet (although, coming as he did from Iceland, that should probably be 'geyser'). What a strange period in our history the aftermath of the takeover turned out to be.

On the pitch we appeared to heading towards a much-needed period of tranquillity. Guðmundsson's first term in charge ended with the Great Escape at Old Trafford – which was anything but tranquil – but after that it promised to be onwards and upwards.

The following year we happily settled for mid-table security under Alan Curbishley, knowing it was only a matter of time before those Icelandic billions had us challenging for a Champions League place.

In March of the 2007/08 season, as we closed in on the serenity of a tenth place finish under Curbs, our owner was number 1,014 on the list of the world's wealthiest people compiled by *Forbes* magazine, which takes an interest in such matters. It reckoned he was worth $1.1 billion. What could possibly go wrong?

Well, for a start, at the beginning of the next season our sponsors, XL Airlines, went bust. Now, I know this probably won't come as a total surprise, but our sponsors and our owner were not exactly unknown to one another. In fact Guðmundsson had provided most of the money to finance XL's buyout from its parent company, which was also part of the magnate's financial empire. In all, it was estimated the collapse cost our billionaire 'saviour' £200 million.

But worse was to follow as the Icelandic economy went up in more smoke than you get from one of its volcanoes, taking with it our dreams of trips to the Bernabeu and San Siro in search of European glory. About this time, *Forbes* revalued Guðmundsson's net worth slightly ... to $0. When we finally parted company he had debts of almost £500 million and was declared bankrupt shortly afterwards. Be fair, that's a spectacular decline even by West Ham's standards.

Perhaps we were just unlucky. As we have seen, some billionaires actually manage to hang on to their cash long enough to make a significant difference to the fortunes of the club in which they invest.

Financially, West Ham's present owners are pretty comfortable by most people's standards, but they aren't in the same league as

Abramovich. (I suspect Arnold Hills would not have approved of how they made their money, though – 'missionary zeal' is not to be confused with the missionary position.) However, they are going to be a good deal richer when they sell off the Boleyn Ground and move to rented accommodation in Stratford.

As supporters we are supposed to be consoled by the thought that the destruction of our home ground will provide the funds for better players and more success. So, will the rubble of Upton Park mean we can match the roubles of Stamford Bridge? I doubt it. And even if it does, there are some things money can't buy. I have a lifetime of memories invested in Upton Park. And I'm not selling those to anyone.

Chapter 13

Unlucky for some

EVER HAD ONE of those days that make you wish you'd
never got out of bed in the first place? Of course you
have – you're a football supporter.

For me, 13 November 2004 was just such an occasion. I realise
now there were some things I could and should have done differently, but when the unfathomable cosmic forces that decide
these matters decree you're going to have a thoroughly miserable day, you're sort of stuck with it.

It all started well enough. Saturday always means a lie-in,
even on match days, but the bright, sunny winter weather
meant there was no hardship in getting up. Besides, I wanted
to make an early start. This was the weekend before Geoff's
birthday – his thirteenth birthday – and he had money from

his nan that needed spending in the club shop. It was new shirt time.

Uncharacteristically, my son needed no second invitation to leave the comfort of his bed and we were on the road in plenty of time. Correction: we would have had plenty of time if the section of the M25 we required hadn't been closed because of an accident the previous day, in which a petrol tanker had overturned and deposited its potentially lethal cargo all over the motorway. Of course I should have checked the traffic reports before I left home – the accident had made national headlines the night before and there had been dire warnings of disruption on the roads. But, hey, we all make mistakes.

The enormity of the problem only became apparent when we pulled off the M23, took the M25 slip road and discovered we weren't the only ones who'd failed to check the travel news before setting out. There was a queue of traffic at dead stop, and it showed no signs of moving any time soon.

West Ham were at home to Brighton that day and, judging by the selection of shirts on display in the stationary cars, it was obvious that many of the occupants were on their way to the game as well. I'd say that for every set of blue and white stripes there was a claret and blue equivalent.

You'd be surprised how many West Ham supporters live in Brighton and Hove. It was first brought home to me by an interesting piece of legislation known as the Football Spectators Act of 1989. The centrepiece of this particular law was something called the National Membership Scheme, designed to combat hooliganism by ensuring the only way you could get into a football ground was with an identity card.

Leaving aside for now the civil rights issues involved in this sort of thinking, there were some practical problems too. The technology wasn't fit for purpose and queues built up at the turnstiles as frustrated fans waited to be admitted. A similar scheme had failed in Holland. And most of the sporadic violence that still took place occurred outside the grounds rather than in the stadiums themselves. But Margaret Thatcher was not a woman to let small details like that get in the way of a headline-grabbing initiative.

No longer could you go to an occasional game as a casual spectator. So, unlike previous years when we'd gone to the Goldstone Ground to watch West Ham in our home town, we now had to become signed-up members of Brighton and Hove Albion FC or risk the lottery that goes with trying to get one of the few tickets in the small area set aside for away supporters.

When I turned up with my best mate Simon, and the necessary documentation to prove we were solid citizens who lived in East Sussex, we were asked if we required tickets for any of the forthcoming games once the formalities of becoming members had been sorted out. We said we wanted some for the West Ham game. It seems we weren't the only ones. And, we discovered, the other new recruits to the membership scheme wanting to watch the Irons didn't seem interested in any of the other Brighton fixtures either. The woman who told us this couldn't understand it at all.

We opted for the main stand, right on the halfway line. And, come the day of the game, we took our seats behind a couple of pensioners who'd clearly been supporting Brighton from the days when the Goldstone was used as a venue in the post-war Olympics. Flat cap, blanket, Thermos flask – they might actually have been sitting there since 1948.

The travelling West Ham supporters were on the opposite side of the ground, standing on an uncovered terrace and getting soaked in a downpour. The local West Ham support was seated and sheltered from the driving rain. Just how many of us were in those dry, comfortable seats became apparent when the players came out and the rival fans declared their allegiance. Rarely has 'Bubbles' been sung by so many in the opposition's main stand. The look of alarm on the faces of that nice old couple in front as they huddled together and peered around to see the extent of the invasion has haunted me to this day. Remember – you could only be in that stand if you were a member of their club. Mind you, they had the last laugh. The Seagulls were 3–0 up within twenty minutes and never looked like losing. By the end we'd all given up with 'Bubbles' on our side of the ground and were giving the Brighton fans a helping hand with 'Sussex by the Sea' instead. Don't look at us like that. We're allowed – we live there!

Meanwhile back in the traffic jam there was an impromptu conference between several drivers and the majority of us decided the only way out was to inch back slowly until we were in a position to take the other half of the slip-road fork and head north west. It was high risk but, mainly thanks to the generosity of other motorists who recognised our predicament, we all got out of there safely.

The choice now was to bomb all the way round the M25 going clockwise or come off and fight our way through the capital's southwest suburbs before driving through central London. I opted for the latter, but this was before I had been convinced of the merits of a satnav (as I say, we all make mistakes). The riddles posed by the likes of Epsom, Ewell and Sutton are not to be solved quickly and the diversion meant there was no chance of getting to Upton

Park in time for Geoff to buy his shirt before kickoff. In fact, rather than have a leisurely couple of hours to browse in the club shop and grab a bite to eat as planned, we barely made it into the ground before the game started. We only managed that through some highly unorthodox parking and a brisk jog through East Ham's Victorian side streets.

Right from the start we battered Brighton – creating chance after chance. Inexplicably, they all went begging.

Judging by the groans it seemed the more perceptive members of the West Ham crowd began to suspect it was going to be one of those days when Carl Fletcher botched a decent opportunity shortly before half time. This came after Marlon Harewood, Don Hutchison and Luke Chadwick had already been profligate in front of goal.

Shortly after the interval Matty Etherington had a shot saved and then hobbled off with an injury. I heard a nearby Jonah tell his mate that, the way things were going, it was only a matter of time before our opponents went down the other end and nicked one. I wasn't having any of that – we were by far the better side. Defeat was unthinkable.

In fact, I was convinced we'd take all three points when Bobby Zamora came on as a sub for Etherington. The script practically wrote itself. He made his entrance to a huge reception from the Albion fans and indifference bordering on contempt from a large section of West Ham supporters, who still hadn't warmed to him. What better way than to make his exit having proved the doubters wrong by scoring against the club where he had made his name?

Barely twenty minutes later, Jonah was proved right as a large lump of Brighton rock called Guy Butters got his head to a hopeful cross into our box and put the astonished visitors ahead. This was nothing short of floodlight robbery. We were favourites for promotion while their form was so poor they had signed a 38-year-old Steve Claridge from non-League Weymouth to dig them out of a relegation hole. We simply could not lose this game.

But we did. In all we created seventeen clear-cut chances. They didn't have a single corner in the entire match. Yet West Ham lost 1–0. Gutted does not even begin to cover it.

Geoff, however, still wanted his shirt. And not only did he want his name on the back, he had his heart set on a giant number thirteen as well to mark his birthday. Now I'm not superstitious you understand, but there is such a thing as pushing your luck too far…

The journey home was never going to be fun. The south-east quadrant of the M25 was still closed so the only option was to head back into central London, cross the river at Blackfriars, and endure the long crawl south as best we could. My son, who had naturally insisted on wearing his new purchase straight away, coped by going to sleep. Which was probably just as well considering what was to happen on the A23.

The traffic was nose to tail and all three of the southbound lanes were choked with cars. Then the guy behind started to flash me. I couldn't have got out of his way, even if I'd wanted to. This went on for several minutes before he forced his way into the outside lane. As he inched past me I got the treatment from the driver and his three mates. I'm no lip-reader, but I got the gist of what they thought of me. Besides, the hand gestures that accompanied the abuse filled in the blanks.

I should have let it go at that, I suppose. But when he'd got past me I flashed him back, which was probably the biggest mistake

I made all day. He immediately cut back into the middle lane in front of me, forcing me to brake hard as he did so. And now the hand signals from his mates in the back were less of a sexual nature and more on the lines of, 'Come and have a go if you think you're hard enough'. Oh yeah – thanks for the invitation, guys. Thanks, but no thanks.

I'd never been involved in a full-blown road rage incident before. This really was turning into the perfect day. I wasn't entirely sure what my next move should be, but I was pretty certain that it didn't involve pulling over to discuss the matter in a civilised manner with these four upstanding young gentlemen.

By now the traffic was starting to thin out and if the guy in front really was in a big hurry he could have easily pulled into the out-side lane and, by bullying other motorists to get out of his way, made the rapid progress he was obviously hoping for when he first encountered me. Instead he slowed down. Effectively he was inviting me to overtake him. Once again, thanks but no thanks. I had no intention of going alongside him and running the risk of being rammed, or getting in front and have him on my tail in some weird and highly dangerous re-enactment of a First World War aerial dogfight. So I slowed down too.

His next move was to pull over into the nearside lane. Again I declined the opportunity to overtake and pulled in behind him. Judging by the looks I was getting from the back-seat passengers I had deeply offended these people. OK, so I had flashed them, but that hardly explained the desire for mortal combat. Parts of the A23 are quite well lit and I wondered if they'd spotted Geoff's West Ham shirt. Was that the cause of their fury? I really could not fathom out why they were all quite so angry.

As I changed down into second I checked the speedometer. We were barely doing 15 mph. Next to me Geoff stirred briefly. I really hoped he wasn't going to wake up. No father wants their son to see him as scared as I was just then. Then I hit on my plan. We weren't far from where the A23 turns from three lanes to two, with a slip road up to a roundabout. I would sit in behind these headcases until we got to the junction and, when it was too late for them to react, I would pull off sharply at the last minute and take an alternative route home across country and come into Brighton via the Devil's Dyke. My heart started to beat a little slower now I had a workable strategy.

I was down to first by the time we were approaching the turn-off. With apologies to the car behind me, who must have thought I was on tow we were going so slowly, I had no intention of signalling my intentions. Nice and easy does it; don't go too soon; leave it until your opponent has passed the point of no return. Relax … wait … any second now … Bollocks! The bastard had done exactly what I had in mind and shot up the slip road – clearly planning to rejoin the A23 on the other side of the junction and then intimidate me from behind. I had an instant to make a crucial decision: follow him to ensure I kept my positional advantage, or hit the throttle and hope the time it took him to get back on the main road would give me the vital minutes I needed to make my escape.

I changed up and put my foot down, going through the gears like a racing driver. I would have been more confident of disappearing into the traffic if I had taken the time and trouble to remove the roof box after our summer holiday months before. How I was regretting that particular piece of idleness now. It felt as if I was carrying around a giant beacon announcing my whereabouts to a group of homicidal maniacs who were intent on giving me a good hiding and possibly more besides.

But you've got to give the Golf its due: when you ask it to get cracking it rarely lets you down. Einstein convinced the world that it is impossible to travel faster than the speed of light. However, you can get pretty close when the occasion demands. There will be a number of drivers on the A23 who've seen a rusting VW with a box the size of a small house bolted on to the roof blur before their eyes as it vanished into the distance who can testify to that.

Never have I been so relieved to get home. By way of celebration I poured myself an extremely large glass of red wine while Geoff showed off the birthday shirt, complete with his name and a large number thirteen on the back, to his mum. She poured herself a glass about the size of mine when he told her how much he had paid for it.

Now, if I'm going to be perfectly honest, I'm not keen on replica shirts. In fact I think that of all the rip-offs the football industry has dreamt up in an effort to separate long-suffering supporters from their hard-earned money, this is the most cynical. They cost buttons to produce yet retail for a small fortune; they become redundant every time a club alters the design; and they look ridiculous on middle-aged men with flabby beer bellies (I know this because there is no shortage of mirrors in our house). However, I was thirteen once and understand that a young man wants to wear his West Ham colours with pride.

Quite how we came by those colours is something of a mystery. There is a wonderful story that we acquired them from Aston Villa as a result of a bet but, sadly, there's not a shred of evidence to support the tale.

This particular legend has it that a man named Bill Dove, who helped train the Thames Ironworks team and was the father of one of the better players, was at a fair in Birmingham when he was challenged to a foot race by four Villa lads who were there as well. What's more, they wanted to have a few quid on the result.

Unfortunately for them, Bill was a top-class sprinter and romped home a clear winner. More unfortunate still, they didn't have the cash to honour their debt – and no one took plastic in those days. Just as it was all on the point of turning ugly it transpired that one of the Villa boys was responsible for doing the club's washing and he offered a complete set of kits by way of payment. The story goes he later told his incredulous bosses that the gear had mysteriously 'gone missing'.

Remember historian John Simkin? He's the man who poured cold water on the Pears soap association with 'Bubbles'. He doesn't believe the Bill Dove story either – but he reckons there might be an Aston Villa connection. He says: 'They were the most successful club side during this period having won the League title five times in seven years. It has been argued that the Hammers might have adopted Villa's colours partly to be associated with the success of the club.'

So when did West Ham first play in claret and blue? 'The earliest photograph I have been able to find showing West Ham wearing today's colours was taken on 16 January 1904,' says John. 'The game was against Plymouth Argyle at the Memorial Ground.'

And before that? 'Thames Ironworks' first match was a friendly against Royal Ordnance on 7 September 1895. The result was a 1–1 draw. I have been unable to discover any written documents that reveal the colours that the team played in. However, there is a photograph taken in 1895 that shows the team wearing dark shirts and trousers. If we assume that Arnold Hills selected the colours, I would think that they played in dark blue. These were the colours of Oxford University, the team Hills represented in the Varsity Match and in the 1877 FA Cup final.

In 1896 Thames Ironworks won the West Ham Charity Cup. A photograph of the team shows that they are still playing in dark shirts. The first detailed description of the kit appeared at the beginning of the 1897/98 season. The strip consisted of light blue shirts, white shorts, red cap, belt and stockings. These kits were probably inherited from Castle Swifts FC, the works side of the Castle Mail Packet Company, which was the first football club to be formed in Essex, and had gone bankrupt.

There are photographs of the Thames Ironworks taken in 1897 and 1899. Although in black and white, they lend support to the idea that the team continued to play in light blue shirts, white shorts and scarlet socks.

Thames Ironworks was renamed West Ham United in September 1900. A team photograph taken that year suggested that the club had retained the light blue colours.

If only the Bill Dove story were true – there would be a delicious irony in receiving stolen goods from the Villains. Although in this case Aston Villa may not be the villains of piece – they could even be the heroes. Simkin says:

What we do know is that the directors of West Ham were seriously concerned about the financial situation of the club at the beginning of the 1903/04 season. Given their perilous situation, did the wealthiest club in England take pity on them and donate them a set of claret and blue shirts?

I guess we'll never know.

You'd think that no shirt would be complete without a badge, but study the old photos and you'll see that West Ham teams of the past often played without wearing one (a badge, not the shirt – this isn't Newcastle). And when they did there was no castle. Early shirt badges merely had the two crossed hammers that represent our ship-building heritage. The highly stylised fortress which is supposed to be the Boleyn Castle didn't appear until later.

The awesome website theyflysohigh, the brainchild of Steve Marsh, has a terrific display of photographs featuring various items sporting the club badge. 'A castle was added to the official match day programmes from the start of the 1921/22 season,' says Steve.

> Up until West Ham United gained promotion to the first division at the end of the 1957/58 season, both the castle and crossed hammers were seen as separate elements. The players' promotion souvenir handbook issued in 1958 was the first time that both the crossed hammers and castle were seen as one combined image.

Interestingly, though, the first picture I can find anywhere of a shirt badge that includes the castle is taken at the 1964 FA Cup final against Preston.

The move to the Olympic Stadium has prompted another redesign and the Boleyn Castle has got the chop once more. In the supporters' poll that preceded this decision I suggested that on the new badge we replaced the castle with a wrecking ball, but nobody seemed very interested in that idea.

The revamped crest also includes the word 'London', which I guess is handy if at any time you forget where you are. But I can't help thinking we've missed a trick here.

Rather than merely listing the name of England's capital city, we could have given the badge an extra touch of class by adding a motto. If we're going to be a superpower in European football as a result of taking up residency in such grand surroundings at Stratford we might as well have all the trimmings. Not that we have to waste a lot of time dreaming up one of our own – we can simply borrow someone else's. It doesn't matter much what it says, but it does have to be in Latin. It's just not a proper motto otherwise.

There are a few to choose from. Tottenham go with *Audere est facere* (to dare is to do) but we don't want anything from them, thank you very much. Man City's motto is *Superbia in proelia* (pride in battle) while Everton's is *Nil satis nisi optimum*. That translates roughly as 'only the best is good enough' – but for my generation those words will always be preceded by the line, 'The Milky Bar Kid is strong and tough', so it doesn't quite fit the bill.

For Blackburn the way forward is *Arte et labore* – by skill and hard work – but look where that has got them; Bolton's *Supera moras* (overcome delays) sounds as if it was created as an early radio traffic bulletin for anyone using the M6; and, despite the best efforts of several managers in its recent history, Sunderland still have some way to go *Consectatio excellentiae* – in pursuit of excellence.

I've always had a soft spot for Queen's Park, the Scottish outfit whose home ground is Hampden Park even though they themselves are amateurs. There's nothing like thinking big in my book. Their motto, *Ludere causa ludendi*, means 'to play for the sake of playing' – and while that may not quite tie in with the club's ethos of recent years, I reckon it sums up what West Ham are all about.

Incidentally, if there are any Jesuit scholars reading this who quibble with the Latin translations I suggest you take up the matter with my learned friend who provided them, Professor Vic E. Pedia.

As I say, I'm not a great one for replica kit. Admittedly I did buy the BAC away shirt before the Keith Hackett semi-final against Forest, but we all know what happened there. Needless to say I never wore it to another match – home or away.

On special occasions I dust off the Wembley 1980 commemorative number (it's white with claret and blue trimming and a nicely understated FA Cup motif). I was lucky enough to be at the Cup final against Arsenal. Looking back on that game it is apparent that replica shirts had yet to make their appearance in the stands. Back then we contented ourselves with scarves.

There's a lot to be said for a scarf. They look fantastic when held aloft by massed ranks of supporters, they don't cost the earth – and they keep you warm on a chilly winter's afternoon.

Be honest, the replica shirt poses problems when the weather turns nasty, doesn't it? There's no point spending all that money and not displaying your expensive purchase, so you don't want to wear it under a fleece. You either have to wear it on top of something else, which looks silly, or you go with just the shirt and freeze your bits off.

The scarf, unlike the replica shirt, can be displayed in all weathers – leaving no one in doubt which team you support. Although, as I discovered many years ago, that can sometimes cause problems.

My mum knitted my first West Ham scarf – alternate squares of the sacred claret and blue with tassely bits of wool at both ends. I loved it. Sadly, the other kids with whom I went to school didn't – especially the ones who supported Chelsea. Things came to a head in the playground one day when some of these boys in blue tried to part me from my precious knitwear. But we all know these colours don't run and I had no intention of giving them up (although I have to admit now it was not because I have ever been particularly brave – the truth is there was no way I was going home to face my mother without that scarf, which she had sweated over for hours).

I'm not going to exaggerate here – this wasn't the Rumble in the Jungle. Nor was it the Thriller in Manila. This was the Tussle with the Tassels. Even so, with a couple of kids pulling one end and me desperately clinging on to the other the immediate future was looking decidedly bleak for my scarf.

My mum wasn't the world's most enthusiastic knitter (I'd had to beg for months before she got cracking with her needles) but she obviously knew what she was doing. As the tug-of-war became more intense it seemed inevitable her creation would come apart in our hands. Amazingly, it didn't. But it did stretch. By the time my assailants lost interest that scarf was about 12 feet long. The squares, so carefully created, were no longer square – they were distinctly rectangular. However, they were still in my possession and now I had an item of clothing that I could wrap around more than just my neck. I could have mummified myself in it.

This was some years before Tom Baker became Doctor Who (I think it was Patrick Troughton at the time). But I did wonder in later years if one of the small crowd who had witnessed my rather undignified struggle had gone on to be something in the BBC's wardrobe department and convinced the producers that what a Time Lord really needed was a scarf as long as the District line.

Not that replica shirts were unheard of when I was kid. It was just that we used to wear them to play football rather than to watch it. Anyone who has seen Brian Glover live out his Bobby Charlton fantasy in the classic film *Kes* will have some idea what the pitch at our school looked like at the end of the '60s.

Perhaps I was ahead of my time, but I wanted something that I could wear on all occasions that would demonstrate my undying love for West Ham United FC, so I persuaded my mum to find her knitting needles again. No – I didn't ask for a bobble hat to match the scarf (I had my suspicions the Chelsea mob would try to do something with that which would not be to my advantage). Instead I talked her into making me a tank top in light blue with two claret hoops – our away colours at the time and a design which is still regarded as a classic by those with an eye for fashion. How classy is that!

There were three problems with my new pullover, however:

1 – We always lost when I wore it.

2 – The Arsenal boys who had hitherto left me alone joined the Chelsea lads in making fun of me.

3 – I outgrew it remarkably quickly.

That's the trouble with teenage boys and their sleeveless jumpers: one grows and the other doesn't. By the time I was fifteen I knew exactly how Dr Bruce Banner felt when he had one of his turns. (Not that I see myself as the Incredible Hulk, you understand; I never had his physique and the only time I've ever turned green is on a cross-Channel ferry.)

As a parent myself I do realise that it would be impossible to fob off your kids with a bit of homemade knitwear these days. You've just got to smile bravely and visit the club shop knowing full well you are going to have to put your hand in your pocket.

However, if you are in that awkward position yourself you may like to use the following piece of football trivia as a way of recouping some of the outlay.

Wait until you on are on a long drive home from an away game and tell your travelling companions that the game which led to teams having to wear different colours in a match took place in 1890 when two sides confusingly turned out in red and white stripes. Be generous and inform them at no extra cost that the home team was Sunderland. (If you're stuck in a traffic jam and really want to spin this story out you could add that when differing kits became compulsory in 1892 it was the home side which was compelled to change if there was a clash, a rule that was in place until 1921. I'll leave that up to you.)

Providing your mates are still awake, you now raise the prospect of making this discussion more interesting by suggesting a small wager that no one can name the other side in red and white stripes at this historic encounter. Give them three guesses – the chances are they won't come up with the right answer. It's Wolves. Unless you've got a right clever dick in the car it's got to be worth a punt that none of them will know that. Just don't put your shirt on it. And if you do, make sure it hasn't got a gigantic 13 on the back.

Chapter 14

Box to box

S ECOND ONLY TO the insult of 'glory-hunter', the greatest abuse you can heap on the head of a fellow supporter is
to call them an 'armchair fan' – which is a bit harsh, really,
seeing as most of us spend an awful lot of time sprawled over some
part of the three-piece suite watching football on the telly.

The point of the barb, of course, is the suggestion that the
recipient never actually goes to a match and therefore can't feel
the pain and the pleasure of true supporters, who regularly pay
to go through the turnstiles. But, as we all know, watching your
team lose can hurt every bit as much when it's televised as when
you're there in person.

Winning, perhaps, isn't quite as pleasurable. Jumping around
the sitting room making loud guttural noises as you celebrate a

goal and startling the cat who had been dozing peacefully in the other chair cannot compare with the collective thrill of being part of a crowd that rises in unison to salute that sublime joy of the ball hitting the back of an opponent's net. But it does ensure that the moggy gives you a wide berth for the rest of the day and pesters another family member when it requires feeding.

There was a time when live televised football was about as rare as a John Radford goal in West Ham colours (actually, that's a bit unfair – nothing is as rare as a John Radford goal in West Ham colours). We got the Cup final and the occasional international, but not much else. What armchair fans did have, however, was *Match of the Day*.

As with my West Ham love affair, it too can be traced back to 1964. The first game shown, in August of that year, was Liverpool v. Arsenal. Unfortunately for the home fans it was shown on BBC Two, which at that time was unavailable in much of the north of England. The television audience was estimated at just 20,000 – half the number of people who were inside the ground to watch the game live.

By 1969 the programme had moved to BBC One and in November it screened its first game in colour – West Ham at Anfield. One of the reasons later cited for the choice was the vivid contrast of the team strips: Liverpool in their traditional all-red; the Hammers in the classic light blue with two claret hoops. We'll draw a veil over the result, but it was generally agreed among fashionistas that West Ham were simply gorgeous, darling.

Perhaps I'm being over-sensitive here but I don't think *MOTD* likes West Ham very much. By my reckoning, unless we are playing one of the so-called big clubs, we seem to be last up every week.

I always preferred ITV's *The Big Match*, which began in 1968 and was the perfect antidote to the Sunday lunchtime purgatory of *The Clitheroe Kid* and *The Navy Lark* which, as nippers, we were compelled to listen to as we sullenly chomped our way through cheap fatty lamb from New Zealand while our parents laughed like drains at the rubbish coming out of the radio. *The Big Match* went out on Sunday afternoon and it regularly showed West Ham as its main match.

These days we all record the matches we go to, allowing us to replay that wonder-goal or re-examine the dodgy offside decision over and over again when we get home. But, believe it or not, there was a time before video recorders when, if you missed a crucial moment at a game, you missed it for ever. *The Big Match* allowed you to lollop on the couch, let your roast dinner go down and relive the match you'd seen the day before.

What's more, it boasted the wonderful Brian Moore as its principal commentator. Forget David Coleman and his 'Lorimer, Bremner, Giles, Clarke ... 1–0,' routine – likewise Kenneth 'they think it's all over' Wolstenholme. Brian Moore was to TV commentary what Bobby Moore was to football itself. Both had no equal.

The one time I watched a match from start to finish with my dad it was on television. West Ham weren't playing but they were there in spirit, as my grandma used to say. This was the England World Cup team of 1982, managed by Ron Greenwood and starring Trevor Brooking (well, it would have starred Sir Trev if he hadn't been laid low by an injury that kept him out of the side until the dying minutes of what turned out to be our final game in the tournament and his last as an England international).

Despite being in my mid-twenties I had accepted an invitation from my parents to join them on a family holiday in the south of France. While we were there the World Cup finals were being held in Spain. England's first group game was against the French and I had spied out a little bar with a TV that was going to show it. I had mentioned a couple of days beforehand that I would be watching the match so count me out of any family plans until England had concluded their business in Bilbao. I knew that no one would be surprised, but I didn't expect anyone to be interested in joining me.

My dad had taken me to cricket on a number of occasions when I was a kid, but we'd never gone to football together. So I was astonished, on the day of the game, when he asked if he could come with me. I was highly suspicious about his motives, to be honest. He loved everything about France (including the French) and I thought there was every chance he planned to support Les Bleus. How wrong I turned out to be. (About as wrong, in fact, as he was at the first Test match he took me to at Lord's and after first assuring me the weather was going to be glorious, therefore I needed no more than shorts and a tee-shirt, was then adamant that the rain which had started to fall was nothing but a shower and would stop soon. Several hours later, having traipsed around the sodden home of cricket wearing his oversized plastic pac-a-mac that trailed behind me through the puddles as I trailed behind him like a vulcanised Wee Willie Winkie, I realised, at a painfully early age, parents are far from infallible.)

In the bar I had reconnoitred earlier we nodded politely to the locals, ordered ourselves a couple of *pression* beers and found two seats towards the back of the packed room. It was clear the French were confident. It had been twelve years since England had been to the finals and our participation in these had been touch and go

at one stage. In the qualifying group we had only managed to finish as runners-up to Hungary, despite doing the double over the
Magyars. In the away tie Trevor Brooking had scored twice, one
of which was a bullet of a shot that was hit so hard it stuck in the
top corner of the oddly designed Budapest goal-frame. But Brooking wasn't fit to play against France, and neither was Kevin Keegan
with whom he had formed a formidable strike partnership. The
other half of the entente cordiale, however, were a decent side cap-
tained by Michel Platini and they had high hopes of going all the
way in the tournament.

The anthems completed, England kicked off with every French-
man for miles around surrounding me and my Francophile father
fully expecting to avenge their humiliation at Agincourt 567 years
beforehand. Twenty-seven seconds later it became clear they would
have to wait a little longer. That's how long it took Bryan Robson
to score what was then the quickest goal in World Cup finals history after being given the freedom of their 6-yard box and hooking
home a Terry Butcher flick-on. The French were stunned. But they
weren't as surprised as me at my dad's reaction to the goal. He celebrated as if we'd just won the World Cup itself.

Never having been to a football match, he simply didn't understand the etiquette required of an away supporter sitting among
the home fans when your side takes the lead. (Nor, I suspect, did
he appreciate the health and safety issues involved.) He thought
that the French were all jolly nice people who would enjoy a good
ribbing over something as trivial as a game of football. And he
didn't let up for the full ninety minutes. Fair play to my old man,
he applauded sportingly when France equalised. But when Robson
restored our lead in the second half he ripped *le piss* out of our hosts

even more mercilessly than he'd done before the interval. What's more, he had the French to do it, having studied the language at night school for years. It was good to see that all that effort didn't go to waste. Paul Mariner put the game to bed with seven minutes left, and the scrape of chairs on the tiled floor could be heard in Paris as the French contingent in the bar stood as one man to leave. I'll never forget the delighted beam on my dad's face as he peered through the Gauloise smog and wished them all au revoir. He hadn't had as much fun in years.

Twenty years later I found myself on another family holiday in France, with children of my own. It was the back end of the school holidays – and the start of a new football season. Little did I know at the outset, but this too would be a campaign that featured Trevor Brooking – in circumstances that no one would have wished for.

Our first game that year was away at Newcastle. Always a tricky fixture, I know – yet one where I had high hopes. This time there was no bar showing the match, however. The part of rural France where we were staying had clearly failed to get the email telling it the entire world was fascinated by the English Premier League and it was their responsibility to keep visiting Brits fully up to speed about events on and off the pitch as they happened. I couldn't even get a commentary on the car radio.

The Newcastle game was on a Monday night – and we weren't due to go home until the following weekend. All I could do was imagine what was going on at St James's Park while my family debated the pressing matter of whether we should go for second-rate pizza again or suffer in the silence of a provincial French restaurant that believes the mysterious parts of unidentifiable animals it serves up really constitutes the finest cuisine in the world.

The following day I persuaded my wife and kids to make the 20-mile trek to a reasonably large town on some false pretext I made up at the time which was really no more than a thinly disguised excuse to find a shop that sold English newspapers. And we found that shop! The only trouble was, the papers it was selling on the Tuesday were Sunday's. It was clearly going to be some time before I got the result of our opening game of the season.

I'm not saying I spent the entire week fantasising about the match, but in the absence of concrete information I would occasionally lie back on a hard-won sunbed by the caravan park pool and allow my mind's eye to picture a Joe Cole free kick crashing into the back of the Newcastle net, followed by a Jermain Defoe tap-in and a wonder save from David James. As I gave my imagination free rein it became obvious that Glenn Roeder really was the messiah we had been waiting for. (I would just like to make it plain at this point that never did I picture myself being called out of the crowd as a surprise substitute and snatching a hat-trick in the last minutes to turn a 2–0 deficit into a glorious away win – I admitted to myself a few years ago that is unlikely to happen now.)

As it turned out we'd lost 4–0. And had I known what the rest of the season had in store for us I probably would have stayed in France – the miserable food notwithstanding. Even those awful green beans they insist on serving with everything would have been more palatable than the prospect of Sir Trev, having taken over from the desperately ill Roeder, presiding over a forty-two-point relegation after coming within a hair's breadth of avoiding the drop.

Now, of course, I wouldn't have had to put myself through the agony of expectation. I could have witnessed the slaughter on Tyneside as it happened, courtesy of the internet and live streaming.

Thanks to the wonders of broadband it is possible to watch any Premier League game, no matter what time it is being played. As a UK citizen you cannot view a 3 p.m. Saturday kickoff live on television, but somebody somewhere in the world will be getting it beamed into their living room – and that transmission will, in turn, be streamed via the net.

True, reception isn't always all that clever. Watching a streamed game can be very frustrating as the broadcast breaks up into a series of still shots that jump one to another at random intervals until the whole picture freezes and you're left with the dilemma of quitting and trying to find a better stream or hanging on in the hope the one you've got will jump back into life.

Even when it doesn't grind to halt, the picture quality has a certain jerkiness about it. It's reminiscent of the flick-books we used to make as kids. What do you mean, you don't remember flick-books? Don't tell me you never took an exercise book and painstakingly drew a picture of a stick-man kicking a ball in the corner of each page – altering each illustration slightly so that when you folded them back and let the whole lot cascade off your thumb you got the animated effect of the ball going up in the air and back down again (or whistling into the Spurs net if you went to a little extra trouble with the drawings). Next you'll be telling me you've never made a clothes-peg crossbow or a cotton-reel tank. It's tragic that these old skills have been allowed to die. No wonder this country is going to the dogs.

The other problem with streaming is that there is a delay between what you are watching and when it actually happened. So if your wife is doing the washing up and listening to the radio at the same time (I still marvel at people who are able to multi-task) while you are watching a game on the laptop she will know if West Ham have scored (or conceded) a good couple of minutes before you do. Which makes it particularly disconcerting when your significant other vacates the kitchen and joins you in the sitting room for no obvious reason. You try to read her face for clues as to whether you are about to be delighted or dismayed, but she has learned to remain impassive over the years. Don't worry – you'll know when the time is right.

Watching your team with fellow supporters on a television in a foreign bar is one of the great pleasures in life. At least it is if you support West Ham. I never fail to be amazed by the fact that wherever you go in the world the chances are you'll not be the only one in claret and blue when the Hammers are on telly in some far-flung part of the planet. And, for a couple of hours at least, there's a bond between otherwise disparate Irons who have been drawn together by the magnetism of our team, which is truly special.

My fondest memory of a televised West Ham game overseas is the 2005 play-off final against Preston North End. This time we'd taken the family to America. France, we felt, had been given every chance to impress by then and had failed to deliver. It was time to give someone else a shot.

After the events of the previous year I really wanted to avoid the play-offs. In the 2004 final, West Ham froze at the Millennium Stadium and blew the chance of an instant return to the Premier League by losing 1–0 to Crystal Palace. I'd had the sniff of a ticket in the Palace end, but I didn't fancy it that much. So, as we couldn't get tickets for all the family, we watched the game on television. That's how I know witnessing a crushing defeat on TV can hurt just as much as if you were there in person. That particular loss cast a massive shadow over my entire summer – and I know every West Ham supporter felt exactly the same way no matter whether they were in the ground or saw it on the box.

In the event, I was glad to make the 2005 play-offs. Hopes of automatic promotion had vanished long before the final fixture of the season at Upton Park. In fact it was our opponents, Sunderland, who secured the Coca-Cola Football League title that night after coming from behind to win 2–1 in front of the biggest home crowd of the campaign. As Geoff and I trudged back to the car and the inevitable first-gear crawl to escape the back streets of East Ham it looked as if the chance to haul ourselves out of the quicksand of second-tier football had gone for another year.

That was a Friday night. The following day, Wolves did us a massive favour by surprising everyone and beating Reading, our rivals for sixth place. On the final Sunday of the regular season we capitalised on that by winning at Watford while Reading lost to Wigan – enabling us to sneak into the play-offs. It was through the back door admittedly – but we were there.

Our opponents in the semi-finals, as they had been the previous year, were Ipswich. This time we were at home in the first game, but we couldn't get to Upton Park because friends were getting married and we had been invited to their wedding. We couldn't watch it live on TV either – the game, which kicked off at the ridiculously early hour of 12.15, coincided with the ceremony. So thank you, Guglielmo Marconi, for taking the time and trouble to invent radio all those years ago. There can't be a football supporter in the world who hasn't had cause to be grateful to you over the years, just as we were that day.

Along with the rest of the congregation, we witnessed our friends declare their undying love for one another and shared their joy. But tucked towards the back of the register office my son and I also managed to share a set of headphones and experience some private joy of our own as Marlon Harewood and Bobby Zamora put us 2–0 up in the first quarter of an hour. A Jimmy Walker own goal and a late equaliser rather took the gloss off things, but by then I had handed my half of the earpiece back to Geoff and was enjoying the reception.

On balance, I wouldn't recommend listening to a football match while you are at a wedding. It takes a good deal of self-control to restrain yourself to a silent fist-pump when your team scores. It would be all too easy to forget where you are and jump to your feet with a celebratory 'Yes!' at news of a goal. As my son pointed out at the time – showing, if you'll forgive a certain amount of parental pride here, a remarkably well developed sense of humour for a thirteen-year-old – that would be most unfortunate if it coincided with the traditional question of whether anyone knows of a good reason why this man and woman should not be joined together in the holy state of matrimony.

Zamora scored twice in the second leg at Portman Road to ensure West Ham were going back to Cardiff. The Williams family, however, were going to the Gulf Coast of Florida. But before we went my brilliant wife had tracked down a bar in the sleepy little resort where we were due to stay which was promising to show the game live. You can see why I married this woman: ask yourself, would your wife go to all the trouble of ensuring the holiday itinerary included a televised football match? It took some doing as well. The internet was in its infancy then – we didn't have broadband in 2005 – and it really was no mean feat to locate somewhere on the other side of the Atlantic that was accessible from our beach-side apartment which was going to televise a game of English soccerball.

We stayed in a place called Clearwater Beach which, it turns out, is something of a favourite with Tom Cruise. A lifetime of working in journalism has made me cautious about grandiose claims, so I was sceptical when the nearby diner showed me a written testimonial from Top Gun Tom claiming the establishment served the best pizza he had ever eaten. It seemed a long way for him to have gone for a quattro stagioni – Hollywood is well over 2,000 miles from Florida. Later we discovered that the adjacent town of Clearwater is home to Scientology, which explained Tom's trip east. It is tempting to be rather scathing about a wacky religious cult that reckons the galactic ruler Xenu visited Earth in a spaceship 75 million years ago, but you'll hear no word of criticism from me. Who am I to judge others' beliefs? I believe West Ham will reach a European final again one day.

The bar Di had pinpointed was called The Big Ben British Pub and it has a special place in our family history. For us it was a 10 a.m. kickoff – but for once nobody was complaining about getting up early. We were in front of the telly with time to spare.

Geoff recalls much of the day better than I do. 'It was probably the first time I got a sense that West Ham really was a big club,' he told me.

> Here we were, thousands of miles away from home in a little beach resort, yet this pub was full of West Ham fans. I was surprised we weren't the only ones in there. It made me

realise this club means so much to a lot of people around the world.

And the opposition? 'There was a little table with two Preston fans on it and, obviously, they were pretty quiet throughout the whole thing.'

My son, of course, is some years older now than he was then. 'As a computer scientist I tend to pride myself on my logical reasoning,' he says. So?

Football is pretty much the one thing where that all goes out the window and superstition takes over. Towards the end of that season I'd established a lucky outfit which saw me through the run-in and the two play-off games. There was a cap involved, but on the morning of the final I couldn't find it. I was terrified about that.

Looking back, Geoff thinks the early start was a good thing.

A game like that, you just want to get it out the way, don't you? All that time spent in the build up is really nervous so a ten o'clock kick off worked out well. And I was too young to drink, so for me the alcohol couldn't play its part.

Personally, I'm not so sure. Defeat would have been disastrous for West Ham. The parachute payments that come with relegation from the Prem were about to run out and financial ruin beckoned. A drink would have settled my nerves, but 10 a.m. is a bit early – even for a journalist. As I sipped my orange juice I tried to put the thought from my mind: lose this game and we are looking at years in the wilderness of lower-league football.

My extremely sober friend and erstwhile colleague Matt Scott reckoned my disquiet was unfounded. In his match report for *The Guardian* he wrote:

> After defeat by Palace at this stage last season West Ham were better prepared than Preston and, despite the relative youth of players such as Elliott Ward, Marlon Harewood and Anton Ferdinand, seemed more at ease with the pressure of a 70,000 crowd.
>
> It took only four minutes for West Ham to hit Preston's woodwork. Shaun Newton spotted Tomas Repka's sprint down the right wing and played a defence-splitting pass for the Czech, whose well-struck shot rattled the post.
>
> West Ham sustained the momentum, Harewood glancing on a clearance from Jimmy Walker for Zamora, who fed Etherington. The winger took it into Carlo Nash's area and forced a fine save.
>
> With the London side defending well in numbers, Preston created next to nothing from open play but their threat lay in well-worked set-plays. West Ham wobbled when free-kicks and corners found their way into their box: had Chris Lucketti's header from Eddie Lewis' corner been delivered with more force Walker might have been hard pushed to stop it.

One of those set-plays nearly brought Preston a goal at the start of the second half; Newton had to clear off the line to prevent us going behind. We hit back immediately – Zamora should have scored from the rebound after Nash could only parry a Harewood shot. Then came the moment we had all been dreaming of.

Over to you, Matt: 'With a looping ball, Zamora put Etherington down the left wing. His pace took him past Mawene and, as Claude Davis slipped, his cross allowed Zamora to hook in his fourth goal in three play-off games.' *When the ball hits the net like a fucking rocket, that's Zamora!* (For the avoidance of doubt I should point out the italicised bit is mine, not Matt's.) The bastardised version of 'That's Amore' – admittedly more popular with Zamora's adoring Brighton fans than us – flashed into my mind, but I didn't sing it. There were children present. But it's fair to say that we West Ham fans gathered in a quiet corner of the Sunshine State did our bit to celebrate that oh-so-precious goal in the manner befitting.

Matt's report makes it sound as if West Ham played out the rest of the game in relative ease, but it didn't appear that way from where we were sitting. Especially when Walker handled outside the area, twisting his knee so badly in the process he had to be carried off and replaced by substitute keeper Stephen Bywater – whose first job was to deal with the resultant free kick.

I think the way Geoff felt at the time reflected the way many Hammers saw things: 'It was a real heart-in-the-mouth moment. I thought that if he saves this we'll be all right – if it goes in, we'll lose. They'll go on and get another one.'

Bywater did save it. But Walker's injury meant seven minutes of added-on time. Seven minutes! No one should have to endure that in a play-off final – there ought to be something in the Geneva Convention to prevent torture of that kind.

One minute gone: We're still winning.

Two minutes: They're pressing, but we're holding on.

Three minutes: I really can't take much more of this.

Four minutes: The bloody transmission has gone down!

There was a collective groan, but no one spoke after that. All we could do was look at one another in dumbfounded silence. How could this have happened at such a crucial point in our lives? This was unbearable!

The screen seemed to be blank for an eternity. Then, just as most of us were reaching breaking point, the picture came back. 'There was a close-up of Nigel Reo-Coker and he was looking around as if everything had gone pear-shaped,' Geoff recalls. I remember a shot of white-shirted Preston players running towards one another as if to celebrate a goal. They'd clearly equalised – I felt sick to the stomach. 'Then they panned out and it turned out it was only a throw-in,' Geoff reminds me before I have another fit of the cold sweats over what might have been.

Then the final whistle went, and that was that. Throughout the bar the West Ham fans celebrated in their different ways – some jubilantly; others, like me, sat quietly for a moment or two, savouring the ecstasy of the moment. Geoff jumped off his barstool, punching the air. 'There was a low ceiling and I got a fistful of lightbulb,' he says.

It was early afternoon when we left the dimly lit, air-conditioned pub. The Florida warmth and dazzling sunshine came as a real shock as we stepped outside. It seemed so incongruous after being totally immersed in a football match all morning.

'After the game we went back to the apartment,' says Geoff. 'There was nothing else to do but relive the goal over and over again. I remember sitting by the pool in thirty degrees of heat and asking myself, could this day get any better?'

The answer, my son, is no, it can't. Tuck that one away in the memory bank and don't lose it. Supporting West Ham, you'll need to remind yourself of the sunny days from time to time.

Chapter 15

Local heroes

AFTER THE BULLDOZERS have razed Upton Park to the ground the builders will move in and start work on what has been dubbed the East End 'village' – a development of 700 homes, shops, underground parking and a landscaped garden dedicated to the memory of Bobby Moore.

Clearly no memorial park worthy of the name would be complete without a statue of the person being remembered, which is why sculptor-to-the-stars Frances Segelman has been commissioned to create an effigy of Moore, which – if she stays true to form – will be cast in bronze. While she's at it she's been asked to knock up various other bits of artwork celebrating the heritage of the club to be scattered around the new 'village'. Chances are, there'll be statues of a few other famous players for residents to admire as well.

There was a time when, rather than gazing at sculptures of West Ham heroes in E13, you could rub shoulders with the people themselves.

Bobby Moore once held open the door of a shop in the Barking Road for the girl I would one day marry. It was the stationer's Davidson Back, and Di had barely started secondary school. But the captain of West Ham and England, probably the most recognisable man in the country, still found time to smile and confess that it was his pleasure when she thanked him for the courtesy.

It's hard to imagine a living god buying his own stationery, and my wife admits to being somewhat taken aback at the time. But it's not as if she only ever saw West Ham players on match days. When she was growing up in East Ham she lived two streets away from the fabulous Ronnie Boyce, whose family ran the local corner grocery store.

It is Boyce who has had more to do with me supporting West Ham than anyone else alive or dead. He scored twice in the 1964 FA Cup semi-final against Manchester United, which set the ball rolling for me. It was after this game, which West Ham won 3–1, that the kids at school started talking about who they wanted to win the final itself – and I found myself in a minority of one in leaning towards the Hammers.

It turned out that Sid had gone to Hillsborough for this momentous match. He had supported West Ham since he was a boy but, apparently, this was his first away game. Curiously, his final away game was to be an FA Cup semi-final as well – twenty-seven years later at Villa Park.

Although Sid was more than happy to take Di to Upton Park he felt that, being only eight, she was too young for the rigours of a trip to Sheffield and the hassle that goes with being in a crowd of 65,000 people. But he did take Rosie, the eldest of his three daughters.

Days like that are engraved on the memory for a lifetime. Rosie, aged just fourteen at the time, recalls getting up in the dark to catch the Lacey's coach that took them to the game, the ham sandwiches on the way, her first impressions of Sheffield ('I had never been north of London'), the optimism on the journey there, the ecstasy of the goals, the joy on the way home, the singing, the incessant rain, and the fish and chips when they got back to East Ham.

Of course you never forget moments like those: 'I had spent a wonderful day with the man I loved most in the world, my dad, watching the triumph,' says Rosie. It doesn't get much better than that.

As a father myself I can see why Sid decided not to take his younger daughters. It would have meant carting around with him all the paraphernalia that is involved in travelling with small children. And, in my father-in-law's case, the equipment would have included a four-legged claret and blue stool he had made for his girls to stand on so they could see what was going on whenever he took them to a game. Di, Rosie and Linda – the middle sister – all used it at one time or another. Sid bequeathed that stool to Geoff when he was a lad. Being 6 ft 3 he doesn't use it much these days – but he wouldn't swap it for the town hall clock. Not even if the council begged him.

Boyce justified my initial faith in West Ham United by scoring the winner at Wembley. I have occasionally asked myself if my life would have turned out differently had he not nodded home Peter Brabrook's cross in the dying seconds. If West Ham had lost against Preston North End, would I still have supported them for the rest of my days?

I hate the thought that I might have been tempted by another club; the best outcome would have been for me to have turned my back on football completely and shown more of an interest in my dad's mechanical tinkerings under the family's Vauxhall Victor on a Saturday afternoon. That way I would have certainly saved myself a lifetime of mental torment. And I could well have also saved myself a small fortune in garage bills every time a car of mine developed the slightest fault. Ah well, *que sera, sera.*

The FA Cup team that Boyce was part of was a real oddity by today's standards. The player born furthest from Upton Park was Geoff Hurst, who took his first breath in the Lancashire town of Ashton-under-Lyne – which is not to be confused with Stafford-shire's Newcastle-under-Lyme nor, crucially, the Northumbrian conurbation of Newcastle upon Tyne where, if you can master the language, you will find it far easier to get a bottle of brown ale, a ferry to Stavanger and chlamydia.

But be warned. Should you find yourself in a pub quiz and you're asked the question, 'In which year did West Ham become the last team to win an FA Cup final with a team comprised entirely of players born in England?', do not jump in with 1964. The correct answer is 1975, when we did it again.

The idea of players living among the fans who support them is one that still appeals to me. I love the thought of walking into the original Cassetaris café in the Barking Road and seeing the likes of Bobby Moore, Malcolm Allison and Ken Brown sitting unostentatiously in the corner sipping mugs of tea and devising new strategies using the nippy salt and pepper pots to outwit a lumbering Sarson's vinegar bottle. These days you feel there is more chance of bumping into a Premier League player outside a glitzy nightclub, where the only contact will be either him lighting your cigarette with a £50 note or sticking one on you for making an inappropriate remark about his girlfriend, who is wearing only slightly more than the last time you saw her on Page 3 of a tabloid newspaper.

It's hard to see how players can truly understand the values of their supporters when, rather than live next door to them, they prefer a luxury flat in the fashionable part of town or a gated mansion in the wealthy suburbs where the security personnel will set the guard dogs on you given half a chance.

I can't envisage many of today's squad shopping for their one-pound fish in Queens Market. There are exceptions, of course. Mark Noble, I understand, is no stranger to Goodmayes furniture shop in the Barking Road, run by my wife's cousin's ex-husband (while I don't know Mark personally, I feel a connection through my wife's cousin's ex-husband means he's almost family). And, to be fair, many of the players do get involved in community work and visit local schools from time to time – but that's not quite the same as finding yourself in a neighbourhood pub surrounded by four large dockers who wish to point out that your performance was a tad below par on Saturday and you need to pull your socks up. (OK, I know there are no dockers any more, but you get my point.)

The one place a supporter can communicate with the players directly is at the ground during a game. At least it is if you can get close enough to the idle layabouts to let them know what you really think as, yet again, they fail to track back and give the man they are supposed to be marking a clear run on goal. That's one of the many things that worries me about going to the Olympic Stadium. I may have to buy a megaphone.

Communication is not always easy inside a football stadium. The Stadio San Paolo in Naples is one of those grounds where you and the players are separated by a running track – at least it was when Di and I went there shortly after Italia '90 to watch Maradona and his mates take on Pisa. Our problem was not so much my difficulty in letting the cheating Argentine know exactly what I thought of him (I reconsidered that course of action when I realised precisely how much he was worshipped by the Neapolitan crowd that surrounded us); the trouble was explaining to those in the neighbouring seats what we were doing there in the first place.

As a spectator you go to a football match to watch others, not be watched yourself. But that was what was happening to us. It was most unnerving.

Visit somewhere like the Nou Camp in Barcelona and no one bats an eyelid that an out-of-towner such as yourself fancies taking in a game while they are there. But Naples isn't Barcelona. They don't get passers-by dropping in very often. And when they do, people are curious about why you'd want to watch their unfashionable football team.

The bloke sitting to my left clearly decided early in the piece that, as I obviously wasn't from Naples, I must be there to support Pisa. Actually, he had a point. I love the small, sophisticated city of Pisa with its Leaning Tower and Piazza dei Miracoli – Di and I once had the best meal we've ever eaten there – and my original thought was to cheer for the away side. That went the same way as my planned critique of Maradona when I gauged the nature of the home crowd. Naples is to Italy what the East End is to the rest of

London – and it turns out both sets of poor relations are equally intense when it comes to football.

The fella sitting next to Di was considerably more welcoming than the guy occupying the seat adjacent to me. He spoke no English and Di's Italian didn't quite run to explaining that, for us, being on holiday meant taking in as much of an area as is possible in the time available and, as supporters ourselves, a football match is just as much part of the cultural experience as marvelling at the breath-taking views over the Bay of Naples or visiting the astonishing ruins of Pompeii. So he got his ten-year-old son who'd just started learning English at school to interpret.

I'm not convinced we got our message across in its entirety. But we learned he was a baker. And he'd heard of Bobby Moore.

My man, who was considerably younger and looked a good deal meaner than Signor Bunn the Panettiere, clearly wasn't convinced that my reasons for being there were thoroughly legitimate. In fact, I got the distinct impression he wanted to arrange for me to slip on a pair of cement shoes and take a nap with the fishes.

I tried to put his mind at rest by applauding Napoli at all the appropriate moments, and cheered like a local when Maradona put them ahead from the penalty spot shortly before the interval. He relaxed somewhat and half time was a good deal less tense than it might have been otherwise.

The tension returned in the second half when Pisa equalised just after the hour. Napoli were reigning champions – the previous year Maradona had practically single-handedly won them their first title in ages – but they had started the new season badly. They needed to beat lowly Pisa.

Napoli really went for it, creating chance after chance – missing them all. We were all standing on our seats. The support was fantastic. But my neighbour was not a happy man. Then the brilliant Brazilian Careca received the ball with his back to goal, shimmied, turned, and unleashed an unstoppable shot that had goal written all over it. The bar was still vibrating when we instinctively turned to one another, both equally astonished that the ball had hit the woodwork and not flown into the back of the net. We couldn't speak a word of one another's language, but the expression on his face needed no translation. It was the universal look of the supporter who knows the fates are maliciously conspiring against him. I felt his pain – and he knew that I understood. In that moment we communicated silently as if we were twin brothers with a telepathic link.

The stadium erupted when Careca grabbed the winner in the final minute. Me and my new best friend hugged each other as if we had known each other for years. Again the language barrier came between us and I may have misunderstood what he said, but I think I might have been made an honorary member of the Cosa Nostra as the final whistle sounded.

Alongside Maradona and Careca in the Napoli squad was a young man called Gianfranco Zola. Little did I know at the time that, some eighteen years later, he would become the manager at Upton Park.

Despite his Chelsea connections, I had high hopes of Zola at the beginning – and it was all smiles in his debut game in charge as we had our wicked way with Newcastle and turned them over 3–1. Everyone remembers their first game but not many remember their last. I don't suppose my daughter Katie does either, but this was it. She was thirteen and decided football wasn't for her.

Knowing my daughter as I do, I can't see her changing her mind now it's made up.

The first couple of goals came from Zola's fellow Italian David Di Michele and there were memories of Naples as the chant went up: '2–0 to the Mafia.' I'm guessing the Bobby Moore Lower didn't know I was a Man of Honour.

It was a different story eighteen months later when we put in one of the worst performances I have ever seen at Upton Park – and that really is saying something. It was a relegation battle against Wolves, and we were shockingly awful as we lost by the same score we had won Zola's first game at the helm. All the flair and promise of the previous season had gone – we were a shambles with no heart, no pride and no idea how to combat a side which, like us, was struggling to maintain its Premier League status.

There was no shortage of communication between the crowd, the players and the manager that night – mainly on the lines of 'You're not fit to wear the shirt,' and: 'Sacked in the morning – you're getting sacked in the morning.' In the event, Zola hung on to his job until two days after the end of the season, and West Ham hung on to a place in the top flight … just. (It took the tactical genius of another Chelsea legend, Avram Grant, to get us relegated the following year.)

That night, Geoff and I got a lift back to Brighton with our friend and neighbour Mike, a true romantic who many years ago chose the Denmark Arms to propose marriage to the lovely Jacqui over a packet of salt 'n' vinegar crisps. As anyone who has ever tried it can testify, getting away from Upton Park by car after a game is never easy – although it's rather less anarchic than leaving the Stadio San Paolo, which is akin to stock car racing on the public highway. The mood in Mike's car was grim on the journey home – made more so by the fact we'd had to cross the river at Blackfriars and then endure a slow crawl in the south London traffic because the Blackwall Tunnel was closed. (Tate & Lyle's riverside plant near the southern end of the tunnel was demolished the following year, but I swear I can still detect a hint of the once all-pervasive stench of industrial sugar whenever I drive past.)

We listened to 5 Live on the car radio, half anticipating the news of Zola's sacking. Had it come, it would have been the one bright spot in the entire evening.

There was a time when, ten minutes after a game, I could be sitting on my in-laws' sofa sipping a steaming hot cup of tea and watching the results come in from other games. I still had to face the drive back to Brighton – but it was always so much easier when the traffic had cleared and I had the fortification of my mother-in-law's Rosie Lee.

Grace made a mean bacon sandwich, too – always with a loaf that had to be cut by hand rather than the cardboard bread that makes up a sliced loaf. But that was reserved for before games; if everyone was hungry after a match we'd get fish and chips. I loved my mother-in-law dearly, and she had many sterling qualities. However, it's fair to say a sense of humour wasn't one of them. I once threw her into a complete spin by asking if she had some vinegar to liven up my chips only for her to discover, after searching high and low, that she had run out of the stuff. So the next time we visited we went armed with a dozen bottles which, with Sid's help, we quietly secreted about the house in the most unlikely places we could think of; the bathroom cabinet, the sideboard, her wardrobe (which several years later we sold to comedian Joe Wilkinson via Gumtree – Brighton really is just a media village, sweetie). One by one she found them all over the following weeks – each discovery leaving her even more baffled than the one before. She never did get to the bottom of that particular mystery. But, on the plus side, she never ran out of vinegar again.

For someone like me, brought up miles away from Upton Park, there was something very special about being able to do something as ordinary as watching *Football Focus* and the two o'clock from Kempton Park on the telly before stepping outside the front door and joining the steady procession of supporters on their way to the game. It made me feel like a proper East Ender.

On the walk back to Beverley Road, if we'd been in the West Stand, we'd usually go past the Champions statue on the junction of Central Park Road and the Barking Road. I'd sometimes ask myself what Ray Wilson thought about finding himself in such an unlikely location. The man was a top-notch left back and first-rate undertaker, but he's no cockney. Finding yourself looking up Green Street day after day when you hail from Huddersfield must be a strange experience – and all because Bobby Moore happened to be sitting on his shoulder at the time a lucky snapper took the iconic photograph on which the statue is based. Ah well, don't worry, Ray – not much longer now and you'll be off to Stratford with the rest of us. I wonder what you'll make of that.

Not that East Ham is going to be short of statues after we've moved. So, while Ms Segelman has got her toolkit out, I'd like to suggest another one.

Just as many countries have their monument to the Unknown Soldier, I want to see something dedicated to West Ham's Unsung Hero. I'm not talking about the likes of Moore, Hurst, Peters, Brooking and Bonds here; they're all well sung. What I'm proposing is a statue that reveres the memory of someone who shouldn't be forgotten, but probably will be in all the excitement of uprooting to the Olympic Stadium.

Deciding who gets that privilege is no easy matter, so I've come up with a shortlist – taking a player from each decade in which I have followed the Hammers. Leaving aside for the time being the small matter of how we're going to finance this particular venture – these statues don't come cheap, you know – we'll need a ballot system which will enable you all to vote for your favourite. Perhaps you could drop the sculptor an email at her riverside gallery in St Katherine's Dock.

Given my earlier paean of praise for Ronnie Boyce you may think I'd be nominating Ticker for the '60s. In fact, I'm going for a man who I never actually saw in the flesh.

Dave Bickles, I believe, got a very raw deal from the club. He made his debut in the legendary 1963 victory at Anfield alongside Moore in the heart of the defence. The lean, lanky nineteen-year-old had been called up to replace the ever reliable Ken Brown. It was a big test – which he passed with flying colours. According to one newspaper report: 'New boy Bickles slotted in as though he had been there for years'.

The brilliant theyflysohigh website features a cutting which gives Bickles seven out of ten for his performance in that historic win and carries two fantastic photos of the young centre back. In one, a smiling Moore has his arm round his shoulder and is giving him a few words of encouragement as they prepare to leave London. Another picture shows him tackling Ian St John.

Three years later it was a challenge on the same Ian St John that was to change Bickles' life. In the collision he injured his shoulder and had to go off. The West Ham medical team diagnosed it as a dislocation; painful but not career-threatening. In fact, a piece of bone had broken off and Bickles should have had some major treatment. The pain must have been excruciating every time he came into contact with an opponent. To quite literally add insult to injury, the Upton Park management accused Bickles of not trying in games and after just twenty-eight appearances in claret and blue he was shipped out to Crystal Palace – where they identified the problem.

Further injuries meant Bickles never did fulfil the fantastic promise he had shown as a junior and he drifted out of football, eventually becoming a teacher in East Ham. The tragic story of Dave Bickles ended on 1 November 1999, when he finally succumbed to kidney cancer. I think a small statue tucked away in the Bobby Moore memorial garden wouldn't go amiss now.

As the '70s candidate I'm recommending Patsy Holland. In all he played almost 300 games for West Ham and in every single one of those he never gave less than maximum effort. Holland was one of those players who could never count on his place in the side and in the early days of his career he was in and out like Nigel Kennedy's elbow as he competed for a berth on the right side of midfield. Apparently he lacked confidence in his own ability, although you wouldn't have guessed it when he got his head down and ran at opposition defences. Check out the goal he scored against Hereford and you'll see what I mean.

He could certainly perform on the big stage when required. In a storming second half performance he played a significant role in both goals in the 1975 Cup final – and scored the following year in the final of the Cup Winners' Cup as we went down 4–2 to Anderlecht at the Heysel Stadium.

His first goal in claret and blue comes with an interesting aside. Like most supporters, I had watched Jimmy Greaves make his West Ham debut on *Match of the Day* because it was at Maine Road, Manchester. I wasn't going to miss his home debut though so, along with 38,000-plus other people, I shuffled through the turnstiles (they seemed so much more spacious in those days) and crossed my fingers in the hope Greaves might help us turn over Bill Shankly's Liverpool for once.

This was March 1970. Holland had made his own debut at the end of the previous season but was still struggling to establish himself as a first-team regular. After a couple of decent performances he was given a further chance against Liverpool – and nearly blew it by turning his ankle while having a playful kickabout with his mates in the local park on the council estate in Poplar where he had been brought up. Club physio Rob Jenkins – an unsung hero if ever there was one – patched him up after he hobbled into his clinic twenty-four hours before the game and agreed to keep the injury a secret from manager Ron Greenwood. The swelling went down and Holland duly scored the only goal of the game.

I'm not ashamed to admit I had to consult *The Guardian*'s cuttings library for precise details of that goal. It came on fourteen minutes after Holland nipped in between two blocks of red granite called Smith and Evans and turned in a pass from Geoff Hurst – with Greaves on hand just in case. What I do clearly recall, though, is how the North Bank got a serious case of the heebie-jeebies in the face of a second-half assault from the opposition. It wasn't the last time I was to experience that phenomenon at Upton Park.

In typical Pat Holland fashion, his last significant act for West Ham at the beginning of the following decade came at a high price for himself. In the promotion season of 1980/81 he scored a vital goal in a top-of-the-table battle at Notts County – who were to finally finish runners-up to us in the old second division. In forcing home Trevor Brooking's pass at the far post, Holland injured his knee and although he limped through the rest of the first half he had to go off shortly after the interval. He never played for the first team again.

(Curiosity Corner: That was last weekend for several years that referees in England used red and yellow cards because it was felt the colour-coded system had actually contributed to the number of cautions and sendings-off. They weren't brought back until the start of the 1987/88 season, following intense pressure from FIFA.)

I really liked Patsy Holland. More to the point, so did Billy Bonds, who played a key role in his development. And if he's good enough for Bonzo, he's good enough to be on this particular ballot paper.

For the '80s my nomination is Tony Gale, who was just sixteen years old and still hadn't signed professional forms when he stepped in to fill Bobby Moore's shoes at Fulham after England's World Cup-winning captain finally called it a day. That was in 1977. Seven years later Gale moved to Upton Park and immediately set about forming a high-class defensive partnership with Alvin Martin.

Gale was to play more than 350 times for the Hammers (although, thanks to our friend Mr Hackett, he only played twenty-two minutes of the semi-final at Villa Park). In 1985/86, when we finished third, he appeared in every single one of the fifty-one League and Cup games that made up our finest ever season.

But the reason I'm putting his name forward as an unsung hero has nothing to do with his performances as a player, stylish though most of them were. What sets him apart, for me, was the way he looked after a young lad called Robbi Reardon in a most unusual FA Cup tie.

We had been drawn away at Aldershot, but the fourth division club were refused permission by their local safety committee to increase the crowd capacity at the Recreation Ground so they switched the game to Upton Park.

Technically they were the home side – although they opted to use the away dressing room. We were required to play in our white away strip and the programme was a strange hybrid of our *Hammer* and the Hampshire club's *Shotscene*.

On the back cover of that programme there is a picture of little Robbi and a no-punches-pulled explanation of why he is there.

> Brave Robbi Reardon is our special match day mascot today. Five-year-old Robbi, from the Isle of Dogs, has an incurable brain tumour and sadly doctors believe he has only months to live. But Robbi's parents, Ian and Jean, are determined to make 1991 a memorable year for him, and we are very pleased to make one of his dreams come true as our special mascot for the FA Cup tie.

Gale was captain for the day because Alvin Martin had been ruled out with an injury. Part of his duties were taking care of the special mascot on his special day. And what a special job he did.

'Robbi was really excited to be the mascot but it was evident right from the start that he couldn't run about with the players like the kids normally do,' says Gale. 'He was out of breath in the tunnel, so I carried him out.'

While his team went through their normal routine in the pre-match kickabout, Gale strolled around the pitch with young Robbi safely perched on his shoulders, ignoring everything and everyone apart from the little VIP he was looking after with such diligence.

'I suppose they picked the right captain that day,' Gale says without a hint of conceit. 'I had a little boy about the same age as Robbi, so I could relate to him. He was a smashing lad. Robbi died not long after – it was so sad. I went to the funeral with Ian Bishop. They were a lovely family.'

As Gale put life and sport into perspective by demonstrating a level of humanity not normally associated with professional foot-ballers he had no idea how closely he was being observed in those few poignant moments. 'I couldn't believe that people came up and thanked me afterwards,' he says. 'The chairman's wife had a tear in her eye.' She wasn't the only one, Tony.

I anticipate some objections to my choice for the '90s. I admit that it's hard to describe a former club captain as an 'unsung' hero, especially when he has been voted Hammer of the Year twice. And his seventeen-year stint at Upton Park spanned three separate decades. But I loved Steve Potts and I feel he never truly got the recognition he deserved. (Besides, if the East End 'village' over-shoots the original budget and Ms Segelman has to cut back on materials a pint-sized Pottsy is the obvious solution.)

What can you say about Steve Potts that hasn't been said before? A total of 463 starts for West Ham in all competitions; a grand total of 506 appearances in all; twice runner-up as Hammer of the Year to go with his two wins; unfailingly sound wherever he played in the back four despite being just 5 ft 7 tall; just one red card in all that time. And just one goal to go with it – which to my mind only goes to show that he spent most of his time doing what he was paid to do and stopping the other lot from scoring.

On top of all that, Potts has done the Knowledge and is therefore qualified to drive a London taxi. Just imagine being picked up by Pottsy – how good would that be? It would mean that every time you hailed a taxi you could eradicate the danger of an unwanted diatribe from an opinionated driver by simply sliding open the dividing window and saying: 'Oi, mate – you'll never guess who I had in the front of my cab.' As the man once said – get your retaliation in first.

That often appeared to be Hayden Mullins' preferred method of tackling. Alan Pardew's first signing after becoming manager at Upton Park, Mullins went on to play more than 200 games for West Ham and is a serious candidate for the 'oos.

Not always a crowd favourite, he never shirked his responsibilities in midfield – often getting stuck in where others feared to tread.

So important was he to Pardew's plans, Mullins played in every Premier League game bar one in the FA Cup final season before being sent off against Liverpool – which brought an automatic ban and ensured he missed the bigger game against Stevie Gee et al at the Millennium Stadium as well as having to sit out the last two League fixtures. The only other time he didn't feature was when he was one of six players rested ahead of the quarter-final against Man City for a home game with relegation-threatened Portsmouth – managed at the time by a certain H. Redknapp – in which we got tonked 4–2. Managerial apologies to the supporters who paid good money to see that rang a little hollow, I'm afraid.

Such was Mullins' contribution to the defensive side of our game there is a strong case to be made that we would have held on to win the Cup had he been playing in Cardiff. However, I'm nominating Jack Collison, who courageously put aside the grief of losing his father in a motorcycle accident to pull on the No. 31 shirt in a League Cup tie against The Hated Millwall in 2009. Collison's father Ian had been on his way to see his son play Tottenham two days previously when the accident happened. Emotionally, Jack must have been in pieces when he played in the cup game. But that didn't prevent him trying to persuade the morons who had spilled onto the pitch to confront rampaging Millwall thugs that they should return to the stands if they truly had the club's best interests at heart. The tears he shed at the end of the game speak volumes for the man.

If there is to be a nomination from the present decade it goes to Kevin Nolan, who divided opinion from the moment he arrived in 2011 to take over the role of club captain. On the minus side are a seeming reluctance to chase back, too many misplaced passes and a bloody silly chicken impersonation when he scores. On the plus side are the goals that initiate the chicken dance, a broad smile and an obvious ability to unite the changing room. A controversial choice for statue status, I know – but it would be a dull world if we all agreed about everything.

However, I'm starting to wonder if this statue of the Unsung Hero should be a player at all. On reflection my vote goes instead to the long-suffering supporter – whose games can be counted in thousands rather than hundreds and whose years of service are never-ending.

What I've got in mind is someone who's 6 ft-plus, slightly hunched to avoid looking like the big-I-am and not carrying quite enough weight for his height. His shoes are a bit scuffed and his trousers aren't quite long enough. The jacket is rather crumpled in places and sticking out of one of the side pockets is a packet of fags. Maybe there's a hint of a Ladbrokes betting slip in the top pocket. The cigarettes are Embassy – which he is forever trying to give up but can't – partly because he needs the packet for his constant end-of-season calculations about how many points West Ham are going to need to avoid relegation. The sawn-off ballpoint he uses for these sums came from the bookies and the betting slip may actually be worth a couple of bob; this man is not a high-roller but he's no mug when it comes to picking a horse. (He's not bad with the dogs either – he reckoned an Irish greyhound once gave him a knowing wink at Walthamstow and he never looked back after that.)

We're going to need a pair of spectacles as well – tinted claret and blue, of course.

The tricky part of any statue is the expression, but I'm sure someone as talented as Frances Segelman can handle that (to get an idea of her work, check out her Billy Bremner outside Elland Road).

Ideally any statue of a typical supporter should be able to shake its head in disbelief occasionally. However, I appreciate the mechanics of that aren't going to be easy. Therefore we need to concentrate on the facial features. Joyful? Depressed? Angry? What do you try to depict? My suggestion would be amused bewilderment. What you need to do, Frances, is capture the look of a man who has just been told by his wife of forty-plus years that he has buttered her cream crackers on the wrong side and you'll have nailed it.

Would Bobby Moore object to sharing his memorial garden with my unsung hero? I don't think so. He did, after all, once hold open a shop door for this man's daughter.

Chapter 16

On the spot

E VERYBODY WANTS TO go to Wembley; players, managers and – most of all – supporters. So, when one of the most famous goalscorers in history puts the ball on the spot and steps back to take the penalty that will surely have you queuing up for final tickets, you take a deep breath and wait expectantly for an unforgettable moment of ecstasy. Then the goalkeeper saves it.

In this case the keeper was Gordon Banks, a man who is still considered by many to be the best there ever was in his position. Mind you, the penalty taker was no mug either. You may have heard of him: a bloke called Hurst. Geoff Hurst.

The game in question was the 1972 League Cup semi-final against Stoke, which was eventually settled over four matches and has gone down in the annals as one of the most dramatic encounters of all time.

Picture the scene. We had won the first leg at Stoke 2–1 – one of the goals was a Hurst penalty – and now we are back at Upton Park in extra time; a seething cauldron of an atmosphere and West Ham looking for a late, late winner. Then Harry Redknapp goes down in the box. The inevitable cries for a penalty from all corners of the ground. Anger as we think we've been denied – then delirium when we realise the ref is actually pointing to the spot. He's given it! Wembley here we come!

I am on the North Bank – not directly behind the goal, but still beautifully positioned to see the net bulge when Hurst does what he always does and smashes the ball past the flailing keeper into the top corner. He puts it to Banks' right-hand side, just as he'd done in the first leg, but this time the England goalkeeper gets a hand to the ball – somehow forcing it over the bar. Hurst is stunned. The North Bank is stunned. Upton Park is stunned. The only man in the ground who isn't appears to be Banks, who picks himself up, modestly accepts the congratulations of his disbelieving teammates and prepares to deal with the subsequent corner.

In later life Banks came to see that as the best save he ever made – better even than the more famous effort against Pelé, which is still shown on telly every four years when the World Cup finals roll around. But as we trudged up Green Street to the station, we were not thinking about what happened in Mexico two years beforehand. All we could think about was how close we'd been to a final of our own.

No one remembers the first replay at Hillsborough, which finished 0–0. But the game at Old Trafford, when Bobby Moore had to go in goal for a spell and saved a penalty, is well documented. Moore took over between the sticks after Bobby Ferguson had been concussed in a terrible challenge by Stoke's Terry Conroy. The game was not even a quarter of an hour old when Ferguson went down. He was on the deck for seven minutes – Moore fiercely standing guard over him to ensure he wasn't moved – before being helped to his feet and attempting to carry on. Again Moore intervened, this time drawing referee Pat Partridge's attention to the fact the punch-drunk Ferguson was clearly in distress and in no position to continue.

That's when the keeper was led off and replaced in goal by his club captain. Astonishingly, Ferguson did come back on just before half time (there was only one sub allowed in those days and teams never put a keeper on the bench) but he barely knew what day of the week it was. An angry Ron Greenwood later revealed his goalkeeper had no recollection of the match whatsoever. Had the Scot been fully fit he certainly would have been disappointed with the two goals that saw Stoke come from 2–1 down to claim that precious Wembley place.

I don't think I've been left more dejected by a defeat before or since. And then, just when I thought I'd started to put it behind me, I learned that we could have actually bought the brilliant Banks, but Greenwood had a verbal agreement with Kilmarnock that he would sign Ferguson – for what was then a world record fee for a goalkeeper – and the fact that he could have instead bought the best in the business wasn't nearly enough to make him go back on his word. What price integrity? Several Cup finals and a couple of League titles, I suspect.

Against any other keeper, Hurst would have scored that penalty at Upton Park. I was fifteen years old and I had worshipped this man for as long as I could remember. He had missed the occasional spot kick (four, to be precise) since his first successful effort nine years earlier at Upton Park but, in my eyes, Hurst was blessed with superhuman powers. Then it turned out he was fallible after all. I'll never forget the shock of learning that – it was like discovering your dad is a cross-dresser.

It was years before I could trust another penalty-taker in claret and blue. There'd be an incident in the box; a cry for justice from the crowd; players' arms rocketing skywards to endorse their appeals; a moment of hesitation as all eyes turned to the ref; widespread joy as the official's finger lasered in on the splash of whitewash 12 short yards from the opponents' goal. Then my celebration would turn to deep, dark doubt about the outcome of this gilt-edged opportunity.

After Hurst left West Ham – by a strange quirk of fate he went to Stoke – the penalty-taking duties were generally shared by Billy Bonds and Pop Robson. (They let Bobby Gould take one once, but that was part of a hat-trick in a 6–0 drubbing of Tranmere in the League Cup so it doesn't really count.) Normally I would have trusted these men with my life but the miss by Sir Geoff had scarred me and I felt a terrible sense of dread every time we were awarded a pen. It took the arrival of a nineteen-year-old lad from Dundee United to change that.

OK, before we go any further it's question time again:

West Ham have won three FA Cup finals and used thirty players in the process. Of those, only one wasn't English. Can you name him?

Sorry, I'm going to have to hurry you. There is a pretty big clue in the fact we've been talking about penalty-takers. Of course – it's Ray 'Tonka' Stewart. Anyone who didn't get that please stay behind after the lesson so we can discuss some extra homework.

Stewart had played fewer than fifty games in the Scottish top flight when word reached John Lyall that this was a kid who had something about him. Lyall put in a cheeky bid, knowing the pulling power of a glamour club like ours would be irresistible … and the Scottish club turned him down. So Lyall, ever the master negotiator, let them stew for a while before coming back with a slightly improved offer. To be precise, he improved the offer by doubling it, then adding a further 45.7 per cent, making it a world record for a transfer fee for a teenager. Ha-ha, you Dundee doughnuts – you didn't see that coming, did you? I'm afraid you're going to have to get up a bit earlier in the morning if you hope to outsmart a crafty cockney when it comes to dealing with financial matters.

That was at the start of the 1979 season. Stewart made his debut at Barnsley in a League Cup game in the early days of September, and scored his first goal for West Ham later that month at Upton Park in a second division game against Burnley. It was, as you might expect, from the penalty spot.

I regret to say I was not one of the 18,327 people who were there to see it. Neither did I see his second thunderbolt from the spot the following month in the next round of the League Cup against Southend. Nor did I witness his third goal – another spot kick – at Fulham. I kept up this proud record by missing him scoring two penalties in the same match against Cardiff at the Boleyn Ground in November 1979 and got 1980 off to a flying start by being absent for his next successful penalty against Preston North End in January. It almost goes without saying that his next three goals, all away from home, were scored without my help. Only one of those was a penalty though – at Orient in the fourth round of the FA Cup.

I realise that absenteeism on this sort of level would have earned me a written warning had it been at work, and all I can do is apologise and promise it won't happen again. By way of mitigation, though, I would like to explain that there was a woman involved.

Some years earlier I had gone out with a girl who gave me a straight ultimatum: West Ham or her. That was simple to counter; I nodded her a swift goodbye and caught the football special to Port Vale for a third round FA Cup tie. It wasn't *Brief Encounter*, but everybody knew where they stood.

The difficulties that came with the relationship I was in at the beginning of the '80s were much harder to contend with. My consort by then never actually came out and said she disliked me disrupting our Saturdays by going to Upton Park – or, worse still, away games – but you didn't have to be a mind-reader to tell she was far from happy when I did. So I had to choose my games carefully, and the ones I went to all seemed to coincide with Ray Stewart not taking a penalty.

I was there for his next spot kick though. Not that there was much riding on it. We were only in the final minute of a pulsating FA Cup sixth round tie against Aston Villa with the score at 0–0 and Upton Park at fever pitch.

Villa were a good side – they were fifth in the first division and the following season would win the League title. We were a good side, too – but we were fifth in the second division. The general feeling was that if we're going to get to the semi-final we had to get the job done at Upton Park.

The second half seemed to fly by. Urged on by the biggest crowd for two seasons, a West Ham side missing the inspirational Billy Bonds laid siege to the Villa goal in front of the South Bank in an attempt to get a late winner. It seemed the clock would beat us, then we got another corner. Trevor Brooking swung it in, looking for the head of Alvin Martin. Instead, it found the hand of Villa's central defender Ken McNaught. Penalty!

There were people around me in the West Stand Lower celebrating as if we had already won the game. They clearly hadn't been there when Hurst missed at the other end of the ground all those years before. Had I known West Ham's name was on the Cup in 1980 I wouldn't have worried either. But no one tells you that sort of thing in advance, do they?

Stewart, wearing the No. 4 shirt normally worn by Bonds, picked up the ball that had been left unattended on the edge of the area while the Villa players debated with the ref and bounced it once before striding forward to place it on the spot that referee David Richardson had pointed to moments beforehand. Nine paces backwards, a moment to compose himself, a short run-up and then the explosion of power that lifted the young Scotsman off his feet and left Villa keeper Jimmy Rimmer grasping at emptiness as a blur of leather hurtled past him. It was a highly individual style of taking penalties that I would see again and again over the following ten years. I never tired of it. And I never doubted it.

If anyone had any questions about Tonka's ability to keep calm under the most intense pressure, he answered them a year later at Wembley in the League Cup final against the team who a few weeks later would win the European Cup. The game was deep into the second half of extra time when Liverpool opened the scoring with a hugely controversial goal. The fact that a red-shirted Liverpudlian was lying in an offside position when the ball flew past Phil Parkes cut no ice with referee Clive Thomas, a man who was not renowned for doing West Ham any favours. We were left with two minutes to put right this terrible injustice.

As in the Villa game, we won a last-gasp corner which was again aimed at Alvin Martin's head. This time Martin made contact – and the ball arrowed towards the top corner. A hand got to the ball … but it wasn't the keeper's hand. It was a penalty!

The 120 minutes were up when Stewart put the ball on the spot. There was not a West Ham supporter in the world who dared to breathe at this moment. I was listening on the car radio, having failed to successfully negotiate a day-release pass, and wondering if failing to inhale while in charge of a motor vehicle contravenes the Highway Code. We knew Ray would smash it – but would he keep it on target? Was this the one that would go over the bar, or come flying back off the post? Nope. This was the one Tonka chose to stroke down the middle, as cool as an autumn day in Dundee. One-one, and a totally deserved replay.

In all, Stewart took eighty-six penalties for West Ham, missing ten. Of those that didn't go in directly he converted two on the rebound after the spot kicks had been saved (versus Luton and Lincoln) and another – against Burnley – was turned in by Paul Goddard after the ball had been parried by the keeper. Ray himself doesn't consider those three to be 'missed'.

For me he was at his brilliant best – both as a player and a penalty-taker – in the climax to the fantastic '85/86 season, when West Ham actually came within a hair's breadth of winning the League. In the run-in we played seventeen games in fifty-six days, and the excitement grew with each match. No one dared admit they were thinking of the title the night we hammered Newcastle 8–1. Stewart scored in that game (who didn't?) but more memorable was the generous way, when we were awarded a penalty, he handed the ball to big Alvin so the central defender could complete an unlikely hat-trick.

A week later, when some of us were starting to dream dreams about finishing top of the pile for the first time ever, Tonka scored from the spot late on against Man City to keep those hopes alive. A break of just two days and we're back at Upton Park for a crucial game with Ipswich. They take the lead; we equalise; then, with time running out, Mark Ward goes down in the penalty area in front of the North Bank. From where I'm sitting in the West Stand it looks like he's dived. I may not be convinced but the referee is and he's the man who counts. Step forward Ray Stewart, once more shouldering the crushing responsibility he has borne on so many previous occasions. A deep breath to quell the rising panic (that's me, not Tonka) then BAM! ... the ball is in the back of the net and West Ham are going into the final game of the season second in the table.

Although I had missed Tonka's debut, I was there for his final game as a West Ham player. It was against Charlton in 1991, when they were playing their home games at Selhurst Park. By then, injury had taken its toll and Stewart was definitely past his best. My two distinct memories of that game were Mad Dog's goal (we were bang in line with his right foot shot and knew precisely where it was headed the moment he struck it) and the heavy-handed approach of the south London police, who insisted on filming us with hand-held cameras throughout the game.

It was a clear infringement of our civil liberties (yes – even football supporters have civil liberties) and our friend Simon was outraged. Mind you, by then he knew a thing or two about security in football grounds.

The worst-kept secret at Upton Park is the coded message to stewards that there is an incident somewhere in the ground that needs their immediate attention.

There is an almighty cheer every time it is announced that Mr Moon is in the stadium – and an equally loud one when it is revealed that he has left again.

It's such a natural occurrence – like the rising of the tides and the setting of the sun – that regulars don't think to mention it to newcomers when they introduce them to the delights of a Saturday afternoon at the Boleyn Ground. I certainly didn't give it a moment's thought when I persuaded my close friend and best man to come along and see his first home game. Perhaps I should have. Simon's surname is Moon.

We were sitting quietly in the West Stand – me studying Hammer, him soaking up all the atmosphere the second division could offer in the '80s – when the oh-so-familiar announcement was made. As is the custom, the crowd roared as if a pantomime villain had suddenly appeared before us. I roared. My wife roared. My father-in-law roared. And my mate nearly jumped out of his skin.

It takes a lot to rattle a man who has been brought up near Wigan and educated by a sadistic bunch of head-bangers called the Christian Brothers who came over to the north-west of England from Ireland with the primary intention of beating the bejesus out of as many young boys as they could in the hope of educating them in the ways of the Catholic Church. But Mr Moon was clearly shaken by 20,000-plus people cheering the fact he had taken the trouble to come to the ground that day.

His look of utter astonishment will live with me 'til the day I turn up my toes and find out whether or not the Christian Brothers are right after all. Then his expression changed slightly. He clearly thought I had something to do with it! All right, I was helpless with laughter and my denials must have lacked a certain amount of sincerity – but how could I have pulled that one off?

I admit he did have grounds for suspicion. What else is a best mate for if it's not to be on the wrong end of a practical joke from time to time? Simon and I worked on the *Daily Express* back then, and one of our colleagues was an obsessive long-distance runner. He wanted to put together a team to represent the paper in the London Marathon and was looking for volunteers. Somebody (it might have been me) let it slip that my mate had been a champion fell runner in his native Lancashire and would be an ideal candidate for the team. The only problem was that he was ridiculously modest about his achievements and would deny them if pressed. But don't be put off, I told our athletic workmate, you'll talk him round in the end. And, whatever you do, don't tell him where you got your information – he'll never forgive me if he finds out it was me who divulged the glories of his past.

My modest friend did deny his achievements, just as I had predicted. That might have been because I had made them up – I'm not sure they even have fells in Lancashire, to be honest. But that didn't deter Marathon Man, who pestered Simon for weeks, leaving him increasingly baffled about why his pursuer wouldn't take no for an answer.

I readily accept this isn't the funniest prank that anyone has played on a mate, but it amused me. (I like a running gag.) The Real Mr Moon only found out the truth a few days before his first trip to Upton Park, and he was convinced that I had concocted a far more elaborate practical joke than the one he had just endured.

I am happy to report Simon came to see the funny side in time, but none of us who were at Selhurst Park to see Tonka's farewell game were laughing when those cameras were turned on us for no reason whatsoever. In the unlikely event the police still have that footage, they might like to look at it again; I think you'll find we were not amused.

Twenty years after I saw Tonka take a penalty for the first time we were back at Upton Park for another quarter-final against Villa. This time it was the League Cup, and we shouldn't have been there at all. We'd already beaten them to book our place in the semis, then it turned out we'd fielded an ineligible player in the first tie.

His name was Emmanuel Omoyinmi, although that was generally shortened to Dear Manny in the death threats he received from irate supporters when it emerged he'd already turned out for Gillingham in the same competition and was therefore Cup-tied. He'd come on for the last few minutes of extra time and barely touched the ball ... but rules is rules and West Ham had broken them.

That first game was a shocker. After eighty-eight seriously forgettable minutes it is 1–1 – then the visitors appear to win it with a Dion Dublin volley. One last foray into Villa territory brings us a penalty ... which Paolo Di Canio strokes home with all the insouciance of an Italian gigolo on the pull in an old folk's home in Rome. Half an hour later the scores are still level and it's penalty shoot-out time. Five West Ham players step up to the spot – and five West Ham players score. Hard to believe, I know, but true nonetheless. Of the five Villa players who try their luck, however, only four are successful. Gareth Southgate, who England followers will recall has some previous in this department, fails to trouble the scorers and the mighty West Ham United are in the semi-final of a major Cup competition with every chance of going all the way. Or so we thought.

We might have had more chance of getting away with it if two months previously we hadn't played Croatian defender Igor Stimac in a UEFA Cup tie, even though he still had a two-game ban to serve dating back four years to his time at Hajduk Split. UEFA accepted responsibility for the oversight on that occasion. But the Football League weren't so lenient and they ordered a replay – which we lost 3–1 after extra time. After years of failure this was the first time in West Ham's history that we had actually managed to win a penalty shoot-out in a competitive game and then go on and lose the tie. You can see why a lifetime spent following the Hammers gives you a rather jaundiced outlook on life.

The penalty kick itself was devised by an Irishman named William McCrum who played in goal for his village side Milford FC in the Irish Football League. Judging by his first season, in 1890/91, he may not have been the greatest keeper the world has ever seen. Milford finished bottom of the League with no points from fourteen games, having conceded sixty-two goals. However, the village had been built by his millionaire father, who also just happened to run the local linen business, so it was unlikely he was ever going to be dropped.

This was the time when the game was played by amateur 'gentlemen', who never cheated. Only they did – and McCrum, as a keeper, was perfectly placed to see them do it. To counter some of the violence that was taking place in front of him (which could be startlingly brutal at times) he came up with a proposal that went before the International Football Association Board for consideration.

What the man known locally as Master Willie suggested was:

> If any player shall intentionally trip or hold an opposing player, or deliberately handle the ball within 12 yards from his own goal line, the referee shall, on appeal, award the opposing side a penalty kick, to be taken from any point 12 yards from the goal line, under the following conditions: All players, with the exception of the player taking the penalty kick and the goalkeeper, shall stand behind the ball and at least 6 yards from it: the ball shall be in play when the kick is taken. A goal may be scored from a penalty kick.

You will notice that the infringement had to happen 12 yards from the goal line, rather than in the penalty area. There is a simple explanation for this; before McCrum came up with the idea of a penalty there was no need for a penalty area, so it didn't exist. Interestingly, a penalty would only be awarded after an appeal – in the way a cricket umpire cannot give a batsman out without first being asked – and the kick could be taken from any point 12 yards away, not necessarily a central spot.

The idea did not go down at all well at first – particularly with his fellow players who dubbed it, among other things, the 'death penalty'. However, a year after the proposal was first made it was approved, with a couple of amendments, and became the Law 13 we know and love today.

Penalties I can live with. But the penalty shoot-out really is a devilish invention. As a way of settling drawn games it is preferable to the heads-or-tails lottery of the coin-toss that preceded it. But only just. First introduced in England in 1970, the shoot-out began life here in the late, but not-so-lamented, Watney Cup. (West Ham were to lose the first of many shoot-outs in this particular competition when Bristol Rovers proved they were better than us at taking penalties in 1973. *Plus ça change*, as they say in Bristol.)

Sorry, did someone say this would be an ideal opportunity to analyse the penalty-taking techniques of the lads who came up so desperately short in the shoot-out after Stephen Gerrard's last gasp equaliser for Liverpool in the 2006 Cup final? Relive that heartache – are you mad?

This isn't just a West Ham thing. There cannot be an Englishman worthy of the name who doesn't dread a penalty shoot-out. I don't care what team you support, I simply don't believe that anyone who considers George the dragon-slayer to be their patron saint actually believes their team will come out on top if it goes to pens.

It's anybody's guess what Master Willie would have made of the bastard offspring of his noble idea. One man who might have an inkling is my colleague Robert McCrum, a highly distinguished writer on *The Guardian*'s sister paper *The Observer*, who is William's grandson. I thought about asking him but we're all pretty busy at work these days and I didn't think it right to waste his time with silly questions like that.

In the unlikely event my life depended on West Ham winning a penalty shoot-out, and I had to choose five players from any era to take them, I'd go for Tonka, followed by Julian Dicks, Paolo Di Canio, Sir Geoff and Mark Noble. I was tempted to include George Kitchen, who didn't let the fact he was a goalkeeper put him off and scored five times from the penalty spot between 1905 and 1912.

(Apparently he is the only keeper ever to have scored on his debut. No kidding?) However, he also missed three – including one in a game against Brighton on Bonfire Night in 1910 in which he also scored. This all sounds a bit flaky to me, and as it is my life we're talking about here I'm not going to risk it.

The mighty Julian Dicks scored fifty times in his 264 appearances for West Ham, which came in two slices. The unlikely filling in this sandwich was a spell at Anfield, where he will always have the distinction of being the last Liverpool player to score in front of a standing Kop before they made them all sit down. The Terminator reckons that of all his penalties he only ever tried to place two: one hit the post and the other missed altogether. The rest he simply blasted with a ferocity that was staggering to behold. In all, he converted thirty-five of his thirty-nine spot kicks while wearing claret and blue.

Di Canio, of course, was a law unto himself when it came to taking penalties, just as happy to wait for the keeper to dive and cheekily chip the ball into the space he had vacated as place it unerringly in the corner; Hurst – despite the heart-breaking miss against Stoke – was brilliant from 12 yards; and mighty Mark Noble has the assurance of a professional assassin when he puts the ball on the spot. Save a plinth in the West Ham hall of fame for this man – the day he hangs up his boots his place alongside the club's all-time greats is assured.

Marlon Harewood, on the other hand, will have to wait a little longer for an invitation to take his place among the legends of E13.

Quite how he got to take a penalty in a crucial relegation clash against Watford in the Great Escape season when Carlos Tevez was on the pitch is beyond me. But that is in the second half, and we have an opposition penalty to deal with first. Geoff and I are in the Trevor Brooking Lower, in much the same place I had stood all those years beforehand when my son's illustrious namesake was foiled by the Banks of England. Less than a quarter of an hour has passed when Anton Ferdinand pulls back Darius Henderson in the area for a nailed-on pen.

Funnily enough, I never have the same feeling of doubt when we concede a penalty as I do when we're awarded one. I am always convinced our keeper is going to save it. And in all my years of going to Upton Park I cannot recall anyone better at saving penalties than Robert Green. This time, however, my confidence is misplaced and Henderson's effort beats Green's flailing right hand and finds its way into the bottom corner.

We proceed to bombard the bottom-placed club and come close on a number of occasions. Then we get our chance from the spot. Curiously, we have had to wait until February for our first penalty. For reasons of illogical superstition that escape me now, I decide to look away when Marvellous Marlon steps up to do the honours. It is the first time I have ever opted not to watch as we take a pen.

By the nature of things, it is rare to turn your back to goal at a football match (we don't do the Poznan at Upton Park) and it is an interesting experience when you do. If nothing else, it gives you a rare opportunity to study the people who share your obsession. Like you, they will be exultant if this ball finds its way into the net. Similarly, they will be plunged into the gloomy depths if it doesn't. You can work out for yourself which emotion we are left to deal with as we go on to lose 1–0 and sink deeper into the relegation mire.

Having tried it, I won't look away again. Neither will I shut my eyes. From Hurst to Harewood, West Ham will always leave me on the edge of a nervous breakdown when a ref points to the spot. But, unlike them, I will never miss another penalty.

Chapter 17

1966 and all that

WHEN BOBBY MOORE wiped the mud off his hands on the velvet cloth draped over the edge of the royal box and prepared to receive the Jules Rimet trophy from the Queen at Wembley on a glorious July day in 1966 I couldn't have been happier. England were world champions, and the nation's global triumph had been achieved with the considerable help of three players from the club side to which I had given my young heart two years earlier.

Moore, Hurst and Peters – the holy trinity for West Ham supporters of a certain age (the age that means you have to start watching your cholesterol and hills seem steeper than they once did). Not only had West Ham provided the captain of a world-conquering team, we had come up with the goal-scorers too.

Naturally, I had pictures of all three of them on my bedroom wall. By the time the World Cup was won I wasn't allowed posters because my dad didn't like the way Sellotape stripped off a piece of the wallpaper when you took one down for whatever reason (such as an elder brother inking in a Hitler moustache on a favourite player in retaliation for some perceived offence by a totally innocent party). Instead, I had framed photographs. The 10x8 prints were supplied by Typhoo Tea in return for a set number of packet tops. The frames – and the glass that prevented any further acts of sibling vandalism – were provided by my old man, who was a dab hand at that sort of thing.

The pictures, hanging on pukka picture-hooks, were aligned with perfect precision – my father was the sort of man who insisted on using a spirit level for jobs like that.

For me, there was a similar and equally pleasing alignment between my club and my country at that time. With Moore, Hurst and Peters being automatic selections for the national side, supporting England was merely an extension of following West Ham.

The three of them remained on my wall, quite content to be there, for the following four years. West Ham never quite enjoyed the success they should have done in that period but I knew it was only a matter of time before we won another trophy. Besides, all three were such an integral part of Alf Ramsey's plans I happily regarded England as my 'other' team. And a very good team it was too. They were certainly going to win a major tournament again soon.

Had I given the matter any thought as I entered my teens, I suppose I would have told you I expected West Ham's World Cup heroes to remain on their hooks where my dad had hung them for years to come. It never occurred to me that any of them might want to leave Upton Park. And I couldn't have dreamt that I would one day feel very differently about England.

The first picture to come down was Martin Peters. To be honest, I wasn't all that upset. In fact, after I'd removed his photo and filled in the holes left by the hook under the watchful eye of my father – who couldn't understand how I could make such a mess with a little dab of Polyfilla and a trowel – I actually wrote a letter to *Goal* magazine expressing my delight at the deal that took Peters to Tottenham and brought us Jimmy Greaves in exchange.

It certainly didn't change the way I felt about England. This was 1970, and the three lions were preparing to defend the World Cup in Mexico. The fact that Martin Peters no longer played his club football in claret and blue mattered not one bit. I was desperate for England to retain the trophy.

They might just have done it too. It would have meant beating a brilliant Brazil team that boasted the likes of Pelé, Jairzinho and Carlos Alberto. But this was the best England side the country had ever produced – better even than the '66 team – and with the defensive brilliance of Moore and the tactical genius of Ramsey anything was possible. Trouble was, we never got to find out. On a Sunday afternoon that was to graze my soul, Sir Alf's strategic acumen deserted him and after taking a two-goal lead – including one from Peters – some dodgy substitutions, coupled with some even dodgier goalkeeping by Peter 'The Cat' Bonetti, saw England crash out 3–2 to West Germany in the quarter-final.

Two years later the picture of Geoff Hurst came down. My dad, having given up all hope of teaching me how to do handyman-type jobs, filled in the holes himself and finished off the job with a splash of paint that matched the wallpaper.

Hurst left West Ham to join Stoke in August 1972. Not only would he never wear the claret and blue again, he'd played his last international as well. In the April of that year he'd been substituted with twenty minutes to go as England went down 3–1 at Wembley to the nation he had put to the sword in the World Cup final. That was his forty-ninth cap for England. There would be no fiftieth.

That defeat effectively ended England's hopes of being champions of Europe, but the tournament then had nothing of the prestige it does today and supporters of the national side shrugged off the disappointment then turned their attention to qualification for the next World Cup in West Germany.

The good news was that Bobby Moore was still at the helm – both for West Ham and England. His face, now hanging proudly alone, looked out over my bedroom with a knowing serenity that assured me all was well.

On Valentine's Day in 1973 he was awarded his 100th cap for England before we Sassenachs demolished Scotland 5–0 at Hampden Park. There was no telling how many more caps he would win as England sailed through the qualifying games and then set about the more serious challenge of negotiating the group stage of the World Cup finals. Then there would be the knock-out encounters – quarter-final; semi-final; maybe even the final in Munich itself . . .

It didn't appear to be a difficult qualifying group. England, Poland and Wales. Finish top of the pile and book the plane for Germany: what could be more straightforward? England started well, beating Wales in Cardiff. Poland, on the other hand, lost to the Welshmen. This was practically in the bag. The first feelings of foreboding came in the Polish city of Katowice. The great Bobby Moore – the rock upon which the England side was founded – had an absolute shocker, getting caught in possession to gift the home side their second goal in a 2–0 defeat.

When the Poles came to Wembley in October 1973, England had to win if they were going to qualify. Those of us who cared about the nation's prial of lions were nervous, but far from over-awed by the challenge. Then came the bombshell news: Sir Alf Ramsey had dropped Bobby Moore. And that was the moment I fell out of love with England.

Of course I wanted England to beat Poland. The World Cup finals without England was unthinkable. But what was 'England' now? Representing my hopes were players I regularly abused when they turned up at Upton Park to represent the likes of Leeds, Liverpool and Spurs. Norman Hunter; Emlyn Hughes; Martin Chivers – I loathed them when they wore their club colours. Now I was supposed to cheer them on in a side that – for the first time in my life as a football supporter – contained no West Ham players. It didn't feel right at all.

After being told he had been dropped, Moore asked Ramsey if that was the end of his international career – only to be reassured that he would still be required to captain the side when they had made it to the finals. That, of course, never happened.

In the event, Moore played one more game for England – his 108th international appearance – in a friendly against Italy a month after being left out of the side. Five months later Sir Alf was sacked – and any hope that the West Ham captain had of re-establishing his place in the national side went with him. Not that it would have been much consolation to the great man at the time, but

Robert Frederick Chelsea Moore kept his place of honour on my bedroom wall while the rest of the country turned its back on him. He didn't come down until he finally said goodbye to West Ham and retired to Fulham. If I remember correctly, my dad took the opportunity to completely redecorate soon after.

With Moore dropped for the Poland game the only remaining member of the '66 World Cup-winning side still in the England team that night was Martin Peters. He took over as captain, in fact.

This, of course, was the man Sir Alf had famously described as being ten years ahead of his time. Yet I had written to Britain's leading soccer magazine to say I was perfectly happy to see him leave West Ham. That letter has troubled me ever since.

I don't really do football memorabilia. My 'collection' consists of some old programmes, a ball signed by Hurst and Peters and an autographed framed photo of the world's greatest ever defender that hangs in our downstairs loo, aka the Bobby Moore Suite. But if I did I would be a regular customer of the wonderful Matchday Memories, run by a boing-boing Baggy named Dave. It was Dave who patiently sifted through his back catalogue of *Goal* mags and found the issue that featured my letter. You, sir, are a gentleman.

What really worried me was that *Goal* had published my letter in full. Because I was pretty sure that not only had I written in praise of the incoming Jimmy Greaves, but had taken the opportunity to point out Martin Peters' shortcomings as well. In the event, it appears I was saved from myself by a kindly sub-editor who took his red pen to the more extreme parts of my correspondence. (As someone who went on to become a kindly sub-editor myself I am better placed than most to appreciate his intervention.)

What appeared under the one-word headline 'Boom!' was:

> I strongly believe West Ham will be back where they belong
> – at the top – next season. It will not be by strong-arm tactics
> or sacking Ron Greenwood but because of Jimmy Greaves.
>
> His presence on the field inspires confidence in the play-
> ers around him, and that is exactly what West Ham needs.
>
> Jimmy could well be the spark that lights the gunpowder
> – and there's going to be quite an explosion.

I was really proud of that letter – it was the first thing I'd ever had published. I showed it to all my mates at school.

For the record, my prediction fell some way short of the mark. The following season West Ham finished twentieth out of twenty-two, narrowly missing relegation. It's fair to say I'm not all that hot at this forecasting malarkey. Perhaps that's why the country's leading bookmakers send me a Christmas card every year.

On reflection, what I should have done was thank Mr Peters for his fantastic contribution to West Ham. It is often said that he played in every position for my beloved Hammers – including goalkeeper – but in fact he never wore the No. 2 shirt. Not that that detracts from his talent and versatility in any way. He made 302 appearances for West Ham and scored eighty-one times, including a hat-trick against Dave's West Brom that is among my earliest memories.

Peters was the complete player: two-footed, good in the air, an eye for goal and strong in the tackle. Greaves, to put it politely, was in the autumn of his career.

Mind you, that didn't stop him scoring on his debut – just as he had done for Chelsea, AC Milan, Tottenham and England. In fact he scored twice in his first game in claret and blue as we thumped Man City 5–1 in a quagmire at Maine Road. Geoff Hurst got a couple as well. There's a fantastic photograph of the two of them celebrating on the back page of my recently acquired copy of *Goal*. Due to the strange camera angle at which the picture was taken Sir Geoff appears to have three legs! Now that would have gone on my wall if it hadn't been for my dad's poster ban.

I loved *Goal*. Thursdays couldn't come quickly enough. I'd often wait by the front door for the newspapers to drop through the letterbox, hurriedly separate my periodical from the rest and scan it over breakfast before going to school. Then, for the next few days, I'd re-read it time and again – savouring every word and memorising every picture with an application that would have astonished my teachers, who were tearing their hair out at my unwillingness to show similar levels of concentration in French, biology, religious instruction and the similarly pointless subjects I was expected to study while in their care.

When Dave sent me issue No. 91, for 2 May 1970 – in return for a couple of measly pound coins plus postage – I read it with the same devotion I displayed forty years ago. (Although I did resist the temptation to do the spot-the-difference puzzle on page forty-six.)

I turned to my letter first. I had been hoping to win the £2 prize for the Star Letter in Goal Lines but I was pipped by Miss Heather Harrington from Blackpool, who had written in praise of women's football (and, as well as the money, earned herself a very condescending remark from the editor asking 'but who will look after baby on a Saturday afternoon?' for her pains).

It should be pointed out that two quid was not to be sniffed at in 1970; at today's value it's worth more than £25. It would certainly have been enough to buy me a good deal of the merchandise on offer in the magazine's adverts.

There is actually an ad for football boots (or, to use the manufacturer's description, 'soccer slippers') that features Martin Peters still wearing a West Ham shirt – several weeks after he had moved to Tottenham. Advertisers would have a fit if that happened today.

The Goalpost advertising page offered several replica kits for boys. Back then, replica kits were always for boys. Grown-ups didn't wear it. A basic set for a child cost 32s 6d (that's a fraction over £1.60 in today's coinage) which would have given me change of 7 shillings and sixpence from my £2 if I'd won the prize for Star Letter. For that you got the shirt, shorts, socks – and a club badge! Had I wanted the iconic West Ham away strip (the light blue shirt with the two claret hoops) I would have had to fork out an extra 5s 6d (27.5p), which would have still left me two bob to the good if Ms Harrington hadn't written a better letter.

There is loads of other good stuff for sale too – but I had all of it. The enamel badge, the shoulder bag, the pen: everything in club colours, of course.

No one was left in any doubt about who I supported when I went to school. I was a walking advert for West Ham United. Which made it all the more galling when I was called up before the deputy headmaster and accused of defacing a desk in the name of Liverpool FC. It was true that I did have some form when it came to writing on desks, but I'd paid my debt to society over five nights of detention and, as I pointed out to Mr Crittenden, I was hardly likely to write 'Liverpool are Great' when I clearly followed another team.

I pointed to the badge on my school jumper; I showed him my bag; I rummaged around inside it to find my pen. I even offered to go to the cloakroom and fetch my elongated claret and blue scarf. But he was having none of it. I was guilty as charged and should prepare myself for another stretch of staying behind after school with sandpaper and elbow grease to atone for my misdemeanour.

I wasn't unduly worried: I knew who had done it. Naturally, I wasn't going to grass him up but I was certain that when he heard I'd been falsely accused he'd step forward and do the decent thing. We weren't the closest of friends but there is a universal etiquette about these matters. Or so I thought. Miserable toerag – he let me take the rap without the slightest qualm. He went on to play rugby for Wasps. Which just goes to show: never trust a rugger bugger.

Edition No. 91 of *Goal* led on the forthcoming European Cup final between Celtic and Feyenoord, with a confident prediction that the Glasgow side would be victorious. Seems I'm not the only one who's a bit shaky in the crystal ball department.

There were also a number of articles looking ahead to the World Cup in Mexico the following month. A particularly good feature pointed out how Geoff Hurst had become a target for 'the cloggers'. And there was an update on the London-Mexico rally that preceded the tournament. Jimmy Greaves and his co-driver lay tenth at the time. They went on to finish sixth – which was probably the most noteworthy thing Greaves did in his time as a West Ham player. As with any World Cup build-up, there was an underlying air of optimism about English prospects.

The quarter-final exit at the hands of West Germany was, for me, as painful as any defeat I had experienced supporting the Hammers. (As a fourteen-year-old I had yet to see West Ham get relegated; nor had we thrown away a magnificent FA Cup final victory in the final minute.) Gerd Muller's extra-time winner felt like a rusty breadknife had been plunged into my essential organs. I was stunned for days afterwards.

Little did I know then that it would be twelve years before we would see England in the World Cup finals again. By the time Bryan Robson led out the team in Spain in 1982 I felt differently about the three lions. There was once more a West Ham connection – England were managed by Ron Greenwood and Trevor Brooking had been brilliant during the qualifying tournament – but I knew the national side's eventual exit from the tournament wouldn't affect me the way it had in Mexico. And it certainly wouldn't hurt as much as watching the Irons get beaten.

Despite the wrench of Bobby Moore's departure I saw a few internationals at Wembley in the wilderness years that followed the Ramsey era. A more depressing experience is hard to imagine.

Watching England on the telly is one thing. Watching them live is something else. The old Wembley was a terrible place for supporters. The journey up the Metropolitan line to get there was a nightmare: the pitch was miles away from the terracing, the facilities were inadequate and some of the football that was served up by a country that had once ruled the world in the game it invented was woeful.

Three years after Martin had played his last game for England I looked on, more in sorrow than anger, as another Peters scored twice at the so-called home of football. This one was called Jan and he played for Holland alongside the likes of Neeskens, Rep and a certain Johan Cruyff. The Netherlands won 2–0 that night but in truth they could have scored however many they liked. The gulf in class was breathtaking.

Don't ask me to explain precisely why, but I could never feel part of things at Wembley the way I did at Upton Park. There's something very different about an England crowd, which I don't really understand and – if I'm going to be totally honest here – don't like very much. Some countries seem to be able to take their sporting nationalism and turn it into a party. The English can't.

It's been argued that many of the people who follow the national side regularly do so because their club sides are in the lower leagues and international football offers an opportunity for some glory on a bigger stage, but that doesn't hold water for me. Whenever my club has been in a lower division my sole focus is on seeing them promoted – what supporter doesn't want to see their team win whatever division they are in?

If the Genie of the Lamp offered me the alternatives of West Ham winning the League or England lifting the World Cup it wouldn't take me very long make my choice. And I'd be astonished if any serious supporter didn't put the national side's interests second as well.

That's not to say I want to see my country crash and burn in major tournaments. Having lived through a number of World Cups where England have failed to qualify I try to enjoy them when they do. I particularly liked Italia '90, even though there was not a single West Ham player in the squad. We didn't have anyone playing for Scotland or the Republic of Ireland either, but there was one Upton Park favourite flying the flag for London E13. Any takers? You are correct my friend – it was indeed the very wonderful Ludek Miklosko, representing the Czech Republic.

Some years later – in 2006 to be precise – something similar happened. We are now in Germany and again there are no players from Upton Park in the England squad, but the West Ham goalkeeper is there in the colours of another nation. This time it's Shaka Hislop, playing for Trinidad and Tobago. What makes this particularly interesting for me is that he is facing England in the group stages. At the risk of angering the patriots I'll put my cards on the table here – I would have been delighted if he'd kept a clean sheet.

We'll draw a discreet veil over the performance of the West Ham keeper who made headlines for all the wrong reasons in South Africa four years later. Poor old Rob Green has taken enough stick for his howler against the US. Incidentally, there were five West Ham players in that tournament – and if you can name them all you are one serious anorak. Green and Matthew Upson are easy enough. You may even recall Jonathan Spector on the US subs' bench without qualifying for nerd status. However, if you've named Valon Behrami as one of the Switzerland squad you'd better slip on that quilted winter coat of yours. And if you know that Guillermo Franco turned out for Mexico while playing his club football for West Ham I suggest you zip it up, pull the draw-strings of the hood tight and go for a long walk in search of a more meaningful life.

There are those of a mystical disposition who will tell you it is written in the stars that England will only ever win the World Cup again when there are three West Ham players in the team once more. I for one am convinced that this is true. However, it seems the three players in question aren't David James, Trevor Sinclair and Joe Cole, who were all playing for the Hammers when they represented the unsuccessful England side of 2002 in Japan and South Korea.

So until the cosmic prediction comes to pass I will continue to cherish the memory of Moore, Hurst and Peters – even though

I was obliged to remove their pictures from my bedroom wall all those years ago.

Watching them play against West Ham for their new clubs was a strange experience. Seeing Bobby Moore in the white of Fulham rather than the white of England at Wembley in the 1975 FA Cup final was probably the easiest of the lot to take. And, as I told the readers of *Goal* magazine, losing Martin Peters to Tottenham didn't seem like the worst thing in the world at the time. But seeing Geoff Hurst move to the Potteries after playing 499 games for West Ham was devastating.

I was clearly not alone in thinking we had made a huge mistake in letting him go. In his first game back at Upton Park he got a fantastic reception from all parts of the ground. It was really odd to see him in red and white stripes rather than claret and blue and I think we were all still trying to get used to the idea when, just eight minutes into the game, my boyhood hero did what he had done so many times before … and scored with his head at the Boleyn Ground.

This time, of course, we didn't celebrate on the North Bank. Some applauded sportingly. Most of us were speechless. I'd like to say Sir Geoff appeared to be as gutted as I felt, but he clearly wasn't. In fact, he looked quite pleased with himself. It later emerged that he wasn't exactly thrilled by Ron Greenwood's decision to let him go – particularly as he felt the move effectively prevented him resurrecting his England career – and the goal clearly underlined his point.

Ten days after I saw Geoff Hurst score against us I watched Martin Peters return to the Boleyn with Tottenham and do the same thing. Ain't that typical? You wait all your life for a former West Ham World Cup winner to score against you, then two come along at once.

Peters' goal came in the Boxing Day fixture, which used to kick off in the morning. Living as I did in Berkshire, I had to make a distressingly early start to get to the game. The good news, though, was that a few days previously I had copped off with a girl called Sharon at a Christmas party and she had agreed to come with me. If I remember correctly, she had been particularly impressed by my enthusiastic response to Gary Glitter's invitation to join his gang (and that's not a sentence you read very often these days).

My abiding memory of Boxing Day 1972 is not so much Peters' goal, nor the 2–2 result, but the overpowering smell of aftershave that lingered like my mate at the party who wouldn't clear off even though it was obvious I was in with a distinct chance of scoring.

For my Christmas present, Sharon had given me a large bottle of Old Spice (she worked in Woolworths and I think they had an offer running). It was my own fault, really. While chatting her up I had added a couple of years to my age, so she thought I was eighteen and did actually shave.

I didn't want to disabuse her so early in our relationship, so I doused myself in the stuff before setting out to meet her at the station. She obviously appreciated the gesture and gave me a very warm welcome. I had high hopes for the rest of the day.

There was a surprisingly large number of people on the train for a Boxing Day morning and any thoughts I had of rearranging Sharon's hot-pants went right out the window (which in those days used to slide up and down and came with dire warnings about not sticking your head out. Train windows that is, not Sharon's hot-pants).

By the time we got to Upton Park my youthful lust had abated somewhat. But the smell of Old Spice hadn't. It seemed to have permeated my clothes as well as my skin and I just couldn't shake it off.

The trouble was, my dad used Old Spice (I think everybody's dad used Old Spice in 1972) and it was like having my father standing behind me throughout the entire day. And when you're a sixteen-year-old boy who wants to shout rude things at Spurs supporters and attempt even ruder things with a seventeen-year-old girl who works in Woollies, that's not good.

Sharon and I had gone our separate ways when Hurst scored for Stoke a second time against us at the old Victoria Ground in the early part of the following season. And when Peters did it again at White Hart Lane the year after that, she was just a distant memory – although that memory was rekindled some years later when West Ham ran out to Carl Orff's rousing 'O Fortuna', which had been used on the Old Spice ads in the '70s. Every time I heard that piece of music – which, when you translate the lyrics, is basically a medieval version of 'Bubbles' – I had a small pang of guilt over the way I misled Sharon.

When John F. Kennedy was sworn in as President of the US a few years before West Ham and I became an item, he uttered the often-quoted line: 'Ask not what your country can do for you, ask what you can do for your country.' (Apparently he pinched it from his headteacher, who was obviously a rather more inspiring character than my Mr Crittenden.)

Well, I reckon I've done my bit for England. I gave them every chance as a supporter and I feel have been let down badly in return.

I owe a few people an apology: Sharon for fibbing about my age; Martin Peters for questioning his undoubted talent; even Geoff Hurst for stealing the title of his autobiography as a heading for this chapter. But I'm not going to apologise to anyone for doing what most football supporters do and putting my club before my country. I did my best with England. It's not my fault that I can no longer summon up an emotional commitment to the national side. I am the innocent party in all this. Honestly, like Bobby Moore when he was presented with the World Cup by the Queen, my hands are clean.

Chapter 18

Pride and prejudice

THERE ARE TIMES when following West Ham is no laughing matter. Certainly, the bloke I was sitting next to at Loftus Road several seasons ago wasn't smiling when the wiry young man in front of us stood up and abused the supporters behind the goal to our left.

'They are West Ham,' he succinctly informed this misguided individual as he placed a giant hand on his head and, employing a vice-like grip, wrenched it through 90 degrees until a whole new set of supporters came into view. 'They are QPR,' pointed out my neighbour, who then continued to read his programme as if nothing had happened.

Before resuming the task of informing the opposition support exactly what he thought of them, the numpty in front of us turned to confront the guy who had just broadened his general knowledge in such a robust way. Their eyes met; one set angry but curious, the other ice cold and deadly. The younger man had barely blinked twice before he decided he would take the matter no further. He may have been stupid, but he wasn't that stupid.

Funny things, football crowds. You find yourself rubbing shoulders with all sorts of people. It's true that at West Ham we have our quota of loudmouths and idiots, just like any club. And we've got some real hard cases too. But, on match day at least, there is clearly more that unites us than divides us. Does it extend beyond a love of the same football team though?

I like to think so. Perhaps it's a certain way of looking at life. Fear the worst, hope for the best and try to see the funny side whenever possible. (Oh yes, and don't have a row with a bloke who is prepared to twist your head like you're auditioning for *The Exorcist* and then looks straight through you when you think about complaining.)

The humour at West Ham has been well documented over the years. 'We've got Di Canio, You've got our stereo,' may be unfair on the good people of Liverpool – but I'd defy any football supporter to keep a straight face the first time they heard that.

There's a fine line between banter and abuse, and my personal favourite undoubtedly crosses that line. Sung to *The Addams Family* theme tune, this one is reserved for trips to East Anglia: 'My sister is my mother, my uncle is my brother, we all procreate with each other, in our Norwich family' (actually 'procreate with' is generally shortened to one word).

If you really want a song that sums up the West Ham sense of humour it has to be: 'We're winning away, we're winning away. How shit must you be? We're winning away!' And if you want to go one better, try: 'We're coming for you, we're coming for you. Barcelona, we're coming for you.'

What doesn't get mentioned quite so often is the pride that goes with being a Hammer.

It will be a long time before West Ham supporters will forget the way we were taken apart by Man City in the semi-final of the 2014 League Cup at the Etihad. After I'd watched the 6–0 mauling on television I got a text from Geoff that probably summed up in one word how everyone who loves the club was feeling at that moment. 'Jesus.' Somehow, that seemed to say it all.

This humiliation, remember, came just days after we had been embarrassed 5–0 at Nottingham Forest in the third round of the FA Cup when an under-strength side had been sacrificed in the hope of keeping what few senior players who were still standing fit for the two-leg semi and the relegation battle in which we had become embroiled.

The defeat at Nottingham was bad. What happened in Manchester was far worse. Essentially, football is a simple game. As a supporter you don't need statistics to tell you when you've been pissed upon from a stellar height. However, here are a few to be going on with. The records show that they had an astonishing thirty-two attempts at goal, eleven of which were on target, while we had three attempts, only one of which vaguely threatened their net. They had eight corners to our four and almost 70 per cent of the possession. Most damning of all, however, is that over ninety minutes we committed just nine fouls and no one was booked. A six-goal slaughter and only nine fouls? I'm sorry, but that just isn't acceptable. If you are going to get hammered you must at least go down fighting – the supporters deserve nothing less.

On the pitch we were gutless. But in the stands we were magnificent. The support was unwavering – there were shades of Villa Park in '91 about the way those who'd made the trip north refused to bend the knee in the face of overwhelming opposition. Despite the abysmal performance of our team the fans never stopped making a racket. At one point they mocked the home crowd with '2–0 and you still don't sing.' Fair play to the Mancs, though, who came back with 'We only sing when it's 4–0.'

The following day I was still angry at the way the team had performed and the clueless strategy that had been handed down from a manager who, at the time, was steadfastly refusing to play football the West Ham Way. But I was unbelievably proud of our supporters. In fact, I felt compelled to wear my favourite scarf to work as a show of solidarity. It's the white one, with the claret and blue stripes. I wore it to the office when Bobby Moore died. Come to think of it I rarely wear it when I go to games these days, but it still comes out on special occasions.

When I got to work a colleague asked if I was wearing my colours as an act of penance. I just smiled and wished him good morning. I didn't bother trying to explain myself – and I don't think he would have understood if I had. He's an armchair Arsenal supporter.

Sad to say, there are times when a small section of the Upton Park crowd leaves me feeling anything but proud. Over the years that I have followed West Ham, the demographics of the East End have changed beyond all recognition. Many of the club's supporters don't live there any more, having chosen to move to leafier areas in Essex and beyond. But they've taken their loyalty with them and they bring it back on match day. Unhappily, a minority – a tiny minority – return with their prejudices too.

It's no secret that we don't like Tottenham. But that's no justi-fication for the anti-Semitic filth that spews from the mouths of a moronic minority of our supporters.

Notoriously, in our first season back in the Prem under Sam Allardyce, the game at White Hart Lane was marred by anti-Jewish gibberish from a vociferous few in the West Ham end, who seemed inordinately proud of their foreskins. One song that caused par-ticular offence was in praise of Adolf Hitler – the man ultimately responsible for the deaths of six million innocent Jewish people in the Second World War. I wonder if some of those morons had been in the 'choir' at Coventry the previous season singing an old favourite from the xenophobes' hit parade, 'There Were Ten Ger-man Bombers in the Air (Then The RAF of England Shot One Down)'. Maybe they missed the history lesson that explained what the planes were doing in the air in the first place.

Unhappily, this hatred is nothing new. One game that still leaves me depressed by the memory is a sixth-round FA Cup tie against the Lilywhites when Geoff was still at junior school. I took him and his friend Mike – the lad who was later to kick Jordan of Riz-zle Kicks at my behest – who at the time was a Spurs fan (I'm glad to say he supports Brighton now).

We sat in the East Stand Upper, generally considered to be one of the more civilised parts of Upton Park. Civilised? Some of the people behind us would have been considered uncouth in the Stone Age. One guy in particular was so full of loathing his eyes were practically popping out of his head every time a Spurs player had the audacity to touch the ball. Only he was one of those West Ham supporters who can't actually bring himself to use the word 'Spurs' – they were the 'Yids'. And he was very

NEARLY REACH THE SKY

keen that others should stand up to demonstrate they too hated these sons of Abraham.

When Sergei Rebrov scored the first of his two goals the atmosphere was so toxic my instant reaction was to place a firm, restraining hand on Mike's shoulder to ensure he didn't leap out of his seat and celebrate. What sort of environment have we created if a ten-year-old lad can't stand up and cheer his heroes when they score a goal without the risk of reprisal from supposedly grown men?

Still, you've got to hand it to the bigots; they are nothing if not even-handed. These guys clearly hate Islam as much as they hate Jews.

In the home game against Man City in October 2013 a small group of Muslims were filmed on a mobile phone as they quietly observed their ritual prayers beneath the Trevor Brooking Stand. There were still ten minutes to go to half time, but word obviously spread quickly because long before the traditional rush for a pint and a hot-dog had started a largely hostile group had gathered to witness the admittedly unusual spectacle. Stewards looked on impassively as the whole incident threatened to turn ugly, with the bystanders attempting to disturb the sunset prayers with chants of 'Irons … Irons' and 'E, E, EDL'.

Sensibly, the worshippers returned quietly to their seats and did all they could to avoid confrontation with their antagonists. But it didn't end there. The footage was online shortly after the game and the keyboard warriors wasted no time in adding their comments.

Among all the usual 'Paki go home' rubbish were a couple of 'facts' that had been hitherto unknown. Apparently, according to some, West Ham were handing out free tickets to Muslims, and when they got there the ungrateful Jihadists decided to support the away team.

The truth is West Ham make available a number of tickets at greatly reduced prices to various community groups who would otherwise not be able to afford to go to Upton Park. You don't have to be a Muslim to qualify. And, for the record, there is not a shred of evidence to support the accusation that the lads who went to the City game were supporting the Mancs.

Encouragingly, more members of the East End's Asian community do appear to be going to the Boleyn Ground – and they're not all getting cheap tickets. The youngest are often taken by their mothers because dad is working. My mate Nick – who is actually a Hindu and doesn't get a cheap ticket either – is sometimes asked in Urdu to keep an eye out for the youngsters when they need a half-time pee because, obviously, mum can't go with them. I've tried to convince him he should take the requests as a compliment, but I'm not sure he sees it that way!

On the pitch, at least, West Ham has done its fair share in the battle to break down the barriers that ethnic minorities so often have to overcome. It should be a matter of eternal pride to everyone associated with the Hammers that, at a time when black players were struggling to break into professional football, we were one of the first clubs in the UK to field three in the same League side.

Put the date in your diary and make a mental note to celebrate it quietly every year from now on: it was 1 April 1972 and the three players in question were Clyde Best, Ade Coker and Clive Charles. We beat Spurs 2–0 at Upton Park, with Coker getting one of the goals.

Clive Charles' elder brother John had become the first black player to turn out for West Ham some nine years earlier, making it into the first team after captaining the side that won the 1963

Youth Cup. He was also the first black player to represent England at any level, winning five international caps as a youth. Clive was a decent footballer himself, and Coker showed early flashes of brilliance before ultimately moving to the US. But it's Clyde Best who will be best remembered as a trailblazer by my generation of West Ham loyalists.

I loved the guy. Most of us did. Sure, he could be frustrating – he had the build of a boxer, the athleticism of an Olympic sprinter and could cover the ground like a downhill skier. Yes, with his talent and physical attributes he probably should have scored more goals than he did. But when he did get it right, no defender could live with him. Some of his goals were the sort of efforts that stay with you for ever – blistering shots from 30 yards; diving headers in a sea of boots; crisp volleys that left opposition keepers motionless as the ball flew past them. And he understood what the supporters expected from their players.

It's fair to say I can't work up quite the same amount of affection for Karren Brady, who was appointed vice chairman of the club by owners Gold and Sullivan shortly after they took over. She used her column in *The Sun* to big up the fact that, at the end of the 2010/11 season, the PFA – in her words – 'came along and rated us highest of all the ninety-two senior clubs for players doing anti-racism and disabilities work.'

She was rightly proud of the achievement. But she then went and ruined a special moment by writing: 'When you remember that East London was once a hotbed of racism, and a rain of bananas used to greet Bermudan Clyde Best when he first played at Upton Park in the '60s, you understand exactly why the club is so committed and will remain so committed.'

Hang on a minute Karren – sorry, Baroness Brady – 'a hotbed of racism'? That's a bit strong isn't it? Yes, over the years we have had a number of followers whose dislike of their fellow human beings is based on little more than the colour of their skin, but to suggest the entire East End was once a step away from *Mississippi Burning*? Some people could take offence at that.

You're right in saying halfwits did occasionally throw soft fruit at Clyde Best. Others pelted him with peanuts. Some merely contented themselves with making monkey noises. The point is, they weren't usually our halfwits. These clowns were generally supporting the opposition. I do remember one bloke referring to him as Sooty throughout a game, which is undoubtedly offensive but more indicative of an age that laughed at *Love Thy Neighbour* than one that identified with the Ku Klux Klan.

Crucially, the man at the centre of if all has no recollection of being abused by his own side. A couple of years before the Baroness's article, Best had told a newspaper that uses rather longer words than *The Sun*: 'I never had any trouble with the West Ham fans. All I felt from them was love. East End people are good people and they will always love somebody who gives their all. I always tried my best for them.'

Clyde Best, MBE, we salute you for making life just that little bit easier for those who followed in your stud marks.

I'm sorry to report that the same cannot be said of Clyde's more famous namesake. I fully realise that George Best had a serious drink problem, but that's no excuse for the racial slur I once heard him use.

He was on stage at the Fairfield Halls in Croydon as part of a question and answer session with fans of all clubs. It was days after

Andy Cole had been transferred to Manchester United from New-castle and Best was asked if he thought the record British transfer fee of £7 million was a reasonable price to pay. He contemptuously dismissed the suggestion with a description of Cole that began with the letter 'n' and rhymed with 'trigger'.

There were gasps throughout the hall, but Best seemed com-pletely unconcerned that his use of possibly the most abusive word in the English language could cause such offence. I stood to leave but Nick placed a restraining hand on my shoulder, just as I had done with young Mike at the Spurs Cup tie. He'd spent a lifetime learning to live with abuse like this and had the maturity to shrug it off. It was precisely the same sort of racist stupidity that would later cost Ron Atkinson his job as a TV pundit, but Best clearly felt it was all perfectly acceptable.

Ten years later Best died as a result of fatal complications with the drugs that he had been prescribed after a controversial liver trans-plant. Man U's first game following his death was at Upton Park and, while I bowed my head to mark the sorrow of the family and friends he left behind, I couldn't bring myself to join the minute's round of enthusiastic applause that was offered up by way of a tribute.

When, I wonder, will gay footballers unearth a pathfinder cast in a similar mould to the likes of Clyde Best and John Charles?

It is inconceivable that every single professional footballer is het-erosexual – the laws of probability dictate otherwise. I recognise that narrow-minded attitudes in the game, both in the dressing room and in the stands, make it difficult for players to be open about their sexuality. But there has to come a time when the anti-gay abuse will look as embarrassingly stupid as the monkey noises do now.

We dish it out to the Brighton fans whenever we meet – most

clubs do. 'Does your boyfriend know you're here,' and: 'We can see you holding hands,' are dusted off with monotonous regularity. I reckon the Seagulls have come up with the perfect response, though. 'You're too ugly to be gay!'

If any set of supporters is going to get behind gay players, I like to think it's going to be us. In a way we do it already.

At Upton Park, if you hear the cry of 'Come On The Hammers!' it will almost certainly be from a pre-pubescent child attending their first game. What you will hear, often quite loudly, is 'Come On You Irons.' To the uninitiated it simply sounds like we are getting behind the team. Some of the better informed opposition supporters may even know we were once the Thames Ironworks, and think the connection lies there.

What they probably don't know – particularly if they come from north of Watford – is that an 'iron' is also a shortened version of 'iron hoof', which in rhyming slang is a distinctly non-PC reference to the one in ten males who are sexually attracted to their own gender. If it's not a phrase you're familiar with, take a minute or two to work out what 'hoof' rhymes with. It's a rather old fashioned term now, but it's not that difficult. (If you're Phil Brown – Sam Allardyce's former assistant – give yourself a little longer; as the man who believed a player couldn't settle in a foreign country because he was homophobic rather than homesick, you clearly need all the time you can get.)

Incidentally, can anyone tell me what an iron hoof actually is? I know about iron fists, iron lungs, iron horses, the Iron Age, the Iron Duke and even the Iron Cross. But what the hell is an iron hoof? I've always assumed it's an ancient term for a horseshoe, but that could be as misplaced as a James Collins back-pass.

Whatever the explanation, it does rather give a double meaning to 'Come On You Irons.' Could you imagine a fan of any other club urging on their team while simultaneously suggesting that the whole lot of them are a little less than totally alpha-male? Of course not. But we do – and, given the testosterone-fuelled atmosphere inside Upton Park at any given moment, it is another clue to the workings of the claret and blue mind. A case of 'Come On You Ironies', in fact.

If the bigotry surrounding homosexuality in football is to be broken down, it needs gay players to come out when they are at the height of their fame, not wait until they retire as Thomas Hitzlsperger did. One thing has intrigued me since the German international who turned out for us a few times in the dismal 2010/11 season made his announcement. Long before he joined West Ham he had earned the nickname of Der Hammer on account of the explosive shot he packed in his left foot. Had he come out when he was playing at Upton Park would it have been right and proper to rename him Der Iron? I'll leave you to work that one out for yourself.

Given that touching on sexual politics is as risky as attempting to offer a peckish Luis Suarez the temptation of naked flesh, let's take a leaf out of the early Allardyce coaching manual by giving this political football a serious hoof and getting it out to the wings as quickly as possible. The question, at West Ham, is whether or not that is left wing or right wing? The reason I ask is that a friend of mine once suggested his club was essentially left-of-centre – which set me thinking about whether or not football clubs in the UK were political and, if so, how would you categorise West Ham?

As with all the best debates, this one took place in the pub. David, being from Yorkshire, was supping a pint of northern filth with some name like Theakston's Old Knee Trembler when he came up with his theory. I swirled my red wine gently to allow a little more oxygen into the already passable Merlot and listened carefully as he explained.

David, I should warn you, supports Sheffield United:

> It was during the run-up to the February 1974 general election, when chants of 'Heath Out' would regularly be heard from the Kop, notably on the strange occasion when we played – yes – West Ham on a Tuesday afternoon, kickoff 3 p.m., instead of in the evening because of the floodlight ban that accompanied the three-day week. It's possible that we regarded West Ham, being poncey southerners, as somehow representative of the government. Anyway, we won 3–0.

Hmmm. And is there more 'evidence' to support this argument? 'Clubs on the eastern side of their cities have always been more working-class than those elsewhere because the east is where the capitalists built the factories, steel mills etc (so the wind wouldn't blow the pollution in their direction). So United have always had more working-class fans than Wednesday, which is miles away in the suburbs to the west. It's the same with West Ham and Chelsea.'

Back in 1974, of course, the Sheffield United fans got their wish and Ted Heath was ousted as prime minister. Unfortunately for us all he was to be replaced as leader of the Tory party by a certain Margaret Hilda Thatcher, who was no lover of football supporters wherever they came from.

Ten years later, when the most radical Conservative government of the twentieth century was busy ripping the heart out of industrial England, some West Ham fans would wave fistfuls of tenners at visiting supporters of northern clubs such as David's and chant 'We've got jobs, we've got jobs!' No doubt the man who was MP for West Ham South at the turn of the twentieth century was spinning in his grave at that – although mention the name Keir Hardie to most East Enders these days and their initial thought is a large housing estate in Canning Town rather than the first leader of the Labour Party.

Despite David's compelling case, my guess is that most West Ham fans care as little about party politics as the rest of the country. However in Italy, particularly Rome, there does seem to be a clear connection between followers of political parties and the club they support. AC Roma is generally considered to appeal to fans whose political beliefs lean to the left, while Lazio attracts those of a right-wing persuasion.

Lazio is the spiritual home of Paolo Di Canio, who many West Ham fans would like to see back at the club in the manager's office. He himself believes it is his destiny.

He was a wonderful player for our club – one of the best we've ever had. Anyone who has ever seen his astonishing goal against Wimbledon as he morphed into Neo from *The Matrix* to volley home Trevor Sinclair's cross will know instantly what I'm talking about. Goal of the season? That was the goal of a lifetime. There are so many Di Canio memories: the fantastic moment of sportsmanship that won him the FIFA fair play award when, rather than head home into an empty net, he caught the cross and demanded that play be stopped until the prostrate Everton keeper was restored to full health; the time he wrestled the junior Frank Lampard for the ball when we were awarded a penalty in the amazing comeback game against Bradford City in which we turned a 2–4 deficit into a 5–4 victory; the way he had pleaded with Harry Redknapp to substitute him only minutes before in the same game.

And there's no doubting his love of West Ham; he's even got the tattoo to prove it. The trouble is he's got other tattoos as well, and they are a good deal less savoury. His back alone is a tribute to fascism, featuring a symbolic imperial eagle and a portrait of Italian wartime leader Benito Mussolini, complete with military helmet. Mussolini, Adolf Hitler's closest ally and architect of one of the most repulsive ideologies mankind has dreamt up, liked to be known as *Il Duce* – 'The Leader'. If the picture on Di Canio's back wasn't enough, his arm carries a tattoo that says *Dux*, the Latin translation of *Duce*.

In his time at West Ham, from 1999 to 2003, Di Canio wisely kept his political thoughts to himself. Neither did he celebrate any of the forty-eight goals he scored in 118 appearances by hailing the crowd with a straight-armed fascist salute. But he did just that when he returned to Lazio – the club he supported as a boy and notorious for its links to extreme right-wing politics. And he did it more than once.

Di Canio is adamant that he's not a racist, which rather suggests he doesn't fully understand what fascism is all about. A political movement that is based on the idea that the people of one nation are inherently superior to those of other countries and continents is inherently racist – and it doesn't become any more palatable when the believers of this idiocy try to implement their way of thinking with extreme violence.

Politics has no place in football, say Di Canio's supporters. I disagree – politics and money go hand in hand, and there's a lot of money in Premier League football. But even if they were right, there are some things that are just wrong. To appoint a man who has aligned himself so closely to fascism as club manager would do untold damage to the credibility of West Ham.

I should probably be more disapproving than I am of the fact that West Ham's owners made most of their money from pornography, which is not exactly one of humanity's most noble endeavours. But you reach a certain stage in your life when you realise you can't be outraged about everything – your mates stop talking to you for one thing – and while I accept that a significant proportion of the population is offended by porn, I personally don't lose a lot of sleep over the fact some people are prepared to strip off their kit for the amusement of others. Censorship is more dangerous than sex, I reckon.

I do, however, still have it in me to stand up and protest against those who wish to subjugate me and mine. The East End has a proud tradition of resisting fascists. The Battle of Cable Street sent Oswald Mosley and his blackshirts packing as they tried to spread their message of fear and intimidation. And the people of the area withstood the worst Hitler and his air force could throw at them as the bombs rained down during the Blitz. They even coined a phrase to encapsulate their defiance – 'We can take it.'

I think there is something in the DNA of every West Ham supporter that yearns for one of our great players to return as manager and create a side in their own image. But I'm sorry, Paolo, it can never be you. You see, if you were to get the job it would send out the message to those who want to intimidate Jews and Muslims and gays and anybody else they don't like that it is somehow all right to do so. And that we couldn't take.

Chapter 19

Dear Mr Bonds

I HOPE YOU DON'T mind me writing to you like this. You don't know me – we've never met. I've wanted to drop you a line for a long time now, but I've always been worried you'll think I'm a bit daft for saying this. You see, you're my hero.

Is it all right if I call you Billy rather than Mr Bonds? I know it's a bit informal, but you don't strike me as the sort of bloke who insists on standing on ceremony. To be honest, I've always thought of you as Bonzo, but I'm worried that would sound overly familiar in a letter from a complete stranger.

As a supporter you get the feeling some players think of us as nothing more than a bunch of mugs. Perhaps they're right – putting your heart and soul into a football team probably isn't the most intelligent thing in the world. But that's what we do – and you got that, didn't you? You understood the passion, the loyalty and the pride that drives us on. Not only did you understand it – you shared it. In fact, you personified it.

'Legend' has to be the most overused and undervalued accolade of our age. Give your mate a lift to work when his car won't start and all of a sudden you're a legend. But there was a time when to be a legend meant a whole lot more, and it is in that knights-of-the-round-table spirit I would use the word to describe you.

Please don't think I'm trying to embarrass you – that's the last thing I'd want. Having read a bit about you over the years (well, quite a lot actually) I understand that you are a deeply private person who would be horribly uncomfortable at the thought of receiving a letter out of the blue that's gushing with praise for all the things you did at West Ham. I'll try not to do that. It's just that for me – and countless others – you embody everything the club should stand for. We'd like you to know how we feel.

You, Billy, are truly one of the West Ham greats. You may not have had giant Upton Park stands named in your honour, nor are there statues gracing the roads around the ground that you brought to life every time you stepped on to its precious turf – or battled your way through its cloying mud – yet you have a special place in the hearts of every one of us who saw you fight the good fight on our behalf.

Enshrined as you are in West Ham folklore, it's easy to forget now that you didn't begin your career at Upton Park. As you will know better than anyone, you joined the Hammers from Charlton for a transfer fee of £49,500. I put that figure into an inflation calculator and it comes out as being worth a bit more than three-quarters of a million in today's terms. That's the sort of money that gets bandied about in the lower leagues for very ordinary players. I'm no expert – I've never had to wheel and deal in the transfer market – but it's my guess that you'd struggle to get a real-life Captain Marvel for £800,000 in this day and age.

Your first year in claret and blue, of course, was 1967. By then I'd been supporting West Ham for three years but that was the first season I got to see a proper game – so in some ways we started at the same time. Astonishingly, it would be more than twenty years before you finally hung up your boots. Incidentally, do retired players really hang up their boots? I'm guessing they're not the sort of things you'd want dangling on a hook in the shed for years on end – they'd go mouldy. And you couldn't leave them in the house for any length of time; not if you're married. I don't suppose you've still got yours, have you? If so, you should put them on eBay – they'd sell for a small fortune.

You were three months short of your forty-second birthday when you played your final game at Southampton in April 1988. The previous season, when you had clocked up the Big Four-O, you were actually named Hammer of the Year! I am proud to say I voted for you. Normally, the idea with Hammer of the Year is to leave it until the final few fixtures before deciding how you're going to fill in your ballot paper. I made my mind up after watching you against Forest in early September. It was a fortnight before you turned forty – and you were still the best player on the pitch.

Remember Billy Jennings? He was the fella we signed from Watford in 1974 who scored thirty-odd goals for us in something approaching 100 appearances. While you were still flogging yourself up and down the Boleyn Ground at an age when other men are considering taking up bowls he had packed up the game and was running a really nice little bar opposite the *Daily Express*, which was paying my wages at the time. I guess you're not much of a drinker but I have to admit a small proportion of my salary did find itself being spent in Billy's most days. And while I was there I used to pick his brains about the West Ham players he had known.

Billy didn't have a bad word to say about anyone – well, not to me anyway. But he was especially complimentary about you. And he wasn't the least bit surprised that you had been able to carry on playing for as long as you did. According to him, you were the most dedicated individual he ever saw on a training ground in his entire career. Five-a-sides? You'd play like it was the Cup final. Timekeeping? You'd be the first to arrive and the last to leave. A cross-country run? There was only ever going to be one winner. Mind you, when it came to running he reckoned you left the others standing because you had an unfair advantage. Apparently you have a remarkable metabolism. The way Billy told it, your heart beats once every six hours and you barely need oxygen at all.

You probably won't remember this but the year Billy Jennings came to Upton Park a Japanese soldier called Hiroo Onoda emerged from the jungle in the Philippines after he was finally persuaded to lay down his arms and stop fighting the Second World War, which he believed was still going on. At the time it was thought he was the last of his kind. Then, as you were approaching retirement, the story went round that Onoda was not alone – and another Japanese soldier who didn't know that hostilities had ended had been found in a different part of the forest.

Reluctantly he agreed to come out under a flag of truce – but refused to surrender until he was certain that the Land of the Rising Sun really had run up the white flag. His would-be rescuers tried to convince him that the world had moved on since he had volunteered for active service. He listened suspiciously as he was told that since Japan had laid down its arms humankind had been to the moon and flown an aeroplane faster than the speed of sound – and, not only was Winston Churchill dead and buried, Britain had elected its first woman Prime Minister. On hearing all this he shook his head in disbelief, picked up his rusty rifle and headed back to the jungle, pausing briefly to turn and ask: 'What sort of idiot do you take me for? Next you'll try telling me Billy Bonds is still playing for West Ham.'

Sorry, Billy. You must have heard that joke a million times. But, you have to admit, the statistics are pretty remarkable. In all, you were at West Ham for twenty-seven years – twenty-one of those as a player – and you made an incredible 793 appearances for the Hammers. You were captain for ten years. You are the only West Ham skipper to lift the FA Cup twice. You were Hammer of the Year four times and runner-up on three other occasions. You were honoured by being made a Member of the British Empire for services to football (although if it had been me giving out the gongs it would have been a knighthood plus the Victoria Cross and the George Medal). It was an amazing career.

Those FA Cup wins were something special, weren't they? Between you and me I'm starting to have serious doubts that today's generation of West Ham supporters will ever get the chance to experience the same thrill we did. God knows, I hope I'm wrong. And I suppose we did come within a bootlace of beating Liverpool in the final a few years ago. But now the game is all about survival in the Premier League – what manager is going to risk his job by taking a full-blown tilt at the Cup?

By the way, what would you have said to Lionel Scaloni if you'd been his captain when he rolled the ball out like that in the final minute at the Millennium Stadium? I'm all for giving the ball back to the opposition after an injury, but why didn't he make sure they fished it out of the River Taff first? You'd know better than me, of course – but I'm sure even Ron Greenwood would have allowed him an honest-to-goodness hoof on that occasion.

We didn't hoof it much in the '75 final against Fulham, did we? That game was dismissed as boring by much of the media, but it looked exciting enough from where I was sitting (near the half-way line, opposite the Royal Box). Perhaps we did win too easily to make it a classic but I'd take that over blowing a 3–2 lead in the final minute and then losing the penalty shoot-out after extra time any day of the week.

I can only guess what it must have been like for you to receive the Cup. I once got a runners' up medal in a five-a-side tournament, but that's not quite the same thing, is it? I can tell you what it was like watching you do it, though. First, there was the mixed emotion of the final whistle. We were two up and coasting by then: I didn't want the game to end – Alan Taylor might have got his hat-trick (or Billy Jennings might have nicked one) and we were never going to concede. Still, the last shrill note meant victory was ours, and that was a fantastic feeling. It was the triumphant end to a long journey that had begun in January and taken us from Upton Park to Wembley via random stop-off points such as Swindon and Villa Park. Winning was the object of the exercise and we had done just that.

There's always that wonderful confused frenzy for the winning side on the big occasions. You fellas on the pitch are desperately trying to congratulate one another while, in the stands, we are celebrating in our own way. All British reserve goes out the window for once – you raise your arms to the heavens; you dance on the spot; you can even go completely wild and embrace a stranger because, for a few glorious moments, there are no strangers. If they're cheering, they're family.

It all calms down slightly when your captain begins the long climb up the most famous thirty-nine steps in football to collect the trophy, followed by his team. Our team. Ecstasy gives way to pride. It's permissible to applaud, but I kept silent as you scaled that staircase. I was saving myself for the special moment that I knew would come soon. You received the trophy and looked at it briefly. I remained silent. You kissed the Cup and teased us with it before glancing at your teammates as if to confirm you did this together. Still nothing from me. Then you raised the holy grail to the sky – sharing it with us like a priest shares the blood of Christ at Holy Communion. That's when I finally roared my heartfelt thanks for this wonderful gift you had given us.

The descent was far more informal as parts of the trophy were passed from hand to hand and the scarves were draped around your neck. A small point, I know, but I remember you made no attempt to shake them off as you came down the steps as I suspect the immaculate Bobby Moore would have down. These were the scarves we wore. This was our uniform. I had always believed you were one of us, Billy. Now I knew.

I guess when I saw you carry out the same ritual five years later I was starting to become a little blasé. I never thought Wembley would become a second home exactly, but I felt that with a team as good as ours we would appear in a showcase final every few years. Got that one wrong, didn't I?

By rights, Arsenal only had to turn up that day to collect the Cup. But it didn't quite work out like that, did it? Trevor Brooking got all the headlines, naturally. He scored the winning goal. The only goal. That's how headlines work. But you were fantastic, Billy. Next to you in the centre of defence was the man who would eventually receive the captain's armband from you, but in 1980 Alvin Martin was considered to still be a bit raw round the edges and it was felt you might need to look after him. In the event, neither of you put a foot wrong. And it was your well-timed tackle on Alan Sunderland that sparked the counter-attack which produced our goal.

I watched an old video of the game recently. 'Billy Bonds – he seems to grow in stature as the years go by,' observed Motty as you masterminded our second-half rearguard action. I am not Mr Motson's biggest fan, but he called that one right.

What made it all so special was the fact we were such massive underdogs – we were in the second division, for God's sake! It is a matter of eternal pride to me that we were the last side from outside the top flight to win the Cup, and I don't see us giving up that distinction any time soon.

The fact that we were able to do that is a huge testament to the loyalty of men such as yourself and Sir Trev. We had been in the second division for two years by the time we got to Wembley and were facing yet another season out of the top flight. It's inconceivable that players of your stature would stay with a lower-league club for that length of time nowadays, but you did. That will never be forgotten by us, the people who can't walk away.

What's it like for you guys after a big win such as that? Obviously there's the initial elation we all feel, but do you get a sense of anticlimax when that wears off? Perhaps it's just me, but the emotions that come with victory never last quite as long as those that follow defeat. If winning is like a glass of champagne, losing is an all-day hangover. The pain of one lasts far longer than the pleasure of the other. There was a time when I was younger I could barely bring myself to speak to other people until Tuesday after we'd lost on a Saturday – and it seemed to me you felt the same way.

I guess it can't be much fun at the training ground after you've lost a match, but going in to work after a defeat is awful for supporters. School; factory; office; I've had to face them all in the wake of a West Ham loss, and it often feels as if it's you against the world. A run-of-the-mill defeat is bad enough but it's truly humiliating when the team has thrown in the towel. You made sure that didn't happen on your watch. You never backed out of a tackle. You never hid when things weren't going well; you never seemed to tire – and you made sure teammates followed your example. Woe betide anyone who didn't put in a full shift; Ted MacDougall can testify to that!

What really did happen at Leeds in 1973? In your autobiography you say that it was nothing more than a heated argument, but in later years you seem to have let it slip that you did actually lamp him in the dressing room. No one would blame you if you did, of course. Losing 4–1 is bad enough but, as I say, it's so much harder for the supporters to take when you feel the players aren't trying. And that, in your eyes, was MacDougall's crime at Elland Road. The story goes that Ron Greenwood let you get on it with it, which speaks volumes when you consider how much he abhorred violence. He didn't like his defenders kicking opposition strikers but he was prepared to turn a blind eye when you gave his big-money signing from Manchester United a knuckle sandwich. MacDougall was gone a month later; ahead of you there were still fifteen years before the West Ham mast. I think it's fair to say there was only one winner in that contest.

Not that there is any suggestion you were some sort of thug. Hard, yes. Hard as nails, in fact. But never unfairly so. That's why, in time, you even won the grudging respect of opposition supporters – and there aren't many players from any club who can claim to have done that over the years.

By my reckoning you were only ever sent off twice – although the second time it happened it nearly cost you your place in the Arsenal final. That would have been a disaster. It's true that some of the tackles you made in your early days as a right back would have got you into early bathfuls of hot water with today's referees, but it was a different game back then.

I recall how Greenwood's decision to move you out of the back four to provide some much-needed bite in the middle of the park raised a good few eyebrows at the time. But putting you alongside Sir Trev was a masterstroke. You were no mere holding midfielder though – you had licence to go where you liked, which was generally where the action was. The energy and inspiration you brought to the side from midfield were a revelation for those who thought of you as nothing more than a destroyer. I can close my eyes now and still see you flying into a challenge, emerging with the ball and then positioning yourself on the half-turn in the way Greenwood had taught you as you looked around for a better-placed colleague. Because not only could you win the ball and keep it, you could use it, too. You were a terrific passer of the ball, Billy. And you could score goals.

Remember your hat-trick against Chelsea that ended our

relegation fears and resulted in you being our leading scorer in the 1973/4 season? To be honest, I don't – but it was 40 years ago and I must have missed that particular London derby. However, I do know that you never used to hang about when a game had finished, preferring to join the traffic queuing up to get through the Blackwall Tunnel and go home to your family rather than heading off to the pub for a pint with the boys. I hope you hung around long enough to collect the match ball after the Chelsea match though, because that was your one and only hat-trick for West Ham. (If that's in the shed with your boots you could put them on eBay together – you'd have buyers queuing round the block.)

About the time you were lining up with Sir Trev and the hugely underrated Graham Paddon in a midfield that absolutely dripped with class, I found myself kicking a ball about on a beach in Italy with my mate and a bunch of weirdos from the US who called themselves the Children of God.

We were challenged to a game by a group of Italian lads, who clearly thought we were there for the taking. To be honest, we were. On paper, we didn't have a chance. But, as they say, football isn't played on paper, it's played on grass. Or, in this case, sand.

It was clear from the start which side had all the class. They were sleek, tanned and wearing sunglasses. We were a rag-bag of a team: the Americans were energetic but sadly lacking in talent. I hoped they would be able to use their religious connections to summon up some divine intervention, but as the early exchanges unfolded it was evident that heavenly help would not be forthcoming. Which is when I asked myself, what would Bonzo do in these circumstances?

The only way we were going to avoid a hiding in this game was for me to win the ball, my more-than-useful mate to play a bit and the Yanks to make thorough nuisances of themselves.

The playmaker was a decent footballer. You could tell he was good because he kept his packet of Marlborough tucked in the waistband of his stylish swim-shorts. He was the one we had to stop.

I got my opportunity after several minutes of backs-to-the-wall defending. He had moved out wide, received the ball and gone round one of the God squad when I clattered him on the water's edge with the sort of tackle I had watched you make time and again. The impact was so forceful we both ended up in the sea, which was bad news for his Marlborough. I really cleaned him up – you'd have been so proud of me, Billy!

I later read that before one of those great European nights at Upton Park you looked across at the opposing captain as you lined up in the tunnel shortly before kickoff and you could see from his face that the intimidating atmosphere had got to him – you knew then that the game was already won. I think I saw a similar look as that young Italian emerged from the water and contemplated his unsmokable cigarettes. We won ugly, but we won.

Your international career, sadly, is about as notable as mine! Why you never played for England is a total mystery to me. There was an Under-23 appearance and you were on the bench for a World Cup qualifier against Italy in 1977. But at a time when some very ordinary players were being picked to represent their country and you were producing the best football of your life, you never got a full cap.

The England manager for much of the time was Don Revie – who had never forgiven West Ham for thrashing his Leeds side 7–0 some years before. He believed, wrongly, that Greenwood had arrogantly snubbed him after that game. Did that colour his thinking, I wonder?

Revie famously – and controversially – walked away from the England job in '77 to take up a lucrative contract in the United Arab Emirates. The next year I followed him to Dubai to take a considerably less rewarding contract on a newspaper that was being launched there. I was asked to handle the sports pages and, as acting sports editor of the *Gulf Daily News*, tried to fix up an interview with Revie. Why he chose not to give you a game was one of the questions on my list. But he never returned my calls.

I know you don't really like to talk about your time in management – or certainly not the way it ended at West Ham. As Jimmy Greaves used to say: 'Funny old game, innit?' You presided over our longest ever unbeaten sequence, won promotion twice and took us to an FA semi-final, yet in many ways your time in charge is still best remembered for the controversy off the pitch rather than success on it.

It all started well enough, with promotion in your first season. Then came that harebrained bond scheme, which provoked huge unrest and resulted in disastrous performances. What were they thinking of? Asking people to pay anything from £500 to £950 simply to give them the privilege of buying a season ticket – with the implied threat that if they didn't pay they would forfeit that right – was never going to go down well. The fact that 808 people did take up this dubious offer proves Abraham Lincoln was right and that you can fool some of the people all of the time. But most of us weren't having it.

Still, at least there wasn't some clever-dick marketing executive thinking the sort of thoughts that now reckons we are 'Moore than just a club'. How puke-making is that? The only stomach-churning slogan that could possibly be worse than the present Barcelona rip-off is if, back in '91, some overpaid clown in a sharp suit had come up with: 'Not just a Bonds'.

Your time at West Ham finally came to an end at the beginning of the '94 season, and it still leaves a nasty taste in the mouth. Harry Redknapp has had his say about the circumstances that led to him replacing you in the manager's office on several occasions, but you chose to maintain a dignified silence until relatively recently when you let it be known you don't exactly agree with H's recollection of events.

What a shame your friendship went up in smoke as a result of all that. As a kid I used to watch the two of you bombing up the right-hand side – him as a winger and you as the overlapping full-back – and sing my heart out. 'Harry, Harry Redknapp, Harry Redknapp on the wiiiiing,' and 'Oh, Billy, Billy – Billy, Billy, Billy, Billy, Billy Bonds,' seemed to go together like Fred and Ginger. I'd love to hear your side of the story one day – we all would.

These days we are West Ham's claret and blue army. When you were the gaffer we were your army. I doubt we'll ever sing another manager's name the way we sang yours. Shamefully it took the 'Moore than just a club' the best part of twenty years before it got round to officially recognising what you did for us. But the supporters never forgot, and I hope the reception that greeted you at the Cardiff game when you were given the Lifetime Achievement Award gave you an inkling of the limitless admiration Upton Park has for you.

As I said at the beginning I don't want to embarrass you, but I reckon I speak for everyone with claret and blue in their heart when I tell you that your place in West Ham's history is assured. It wasn't just your ability, it was all the qualities that went with it: loyalty, honesty, leadership, dignity, courage, humility – you are everything we all strive to be, knowing that all too often we will come up short.

Moore, Hurst, Peters, Brooking, Greenwood, Lyall, Bonds; your place alongside the West Ham greats is guaranteed. You, modestly, would probably disagree. But you'd be wrong. In fact, Billy, in the eyes of so many of us, you are actually the greatest of the greats. And we thank you for it.

Yours respectfully,
Brian Williams

Chapter 20

Let there be lights

I**T'S A FEW** minutes before 3 on a mid-winter's afternoon and what little daylight that's left is fading fast. You've been looking forward to Saturday all week, and here it is at last. Now you are impatient for the game to get started.

Perched towards the top of the Bobby Moore Stand you shift your gaze beyond the confines of the rapidly filling stadium to the north east, where the grey sky has merged seamlessly with the colourless landscape below. And, with a sudden chill in your heart, you are gripped by the terrible realisation that everything is about to go horribly wrong.

There's no logical reason for this surge of pessimism. Everything up to this point has been fine. The players looked sharp enough in the warm-up. There are a couple of injuries, but that's to be expected at this time of year. The opponents are mid-table and their away form is woeful. Even the ref is one you can live with.

You are prone to the odd superstition but have done nothing to anger the fates – you even put on your lucky claret socks in the right order. What's more, things augured well on the way to the ground. It's not as if the Tube let you down again. Sure, there was the usual hold-up waiting to get into the station but it was nothing out of the ordinary. Better still, you actually managed to smuggle that can of lager past the security guy on the turnstiles for once and you're grateful for a swig of it now. You thought your mouth was dry because of the salty bacon in the sandwich you bought from the burger stall. But you know the cause is something different. Not panic, exactly. More a certainty that today is going to end in bitter defeat. You've had this feeling before, and you're rarely wrong.

You try to shake it off by singing 'Bubbles' at the top of your voice. You give them an ear-shattering 'Come On You Irons' before you resume your seat and try to tell yourself that things will be all right. You even brighten up as we win a throw in their half.

Then the bloke behind you starts to moan to his mate. He is of the opinion that we won't have scored even if we're still playing this time tomorrow. You fear he's right, but you don't want to hear him say it. He's still saying it ten minutes later, by which time your illicit can is empty and it's become clear that the last time this man set foot inside the ground Scott Parker was still in the team. What's worse, he's one of those clowns who think Parker was club captain.

You want to turn around and say something but you keep your thoughts to yourself. Another pass goes astray in midfield and, in the defensive scramble that follows, we're forced to concede a corner. You have no doubt that this is the moment they will score.

We're still one down at half time and you can't be bothered to fight your way to the bar to get another beer. Instead you remain in your seat, grateful that the idiot behind you has gone – in his words – 'for a pie and mash'. In your day it was an Arthur Bliss, but it's painfully obvious that composers of classical music no longer register in popular culture and it appears Arthur has been aimed out. Time moves on, and you fear it may be leaving you behind.

Sitting alone quietly you try to make sense of it all.

You know that you can't win 'em all and you don't expect the Hammers to sweep all before them. Not these days anyway. Besides, you don't support a club like this one for the glittering prizes. It's been a long time since a West Ham captain hoisted aloft a significant trophy (the piece of Ratneresque crap they hand out for winning the play-off final doesn't count – that game is about promotion, not silverware). And you're not expecting to win anything any time soon, certainly while the finances of modern-day football mean clubs regard Cup competitions as an annoying distraction from surviving in the Premier League.

It's not simply the fact we're losing that has brought on this black-dog mood: you've seen West Ham get beaten before and, while it still hurts, you can cope with the disappointment better than you once could. This is something more fundamental. And dangerous. You are on the point of asking yourself why you do this in the first place – knowing that a failure to answer satisfactorily will make a mockery of your entire life.

You can't invest fifty years of heart and soul devotion into something only to discover that it's utterly pointless.

Things, undeniably, have changed in that time. For a start the football itself rarely excites you in the way it once did. You will concede that the game is more athletic than when you first stood on the Upton Park terraces: the players are fitter, faster and stronger – but brawn is no substitute for brain. You still appreciate a defender throwing his body in front of an opponent to block a shot but it doesn't send a little shiver down your spinal nerve-ends in the way Bobby Moore did when he stepped in to intercept a pass, taking the ball on his chest and instantly bringing it under control before side-stepping an onrushing attacker in his own penalty area and springing a counter-attack with an inch-perfect pass.

There's no place for risk in today's game. Flair has to be sacrificed for points. Get the ball into the channels and then press until the other side makes a mistake. Forget precision passing; now the order of the day is to play the percentages. Get it forward as quick as possible and look for the second ball. It brings results, but it doesn't make the hair on the back of your neck stand to attention.

Not everyone agrees with you though. You've been informed by the younger generation that the West Ham you once knew has gone for good. Now we've got to mix it up: you can't just hope to pass your way through a well-drilled opposition, you've got to be more direct. Get the ball wide and bombard them with crosses.

You counter with the suggestion that 4–4–2 produces a brand of football that's easier on the eye than 4–3–3, only to be told in no uncertain terms that no one plays 4–4–2 these days. It's said in the same way you'd have once told an old bloke with a fondness for the way things used to be that 2–3–5 had been consigned to the dustbin of history along with the dodo.

Fashions alter – you know that. So do tastes. Take clothes: it used to be that you wouldn't wear a pair of jeans unless they were made by Levi Strauss; now you prefer the ones with a stretchy waistband from Marks & Sparks. Or music: as a teenager you were obsessed by Rod Stewart and the Faces – you even had your hair cut like the diminutive Scotsman. The Roundhouse; the Rainbow; Hammersmith – you'd go anywhere to watch them belt out 'Stay with Me', 'Maggie May' and 'You Wear It Well'. Now you wouldn't get out of your armchair to watch Rod the Mod do a gig if he were playing in your back garden. Then there's food: you used to love a sweet and sour; now you only ever eat Chinese when you've been outvoted by the rest of the family who reckon it's time to give the Indian takeaway a miss for a change.

So, while you've moved on in so many other ways why do you maintain this unswerving loyalty to a football team you picked for the flimsiest of reasons when you had barely passed the age of reason? The players change, the managers change, even the shirt changes every couple of years with a view to parting you from large lumps of money in the club shop. All things must pass (except the midfield in a 4–3–3, it seems) but your support never wavers. You'd be well within your rights to hand in your notice – this isn't what you signed up for all those years ago. Not that you'd even think of switching your allegiance to another club; there's more chance of you applying for French citizenship than supporting someone else. But you could let it all go without anyone unfairly accusing you of cowardice in the face of the enemy.

The world didn't stop spinning when you gave up the season ticket, did it? You told yourself that it was a sacrifice that had to be made now you were a family man because you could no longer justify the expense. Yet part of you was secretly relieved that the ball and chain of hauling up to East London from the south coast every other week (regardless of how badly we were playing or who the opposition was) had been sprung from your ankle. Not that you would ever voice that thought in public.

However, you still feel the gravitational pull of Upton Park. You may not go to every game now but it's unthinkable that you'd never come here again. Everything else about the club may be different but the Boleyn Ground is a constant reference point in your life in the way the North Star has been a focal point for navigators over the centuries. But your personal star is going to go supernova when the demolition men's wrecking ball puts an end to a century of football. What the hell will there be to hang on to then?

There are the memories for a start. There are just too many of those to stuff into a suitcase and hide away in the loft in the hope they might be forgotten like the rest of the junk that's up there. There are all those heroes – too many to name, in fact. There are the villains as well – the donkeys are just as much a part of the jigsaw puzzle as the thoroughbreds.

The emergence of home-grown talent still excites you. Watching the youngsters come up through the Academy and force their way into the first team allows you to believe the club hasn't yet lost its heart and soul.

And there are all those intangibles: pride in the club's heritage; the comforting sense of solidarity that comes with being a supporter; respect for those players who exhibit a determination and effort that shows how much wearing claret and blue really matters to them; the unalloyed joy of a goal; the simple silliness of match day rituals. Best of all, occasionally, is the immeasurable pleasure of beating one of your Billy Big-Bollocks London rivals.

The way you feel about your football team can't be compared with your preference for a pair of chinos or a chicken jalfrezi. This isn't a commercial transaction – it's a deeply personal relationship that begins with blind passion and then, if you are among the lucky ones, turns into true love, allowing you to grow together and recognise there are sometimes faults on both sides but being able to forgive one another's mistakes too. A bit like marriage really.

For better or worse you know you are going to be hitched to West Ham until the day you are finally called to the celestial Bobby Moore Stand, where the angels are dressed in claret and blue and you never have to queue for a beer at half time. It's a comforting thought in so many ways.

The second half is under way when the bloke behind returns to his seat, disturbing everyone around him as he does so. He has barely settled down before he starts talking nonsense again. The fella clearly doesn't recognise half the players. True, these days you are a bit hazy about some of the opposition. There was a time when you could instantly identify every player in the division and be able to pronounce all their names, but you don't seem to have the time and enthusiasm to maintain that level of knowledge these days. Still, unlike the bloke behind, you're savvy enough to have bought a programme – and you know how take to a surreptitious shufti at the runners and riders without giving yourself away. More to the point, you can name all the West Ham players. You may be getting on a bit but you're not senile.

It's reaching a point that you're having trouble concentrating on the game. Your brain is drowning in his inane prattle. The muscles in your neck are getting tenser by the minute and your overworked sense of humour has decided to take the rest of the day off. For the second time you consider telling Motormouth to button it but then think better of it. There's no point having a row with someone sitting behind you – their position gives them a strategic advantage that is almost impossible to overcome.

You think back to the good old days when standing made it the easiest thing in the world to gently sidle away from someone in whose vicinity you'd rather not be. For the first time that afternoon you smile inwardly as you think back to the time you told the buffoon selling his inflammatory pamphlets in Priory Road precisely where he could stick his Nazi propaganda, only to find yourself standing next to him on the Chicken Run half an hour later. It was apparent from the way his ape-like forehead knitted slightly when your eyes met that he knew he'd seen you before but couldn't remember quite when or where. By the time he did you were down the other end of the terrace, proud to have struck a blow for free speech. (It was a complete coincidence you opted to watch your football from the other side of the stadium for the remainder of that season – large skinheads with extremist views and a taste for violence don't frighten you.)

When you do manage to focus on the game once more, West Ham are no better than they were before the break. They have days like this sometimes – perhaps all teams do. It's just the opposition never seem to have their off-days when they're playing us. There's no explanation for a performance like this, but you try to rationalise it anyway.

Perhaps we'd have been better if this was live on the telly. Trouble with that is it means one of those stupid start times you hate so much. You're a traditionalist at heart and you believe that three o'clock on a Saturday afternoon is the right time for a football match to kick off. The TV schedules made a mockery of all that with their 12.45s and 5.30s, and you know you should be grateful that your body clock hasn't been jolted out of its finely balanced precision by one of these untimely fixtures. That early kickoff is the worst – it completely throws the rest of the day. But this is a dismal performance on a dismal day and you've seen too many of those over the years. Sod tradition. A 3 p.m. start may be great for everyone else but it clearly doesn't suit West Ham.

The bloke behind is off again, stumbling slightly and steadying himself with a hand on your shoulder. You really don't appreciate being manhandled in this way. Why do you put yourself through afternoons like these? Then it's as if a giant filament is suddenly illuminated inside your head. The answer is so simple you wonder why no one has ever thought of it before: don't play in the afternoon – play in the evening. All our games should be under lights!

You get a different crowd at evening kickoffs – not quite the uncompromising support of an away game but certainly not as many whingers. There's a totally different feel about the whole experience. The team simply plays better.

If only that bloke hadn't shambled off again; you might turn around after all and astonish him with your encyclopaedic knowledge of floodlighting at Upton Park, which you picked up from the brilliant book your wife got you for your birthday. (You must remember to see if the author has written anything else and ask for it at Christmas.)

You could recount, for a start, the fact that West Ham first played under lights at Upton Park in April 1953 when we beat Tottenham 2–1 in a friendly. At that stage, floodlighting was still considered too unreliable for League games.

The lights did famously fail more than forty years later but that was down to skulduggery rather than technical problems. We had just come back from 2–0 down against Palace to equalise in the sixtieth minute when the ground was plunged into darkness. No one could find a shilling for the meter, which meant the game had to be abandoned and a crooked betting syndicate based in the Far East who had gone for the draw cleaned up. (Don't be tempted to try this yourself. UK bookmakers do not pay out on games that are called off – unless you've actually backed them to be abandoned, in which case you are liable to find yourself talking to the Serious Fraud Office under caution.)

You could also dazzle the bloke behind with your new-found knowledge that Arnold Hills, the man who made West Ham possible, experimented with floodlighting when he founded Thames Ironworks FC back in 1895. The first night game took place nine days before Christmas. Apparently there were ten lights, each said to have the power of 2,000 candles, and the ball was dipped in a bucket of whitewash beforehand. Come to think of it, you'll dip that guy's balls in a bucket of whitewash if he kicks the back of your seat again when he gets back from the gents.

You savour that thought as you think back to some of those classic encounters under the floodlights at Upton Park. Back in the '70s and '80s you had some fantastic games against European sides with exotic names like Ararat Yerevan, Dinamo Tbilisi and Politehnica Timisoara. More recently there was that 4–0 thrashing of Man Utd in the snow when Jonathan Spector played like Pelé. And there was the 2–0 victory in the second leg of the play-off semi-final against Ipswich that took us to the Millennium Stadium – God, the ground was rocking that night.

Then you recall an evening that helps to explain why the bond between you and West Ham will never be broken.

Your parents-in-law lived a five-minute walk from the ground and you often went to games from there. Your mother-in-law wasn't as young as she used to be, so you offered to cook the evening meal she insisted you ate before going to football. You did a shepherd's pie – one of her favourites. She wasn't an easy woman to please and looked suspiciously at some of the things you threw into the mix. But she loved it! You got a hug and were told that you were a mate. Compliments from your mum-in-law just didn't come any higher than that! As you dodged the traffic crossing the Barking Road on the way to the game it was as if you were a winner already. When Stuart Slater went on to inspire a sixth-round FA Cup victory against Everton, the bloke in the seat next to you forgot the usual English conventions about how total strangers are supposed to behave towards one another and you got your second hug of the evening in celebration of the winning goal. He bent your glasses, but you didn't mind. Life doesn't get much better than that…

My favourite game under lights? Sorry, I was miles away there. Nice of you to ask. Actually, it was a League Cup tie against the all-conquering Liverpool. It was many years ago now but I can still picture the goals as if the game were played yesterday. More interestingly, perhaps, I recall the feeling of total confidence that we would win. Without wishing to wax too lyrical here, it enveloped me like a warm blanket on a chilly November evening.

This was Liverpool, right? They were the reigning champions. And back in those days the big boys didn't put out weakened teams in Cup games – they wanted to win. In the League we were deep in relegation trouble. Even so, well before we took our seats in the West Stand I just knew we were going to triumph that night. It wasn't hope – it was absolute certainty. A rare sensation for any West Ham supporter, I admit. But it's a fantastic feeling when it happens.

My optimism was well founded. With Alan Devonshire playing brilliantly on the flank and Liam Brady demonstrating all his old skill in midfield, we took the Scousers apart. The first goal was truly sensational. I was in line with Paul Ince when he hit the volley from the edge of the box – if he'd leapt much higher he would have been considered a danger to passing aircraft – and then struck the ball as sweetly as any ball has been struck before or since. Minutes later we were two up – Ince again, this time with his head. The boy was clearly destined to be a West Ham legend. It was obvious to anyone with eyes to see that only by doing something sensationally stupid would he be denied his rightful place in the pantheon of Upton Park greats. (Oh, I don't know what exactly – being photographed in another club's shirt perhaps? But who'd be enough of a prat to do that?)

Kenny Dalglish's team pulled one back from the penalty spot but my faith waivered not one jot, scintilla or iota. (To be honest, I'm not sure what that adds up to in real money – but, take my word for it, I kept the faith.) Then in the second half we restored our two-goal lead courtesy of Liverpool's international defender Steve Staunton, who deftly headed an aimless David Kelly cross into his own net. And as the red wall formed while Tony Gale lined up a free kick, I was utterly sure this would be the crowning glory of a fabulous performance. Up … over … and in. 4–1. What a truly magical night!

Anyway, I liked the idea of playing all our games under lights so much I did a spot of research to see if the floodlit effect did to our League form what it did in Cup games. I'm sorry to say my findings were not encouraging.

In our Saturday–Tuesday grind of the Championship in 2011/12, we had five home games that kicked off at 7.45 – and we didn't win a single one of them. Four draws and a defeat against Ipswich produced a miserable return from a possible fifteen points. On top of that there were two games in the twilight zone. The 5.20 starts saw us beat Derby 3–1 and draw 3–3 with Birmingham in a real roller coaster of an affair. Those old fashioned three o'clock kick-offs, however, were really good for us. Played eleven; won eight; lost two; drew one. Goals for: twenty-six. Goals against: thirteen. Points: twenty-five.

Since being back in the Premier League we have won a few and lost a few, none more painfully than when Tottenham came from behind to snatch victory in the dying seconds with a wonder goal from Gareth Bale ... which left me wondering why I continue to put myself through this sort of torture after all these years.

Yet who needs ice-cold statistics when your heart tells you something different? Every Hammer knows that floodlights lift Upton Park out of the gloom and transform it into a theatre, where we're entitled to expect a happy ending.

Sadly, of course, there can be no joyous finale for the Boleyn Ground itself. The final curtain will come down all too soon, and that will be that. From then on the drama that is West Ham United will be played out elsewhere. We are told the Olympic Stadium will provide the perfect stage for a club that is on the verge of greatness but I'm not buying a ticket for that particular piece of fiction.

We're going to Stratford, not Stratford-upon-Avon. And the key difference between a football match and a Shakespearean play is that the crowd at a game are not merely spectators – we are actually part of the ever-changing plot. Without us, or at least our active and vociferous participation, what happens on the pitch is – to borrow a few words from Macbeth – 'a tale told by an idiot … signifying nothing.' Worse still, it's missing the sound and fury that makes it all worthwhile.

The OS is an impressive-looking arena (I bet the floodlights are second to none). No doubt, on occasions, it will be packed with bubble-blowing supporters who will sing their hearts out as they dream dreams and scheme schemes. But I can't believe a stadium like that will ever be able to generate the passion and the involvement of the people who have made the club what it is in the same way as the Boleyn Ground.

Yes, in property terms we're trading up to posher premises, although I wonder at what cost to us as supporters? East Ham, meanwhile, will have a few new flats and a statue where it once had a heart. I fear for its future, as I fear for ours.

Still, there's no rewriting the script now. As supporters we have pledged to follow West Ham over land and sea – which, I guess, includes a couple of miles on the 104 bus to Stratford. There is one thing I'd ask, though. Will the last person to leave Upton Park please turn out the lights?

Thank you.

Acknowledgements

HAVING WRITTEN THIS book I now feel like a total fraud. It was inspired by my very good friend Angela – who reminded me how I felt about all things claret and blue when I was having a moan about the move to the Olympic Stadium and wondering if that would be a step too far for me. 'But you love West Ham,' she said simply. She's right – I do. However, I now realise I didn't know nearly as much about the club I have followed for fifty years as I thought. That's why I am so grateful to all those people who have helped me with my research.

Thanks in particular must go to Steve Marsh, the encyclopaedic brain behind the theyflysohigh website, and two historians: John Simkin, who I quote at length, and Charles Korr, whose official history – *West Ham United* – is essential reading for anyone with the faintest interest in the club. Steve is also one of the contributors to John Farley's westhamstats website, which has been invaluable. I'd like to thank John and the rest of the team as well: John Northcutt, Roy Shoesmith, Jack Helliar, John Helliar, Tony Hogg, Tony Brown, Fred Loveday, Andrew Loveday and Steve Bacon. If there are mistakes in this book they are down to me, not them.

Likewise, I'm grateful to Geoff Hurst, Jeff Powell and Graham Murray for all the information I have gleaned from their excellent publications: *1966 and All That*, *Bobby Moore: The Definitive Biography* and *The 'Bubbles' Legend*, respectively.

I'd like to thank Tony Gale for taking the time to talk to me, and *The Guardian* (particularly Richard Nelsson) for all the help with cuttings and copyright.

I also owe a debt of gratitude to friends, family and colleagues who have let me share their stories with the rest of the world. And thanks, too, to the West Ham supporters among whom it has been my privilege to number myself for half a century. If you recognise yourself, I hope I have done you justice.

My son Geoff deserves a special mention for putting up with my many grumbles about West Ham for his entire life. Katie, my daughter, must be thanked for putting up with all other grumbles. And finally I want to say thank you to Di, my beautiful wife. Without her, nothing would make sense. COYI!

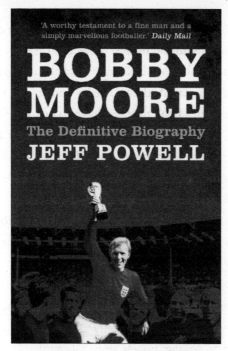

352PP PAPERBACK, £9.99

The new edition of the bestselling biography.

Bobby Moore was the embodiment of all that was great about English football. Captaining England to glory in 1966 and West Ham to victory in several major tournaments, he was loved and respected throughout the world as football's golden boy.

This definitive and authorised biography illuminates the extraordinary story of a sporting hero, from exciting accounts of his World Cup triumph to candid memories of his friendships with Beckenbauer, Eusébio and Pelé. It also reveals the inside story of a life beyond football, updated to include fascinating new material on Moore's enduring legacy in the years following his tragically premature death.

Award-winning sports writer Jeff Powell, a close friend and confidant to the Moore family, has created a powerful and fitting tribute, honouring the golden era of English football and the exceptional man at its helm.

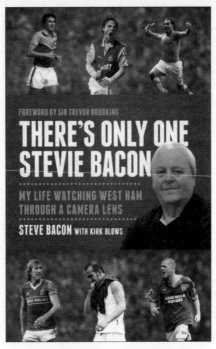

MR MOON HAS LEFT THE STADIUM
Confessions of a Matchday Announcer

JEREMY
NICHOLAS